iPad™
ALL-IN-ONE
FOR
DUMMIES®

Whit
542
Wh

Wile

iPad™ All-in-One For Dummies®

Published by
Wiley Publishing, Inc.
111 River Street
Hoboken, NJ 07030-5774

www.wiley.com

Copyright © 2011 by Wiley Publishing, Inc., Indianapolis, Indiana

Published by Wiley Publishing, Inc., Indianapolis, Indiana

Published simultaneously in Canada

For general information on our other products and services, please contact our Customer Care Department within the U.S. at 877-762-2974, outside the U.S. at 317-572-3993, or fax 317-572-4002.

For technical support, please visit www.wiley.com/techsupport.

Wiley also publishes its books in a variety of electronic formats. Some content that appears in print may not be available in electronic books.

Library of Congress Control Number: 2010941510

ISBN: 978-0-470-92867-7

Manufactured in the United States of America

10 9 8 7 6 5 4 3 2 1

WILEY

About the Author

Nancy Muir is the author of over 60 books on technology and business topics. In addition to her writing work, Nancy runs two Web sites: `iPad MadeClear.com`, which contains up-to-date information on iPads and iPad apps; and a site focussed on technology for seniors called TechSmartSenior. com. She also writes a regular column on computers and the Internet on `Retirenet.com`.

Dedication

To my wonderful husband, Earl, who walks through life side-by-side with me, putting up with every book project along the way.

Author's Acknowledgments

First my thanks to contributing authors Jesse Feiler (iWork) and Bryan Chaffin (iPad Apps) who gave of their time and expertise to make this a better book. Also, I was lucky enough to have Blair Pottenger, the absolute best editor in the world, assigned to lead the team on this book. Blair, I couldn't have gotten through this book without you. Thanks also to Dennis Cohen for his able work as technical editor, and to Heidi Unger, the book's copy editor. Last but not least, thanks to Kyle Looper, Acquisitions Editor, for trusting me to write yet another book.

Publisher's Acknowledgments

We're proud of this book; please send us your comments at http://dummies.custhelp.com. For other comments, please contact our Customer Care Department within the U.S. at 877-762-2974, outside the U.S. at 317-572-3993, or fax 317-572-4002.

Some of the people who helped bring this book to market include the following:

Acquisitions, Editorial, and Media Development

Project Editor: Blair J. Pottenger

Acquisitions Editor: Kyle Looper

Copy Editor: Heidi Unger

Technical Editor: Dennis Cohen

Editorial Manager: Kevin Kirschner

Editorial Assistant: Amanda Graham

Sr. Editorial Assistant: Cherie Case

Cartoons: Rich Tennant
(www.the5thwave.com)

Composition Services

Senior Project Coordinator: Kristie Rees

Project Coordinator: Sheree Montgomery

Layout and Graphics: Samantha K. Cherolis, Joyce Haughey, Brent Savage, Christin Swinford

Proofreaders: Melissa Cossell, Penny L. Stuart

Indexer: BIM Indexing & Proofreading Services

Publishing and Editorial for Technology Dummies

Richard Swadley, Vice President and Executive Group Publisher

Andy Cummings, Vice President and Publisher

Mary Bednarek, Executive Acquisitions Director

Mary C. Corder, Editorial Director

Publishing for Consumer Dummies

Diane Graves Steele, Vice President and Publisher

Composition Services

Debbie Stailey, Director of Composition Services

Table of Contents

Introduction

Slate-style computers have been around for a few years, but it took Apple to make them catch on with the general public in a big way when it introduced the iPad. This small, pound-and-a-half wonder sold millions of units in just a few short weeks for good reason: It's well designed, feature rich, and opens up a world of apps and media viewing in a highly portable format.

About this Book

This book has one aim: to be the ultimate reference on the coolest digital device of the day. If you're reasonably computer savvy, you can use this book the day you buy your iPad to get up to speed quickly, and then pick it up again any time you feel like taking your iPad to the next level. If you've been puttering with your iPad for a while, you'll still find things you didn't know existed between these covers.

Though the iPad is relatively simple to use, there's a lot packed in there, and you can get even more out of it by downloading apps to do seemingly everything under the sun. This book approaches the iPad from every angle: from the basics to powerful road warrior tools and productivity apps to ultra cool games and media.

This book offers step-by-step instruction in the basics, hot tips for getting the most out of iPad, and reviews of apps, to steer you to the best of the best.

How This Book Is Organized

This book consists of easily read chunks of chapters organized in six minibooks. Each minibook handles a different facet of using the iPad, such as having fun or getting work done.

You don't have to read this book in sequence, but if you're new to iPad, it's a good idea to start with the basics in the first minibook. The following sections give you a quick synopsis of what's covered in each minibook.

Book 1: iPad Basics

Here's where you get to know what comes in the iPad box, get an overview of all the built-in apps that come with your iPad, and discover how to set up iPad and sync with your computer. You get acquainted with iPad's touch-screen, and how to make settings for how iPad works. You also get going with the built-in Safari browser and get your e-mail set up, as well as explore some advice about how to take care of your iPad.

Book 11: Just for Fun

Why wait till later in the book to get to the fun stuff? iPad is a fun device but the music, videos, photos, and eBooks you can view on it are a big part of its appeal. In fact, iPad is considered by many to be mainly a content consuming machine. And let's not forget games: There are some absolutely awesome games out there that you may have played on your phone, but that roar to life on iPad's great screen.

Book 111: iPad on the Go

If you travel for business or pleasure, one of the great attractions of iPad is its portability and long battery life, and the chapters in this minibook walk you through going on the road with your iPad. Using Wi-Fi or 3G connections, you can stay in touch with others and with your home office. This minibook also covers great uses of iPad when travelling, from using the Maps app for directions to making travel arrangements or finding that great hotel, restaurant, or the nearest ATM as you roam.

Book 1V: Getting Productive with iWork

Some reviewers say iPad isn't for getting work done, but they'd be wrong. There are apps out there that help you perform the typical office suite functions, including iWork from Apple. In this minibook, you find out about the iWork apps for iPad, including how to share your work on iWork.com. You also discover how to use Pages for word processing, Numbers to crunch those numbers, and Keynote for power presentations.

Book V: Using iPad to Get Organized

There are several built-in apps in iPad that help you organize your life. There's the usual Calendar and Contacts apps to keep your schedule and people in line, as well as a handy Notes app for jotting down quick messages or records for yourself. In this minibook, you also get advice for file management on iPad: how to sync files to your computer, store things online, and print hard copies.

Book VI: Must-Have iPad Apps

Throughout this book, I mention apps that can broaden your iPad horizons, but this is the minibook that is dedicated to apps. In a variety of categories, such as business, travel, education, news, finance, and entertainment, I offer reviews of some of the hottest apps out there. If you want to go beyond the built-in functionality of iPad to a world of possibilities, this is the minibook for you!

Foolish Assumptions

If you want a book that gives you insight into the powerful ways you can use iPad, I just have to assume you are computer and mobile phone literate. You don't have to be an iPhone user to use this book (though iPhone has great similarities to iPad and shares many apps with it). You don't even have to be a Mac person — PC people do just fine with iPad.

I do assume you want to take iPad to the next level, discover great tips and advice as well as great apps for expanding your iPad experience. You may be using iPad for personal pleasure or to get your work done — or both. If you travel a great deal or use iPad to get work done, you'll find extra benefits in the material covered in this minibook.

Icons Used in This Book

Little pictures in the margin of tech books help you find certain types of information such as tips or warnings quickly. Here are the ones you should look for in this book:

Tips are like little advice columns that provide advice about the current topic, or other great things you can do to push your iPad experience to the next level.

Remember icons signal either a pertinent fact that relates to what you're reading at the time (but is also mentioned elsewhere in the book) or a reiteration of a particularly important piece of information that's, well, worth repeating.

Warning icons alert you to potential pitfalls, so don't ignore them. Ignoring Warnings might leave you with lost data, a broken iPad, or lost connection.

Seriously Cool icons draw your attention to incredible features or out-of-the-box ways to use your iPad or an outrageous app.

This icon marks iPad information that goes beyond the basics.

Where to Go from Here

It's time to jump into all things iPad. Go to any chapter in any book, and I hope you'll find something you didn't know about iPad that will up your enjoyment in your new device.

Start by checking out the basics in Book I (you might be surprised what you'll discover even if you've been tinkering with your iPad for a bit) and then jump to any book that addresses where you want to go next. Have fun, get work done, or explore more apps, for example.

Wherever you dive in, you're likely to find some advice or information that will make your iPad experience even greater.

At the time of this book's publication, iOS 4.2 became available as an iTunes update for iPad users. I have included the most important differences within this book, but because space was limited, I provide greater detail on my Web site at www.iPadMadeClear.com. Please check my Web site periodically as Apple makes new software and hardware updates to the iPad.

Book I
iPad Basics

The 5th Wave By Rich Tennant

"It's a docking system for the iPad that comes with 3 bedrooms, 2 baths, and a car port."

*I*t's time to explore the iPad as it comes out of the box and get an overview of all the great built-in apps that come with your iPad. To get you going, the chapters in this part help you to set up iPad and sync your new device with your computer to share all kinds of content.

This is also the minibook that shows you how to make settings for iPad and its various apps so you can get things working just the way you want. You also get up to speed with the built-in Safari browser and get your e-mail set up so you can stay in touch. Finally, in this minibook you get some advice about how to take care of your iPad.

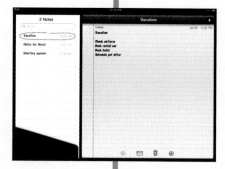

Chapter 1: Buying Your iPad

In This Chapter

✔ **Picking the right iPad for you**

✔ **Knowing where to purchase your iPad**

✔ **Contemplating accessories for your iPad**

*Y*ou've read about it. You've seen news reports about the lines at Apple Stores on the day it was released. You know you can't live without your own iPad to have fun, explore the online world, read e-books, organize your photos, and more.

Trust me; you've made a good decision because the iPad does redefine the computing experience in an exciting new way.

So, where do you begin?

This chapter is for those of you who don't already have an iPad. Here is where you discover the different iPad models and their advantages, as well as where to buy this little gem and the accessories you can purchase to outfit your iPad.

Choosing the Right iPad for You

iPads don't come in different colors. In fact, if you pick up an iPad (see Figure 1-1), you're not likely to be able to tell one model from another. That's because the differences are pretty much under the hood.

Figure 1-1: Silver and black become your newest BFs.

There are two variations in iPad models:

- The amount of memory built into the iPad.
- How you connect to the Internet: Will you just use Wi-Fi or will you use Wi-Fi and 3G/Edge?

Read on as I make a few suggestions that might help you hone in on the right model for you in the following sections.

 Because Apple upgrades and comes out with new versions of hardware and software on a somewhat regular basis (a practice that keeps tech writers on their toes), I've avoided getting too specific on memory specifications and pricing in this chapter. However, you can go to www.iPadMadeClear.com to check the latest details at any time.

Deciding how much memory is enough

You probably know that *memory* affects how much you can store on a computing device (for example, how many movies, photos, and applications you can keep there). Memory can also affect your iPad's performance when handling tasks such as streaming your favorite TV show from the Web or downloading music.

Using video and audio streaming, you can enjoy a lot of content online without ever downloading the full content to your hard drive, and given the iPad has a relatively small amount of memory in any of its models, that's not a bad idea. See Book II, Chapters 2 and 3 for more about getting your music and movies online.

So what are the memory options with an iPad? You can get three levels of memory (the specific GBs will vary as Apple updates models): think of them as small, medium, and large. It's important to choose the right amount of memory because you can't open the unit up and add memory as you can with a desktop computer. You also can't slot in a flash drive to add backup capacity because there is no USB port in the first version of the iPad . . . or CD/DVD drive, for that matter.

So how much memory is enough for you? Here's a rule of thumb: If you like lots of media such as movies and photos or e-books and you want to store them on your iPad (as opposed to experiencing or accessing this content online on sites such as Hulu or Netflix or from your Mac/PC using an app like Air Video), you probably need the iPad with the largest amount of memory. For most people who manage a reasonable amount of photos, download some music, but watch heavy-duty media like movies online, medium is probably sufficient. If you pretty much want to check e-mail, browse the Web, and make short notes to yourself, the smallest memory iPad *might* be enough, but for my money, why bother?

If you bought the first version of iPad, you should know there is no way to expand memory. Memory resides on a micro-SIM card (a smaller version of the SIM card in your cellphone), which is fine for saving your contacts' addresses and similar data, but doesn't lend itself to video storage. Apple is banking on you wanting to stream and sync content. Only you can decide if that will work for you.

What's the price for larger memory? It will cost you about $100 for each step up in memory.

Determining if you need Wi-Fi only or Wi-Fi and 3G

Because the iPad is great for browsing online, shopping online, e-mailing, and so on, obviously having an Internet connection for your device is pretty essential. That's where Wi-Fi and 3G come in. Both are technologies used to connect to the Internet and in case you need a refresher course, here's a quick summary:

- ✔ *Wi-Fi* is what you use to connect to a home network or your local coffee shop network. It's a network that has a reasonably limited range. If you leave home or walk out of the coffee shop, you can't get online. (Though some towns are installing town-wide Wi-Fi networks, and I hope yours is one of them).

- ✔ *3G* is the cellphone technology that allows an iPad to connect to the Internet via a cellular network that is widespread, just as you can make calls from just about anywhere using your cellphone.

You can buy an iPad with only Wi-Fi or one with both Wi-Fi and 3G. Here's an example of how the pricing for these models worked for the original iPad: Getting a 3G iPad cost an additional $130, but that model also includes GPS so you can get driving directions. Also, to use your 3G network you have to pay AT&T a monthly fee. The good news is that there is no long-term contract as there is with your cellphone for a data connection — you can pay for a connection the month you travel to Hong Kong and then get rid of it when you arrive home.

You can use a Verizon or Sprint MiFi router to take a cellular signal and change it into a virtual Hotspot, which means your Wi-Fi iPad model could grab the signal as if it had 3G — and save yourself the cost of the data connection fee. If you feel like toting a router smaller than a deck of cards around, you should also know that you can connect up to five devices to it.

So how do you choose? If you want to wander around the woods or town with your iPad/iPad2 constantly connected to the Internet, get 3G and pay the price. But if you'll use your device mainly at home or in a location which is a Wi-Fi hotspot, don't bother. And frankly, today, there are *lots* of Hotspots out there, including restaurants, hotels, airports, and more.

The 3G iPads are GPS devices, meaning that they know where you are and can act as a navigation system to get you from here to there. The Wi-Fi–only model uses a digital compass and a triangulation method for locating your current position, which is much less accurate; with no constant Internet connection, it's pretty useless. If getting directions is one of the features of iPad that excites you, get 3G and then see Book III, Chapter 2 for more about the Maps feature.

Knowing what you need to use your iPad

Before you head off to buy your iPad, you should know what other devices, connections, and accounts you'll need to work with it optimally. At a bare minimum, you need to be able to connect to the Internet to take advantage of most of iPad's features. It's also helpful to have a computer to allow you to download photos, music, or applications from non-Apple online sources such as stores or sharing sites like Calibre and transfer them to your iPad through a process called *syncing*. You also need a computer to register your iPad the first time you start it, although you can have the folks at the Apple Store handle that for you.

Can you use iPad without owning a computer and just using public Wi-Fi Hotspots to go online (or a 3G connection if you have a 3G model)? Yes. However, to get the most out of a Wi-Fi–only iPad and use many of its built-in features, you should have a computer and home Wi-Fi network available.

Apple's iPad User Guide recommends that you have

- a Mac or a PC with a USB 2.0 port and one of the following operating systems:
  - Mac OS X version 10.5.8 or later
  - Windows 7, Windows Vista, or Windows XP Home or Professional with Service Pack 3 or later
- iTunes 9.1 or later, available at `www.itunes.com/download`
- an iTunes Store account
- Internet access

Apple has set up its iTunes software to help you manage content for your iPad, including movies, music, or photos you've downloaded, and you can also transfer your iTunes calendar and contact information to your iPad. Book I, Chapter 4, covers those settings in more detail.

Finding a Place to Buy Your iPad

Apple doesn't offer iPad through every major retail store such as Sears or through all major online retailers such as Newegg. As of this writing, you can buy an iPad at the Apple Store and through a few brick and mortar stores such as BestBuy (by September 2010 all of their 1,000 stores stocked iPad), and at online sites such as MacMall.com. Some independent stores that specialize in Apple products stock iPads. These are mainly located in large cities or the occasional college town. Amazon also has seller associates that offer a new or used iPad, and you can browse some auction sites such as eBay for new or used models.

If you get your iPad from Apple, either at one of their retail stores, or through their online store, here's the difference in the buying experience:

The Apple Store advantage is that the sales staff will help you unpack your iPad and make sure it's working properly, register the device (which you have to do before you can use it), and help you learn the basics. On the day it launched there were workshops to help people learn about iPads, but even after the hoopla is over, Apple employees are famous for being helpful to customers.

However, Apple Stores aren't on every corner, so if visiting one isn't an option (or you just prefer to go it alone), you can go to Apple Store's Web site (`http://store.apple.com/us/browse/home/shop_ipad/family/ipad`), shown in Figure 1-2, and order one to be shipped to you. Shipping typically is free, and if there's a problem, Apple's online store customer service reps are also known for being very helpful — they will help you solve the problem or possibly replace your iPad.

Figure 1-2: iPad model options are spelled out on Apple's site.

Considering iPad Accessories

Accessories for your iPad can make your computing life easier. You can get them from Apple, or explore the broad and ever-growing world of third-party accessories.

Apple's stable of accessories

At present, Apple offers a few accessories you might want to check out when you purchase your iPad (or purchase them down the road), including:

- **iPad Case:** Your iPad isn't cheap, and being a slate device, it has an exposed screen that can be damaged if you drop or scratch it. Investing in the iPad Case is a good idea if you intend to ever take your iPad out of your house — or if you have a cat or children.

  The official Apple iPad Case has an ingenious little slot on the back. You can flip the front cover back and tuck it into the slot to make the case rest on your desk or counter at a very handy angle for viewing and typing. You can also prop the case up in a kind of U-shaped configuration to give presentations to others.

- **iPad Camera Connection Kit:** Because there's no USB port on the first version of the iPad, the only way to upload photos from your digital camera — without using an accessory — is by sending them to your computer and then syncing them to the iPad (a process you hear more about in Book I, Chapter 4). This handy kit allows you to download digital photos directly to your iPad. It will set you back about $30 for the privilege.

- **iPad Dock:** The iPad is light and thin, which is great, but holding it all the time can get tedious. The iPad Dock (see Figure 1-3) lets you prop it up so you can view it hands-free while you charge the battery and sync content to your computer. At about $30, it's a good investment for ease and comfort.

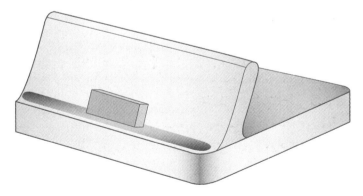

Figure 1-3: The simple, but useful, iPad Dock.

- **iPad Keyboard Dock:** The iPad provides an onscreen keyboard that's passable, especially if you position it to view things in landscape orientation. However, if you're a touch typist who wants to write long notes or e-mails, or you want to use the iPad as a primary computing device, the iPad Keyboard Dock (see Figure 1-4) or a wireless keyboard could be a must have. You get some dedicated keys for brightness and volume control, a lock key, and some iPod controls. However, you can use the keyboard with your iPad only in portrait mode.

Figure 1-4: This lightweight keyboard is remarkably comfortable to use for typing or syncing.

✔ **Apple Earphones with Remote and Mic:** There are two versions of these: in-ear and not so in-ear. They both offer remote control of your audio.

✔ **iPad 10W USB Power Adapter:** This accessory is similar to the 10W USB Power Adapter that ships with the iPad. However, this accessory makes charging easier if you need to place your iPad a bit farther from a power outlet because it sports a six-foot-long cord.

✔ **Apple Dock Connector to VGA Adapter:** Use this to connect your iPad to a TV, monitor, or projector to watch all that great multimedia. You can also use the **Apple Composite or Component AV Cables** to attach iPad to the corresponding audio and video inputs on your entertainment center.

Checking out what others have to offer

If you want to explore third-party accessories, there are many, and more appear all the time. Just perform a search for *iPad accessories*. You'll find that there are suede, leather, neoprene, aluminum, and canvas cases; a variety of stands; carrying bags; screen protectors; and external batteries to supplement iPad's impressive 10-hour battery life. Design Mobel has even come up with a bed called the Pause that goes with your iPad, but let's not even go there . . .

Want to stand out from the crowd by carrying your iPad around in a case with character? The McNally Microsuede case is a good option which folds like the Apple Case so you can use your iPad as a presentation unit. If you're made of money, the Louis Vuitton model at about $400 will make you the envy of your friends. And eBags offers some nice canvas bags if your tastes, and budget, are more down-to-earth.

A good option to Apple's keyboard Dock is McNally's BTKey, a fully extended keyboard with number pad which you can use with your iPad device in portrait or landscape mode. This neat device also works with your iPhone.

There are even a few clothing companies coming up with duds that can hold an iPad. (Steve Wozniak is on the board of SCOTTEVEST, shown in Figure 1-5, so you know they've got a few iPad-holding clothes.) iClothing and iPad Suit are following suit — excuse the pun.

Figure 1-5: Wear your iPad with style.

iPad also supports Bluetooth, to help you connect with nearby Bluetooth-enabled devices such as wireless keyboards, so consider that an option to the Apple-offered iPad Keyboard Dock.

Don't bother buying a wireless mouse to connect with your iPad via Bluetooth — the iPad recognizes your finger as its primary input device, and mice need not apply.

Chapter 2: Getting Started with iPad

In This Chapter

- ✓ Discovering what's in the box
- ✓ Getting your first look at the gadget
- ✓ Charging the battery
- ✓ Powering-on your iPad and registering it
- ✓ Using the touchscreen
- ✓ Becoming familiar with the Status bar
- ✓ Putting your iPad to sleep, waking it up, and turning it off

Once you've got your hands on an iPad, you can explore what's in the box and get an overview of the little buttons and slots you'll encounter — luckily, there are very few of them.

You also need to get comfortable with the touchscreen. If you have an iPhone, you're ahead of the game here, but even if you do, you should take a little time to get comfortable with using the larger format screen.

Finally, after a tough day of playing with your new gadget, you need to know how to put it to sleep. I cover all of these iPad basics in this chapter.

Exploring What's in the Box

When you fork over your hard-earned money for your iPad, you'll be left holding one box about the size of a package of copy paper. Here's what you'll find when you take off the shrink-wrap and open the box:

- ✓ **iPad:** Your iPad is covered in a thick plastic sleeve thingie you can take off and toss. (Unless you think there's a chance you'll return it, in which case you might want to keep all packaging for 14 days — Apple's return period.)

✒ **Documentation (and I use the term loosely):** You'll find a small white envelope under the iPad itself about the size of a half-dozen index cards. Open it up, and you'll find:

  • *A tiny, useless pamphlet:* This pamphlet, named Important Product Information Guide, is essentially small print (that you mostly don't need to read) from folks like the FCC.

  • *A mysterious label sheet:* This contains two white Apple logos. (Not sure what they're for, but my husband and I use one of these stickers to differentiate my iPad from his.)

  • *A small card containing the actual documentation (sort of):* This displays a picture of the iPad and callouts to its buttons on one side, and the other side contains about three sentences of instructions for setting it up and info about where to go online to find out more.

✒ **Dock Connector to USB Cable:** Use this cord (see Figure 2-1) to connect the iPad to your computer, or use it with the last item in the box, which is the . . .

✒ **10W USB Power Adapter:** The power adapter (refer to Figure 2-1) attaches to the Dock Connector to USB Cable so you can plug it into the wall and charge the battery.

That's it. That's all there is in the box. It's kind of the typical Apple study in Zen-like simplicity.

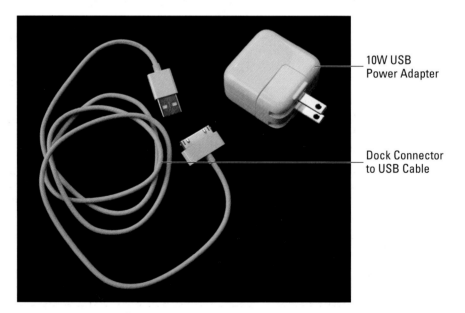

10W USB
Power Adapter

Dock Connector
to USB Cable

Figure 2-1: Some pretty simple gadgets for power and USB connections.

Taking a First Look at the Gadget

The little card contained in the documentation (see the preceding section) gives you a picture of the iPad with callouts to the buttons you'll find on it. In this section, I give you a bit more information about those buttons and some other physical features of the iPad. Figure 2-2 shows you where each of these items is located.

Here's the rundown on what these things are and what they do:

- ✔ **(The all-important) Home button:** Before the 4.2 update to iOS, you had to go back to the Home screen to do just about anything. If you were browsing online and you wanted to open the calendar, you pushed the Home button and you'd exit the Web browser and end up on the Home screen, where you could tap one of the application icons, such as the Calendar app (or whatever app you'd like to use), to open it. After iOS 4.2 added the ability to *multitask* (have various apps open at the same time and switch among them) you didn't have to use the Home button to switch among open apps, but it's still the case that no matter where you are or what you're doing, you can push Home and you're back to home base.

- ✔ **Sleep/Wake button:** You can use this button to power up your iPad, put it in sleep mode, wake it up, or power it down (more about this in the final section of this chapter).

- ✔ **Dock connector slot:** This is where you plug in the dock connector cord to charge your battery or sync with your computer (which you learn more about in Book I, Chapter 4).

- ✔ **Screen Rotation Lock:** In case you hadn't heard, the iPad screen rotates to match the angle you're holding it at. If you want to stick with one orientation, even if you spin the iPad in circles, you can use this little switch to lock the screen, which is especially handy when reading an e-book in bed.

  With iOS 4.2, the Screen Rotation Lock button's function changed and became the Mute button. To find out how to lock the screen rotation in iOS 4.2 see Book I, Chapter 7.

- ✔ **(A tiny, mighty) Speaker:** One of the nice surprises I had when I first got my iPad was the great little sound system it has and how much sound can come out of this little speaker. The speaker is located on the bottom edge of the screen below the Home button.

- ✔ **Volume:** A volume rocker you use like any other volume rocker: tap up for more volume and down for less.

- ✔ **Headphone jack and microphone:** If you want to listen to your music in private, you can plug a 3.5mm minijack headphone in here (including an iPhone headset if you have one, which gives you bidirectional sound). There's also a tiny microphone that makes it possible to speak into your iPad to do things like make phone calls using Internet calling services.

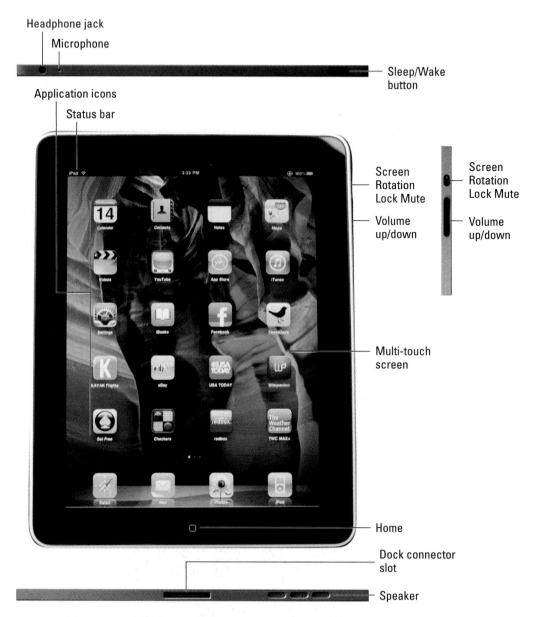

Headphone jack

Microphone

Sleep/Wake button

Application icons

Status bar

Screen Rotation Lock Mute

Screen Rotation Lock Mute

Volume up/down

Volume up/down

Multi-touch screen

Home

Dock connector slot

Speaker

Figure 2-2: There are probably fewer gizmos to get used to on iPad than on your cellphone.

Charging the Battery

You've heard about the awesome 10-hour battery life on your iPad, and it's all true. My iPad showed up fully charged from the Apple Store, but even if you got yours shipped it should have been at about 90% or so. But all batteries run down eventually (the little battery icon in the iPad Status bar will tell you when you're running low), so one of your first priorities is to know how to recharge your battery. This is a pretty obvious procedure, given the few items that come with your iPad, but just in case you need help, you can follow these steps to get that battery meter up to 100%:

1. **Gather your iPad, connector cord, and power adapter.**

2. **Gently plug the USB connector on the end of the connector cord into the power adapter.**

3. **Plug the other end of the cord (see Figure 2-3) into the cord connector slot on the iPad.**

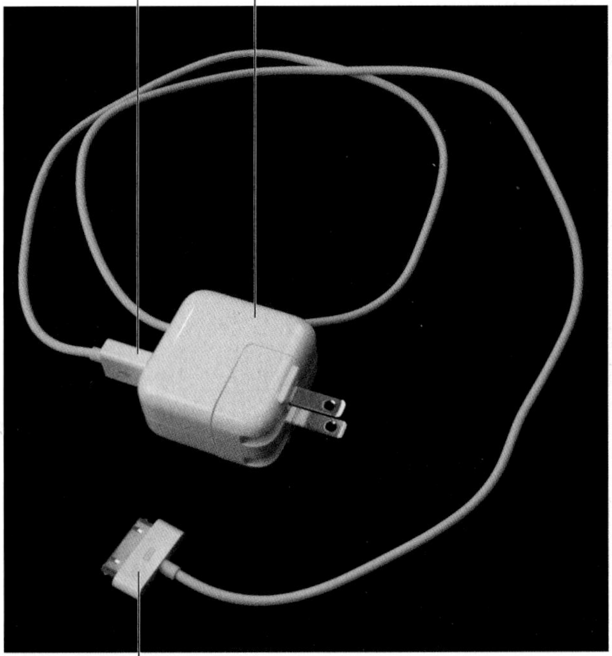

Attach the USB connector...

to the power adapter.

Then plug this end into the iPad

Figure 2-3: Assembling the connector cord and power adapter to charge the iPad battery.

4. **Unfold the two metal prongs on the power adapter (refer to Figure 2-3) so they extend from it at a 90-degree angle, and plug the adapter into a wall outlet.**

If you buy the iPad Dock or the iPad Keyboard Dock accessory, you can charge your iPad while it's resting in the dock. Just plug the larger end of the connector cord into the back of the dock instead of the bottom of the iPad.

Turning iPad On and Registering It

Apple has done a pretty nice job of getting folks to the iTunes store to buy their iPad content, whether they want to or not. In fact, the first time you turn on your iPad you have to register it using a connection to a computer with the latest version of iTunes installed before you can get it to do anything at all.

Once you have an iTunes account (Book I, Chapter 4 provides details of getting set up with an iTunes account if you don't have one), hold the iPad with one hand on either side, oriented like a pad of paper, and then follow these steps to register it:

1. **Press and hold the Sleep/Wake button on the top of your iPad until the Apple logo appears.**

   In another moment, a screen appears, showing a picture of a cord plugging into an iPad, subtly indicating your next step.

2. **Plug the Dock Connector to USB Cable into your iPad.**

3. **Plug the other end into a USB port on your computer.**

   Both your computer and iPad think for a few moments while they exchange some data.

4. **Sign in to your iTunes account in the dialog that appears, and then follow the simple onscreen instructions to register your iPad and choose what content is automatically downloaded when you connect your iPad to your computer.**

   (You can change these settings later; this is covered in Book I, Chapter 4.)

   When you're done, your iPad Home screen appears, and you're in business.

5. **Unplug the Dock Connector to USB Cable.**

If you buy your iPad at an Apple Store, they'll register it for you, and you can avoid getting an iTunes account right away and in fact skip this whole process (though you'll eventually probably want to get an iTunes account to get at their treasure trove of content and apps).

You can choose to have the following transferred to your iPad from your computer when you sync: music, videos, downloaded applications, contacts, calendars, e-books, podcasts, and browser bookmarks. You can also transfer content you download directly to your iPad using the iTunes and App Store apps to your computer. See Book II, Chapter 1 for more about these features.

Meeting the Multi-Touch Screen

When your Home screen appears (see Figure 2-4), you'll see a pretty picture in the background and two sets of icons. One set appears in the Dock along the bottom of the screen. The *Dock* contains the Safari browser, Mail, Photos, and iPod app buttons by default, though you can add other apps to it. The Dock also appears on every Home screen. (You start with one Home screen, but adding new apps creates additional Home screens — up to eleven in all.)

Other icons, the application icons, appear above the Dock and are closer to the top of the screen. (I give you an overview of the functionality of all these icons in the next chapter.) Different icons appear in this area on each Home screen.

This may or may not need saying, but the screen is made of glass and will smudge when you touch it and break if you throw it at the wall, and contrary to Apple's boasts, can also scratch. So, be careful and treat it nicely.

Connecting with the touchscreen

The iPad touchscreen technology allows you to swipe your finger across the screen or tap an icon to provide input to the device. You hear more about that in the next section, but for now, go ahead and play with it for a few minutes. Just as you may have become used to with your mobile phone, you use the pads of your fingertips (not your fingernails) and do the following:

1. **Tap the Settings icon.**

   The various settings (which you hear more about in Book I, Chapter 7) appear. (See Figure 2-5.)

2. **To return to the Home screen, press the Home button.**

3. **Swipe a finger or two from right to left on the screen.**

   Because the iPad has a few additional Home screens available (11 to be exact) that you can fill up with all the applications you'll be downloading, the screen shifts slightly to the left. (If you have more apps downloaded, filling additional Home screens, this action moves you to the next Home screen.)

With multiple Home screens in use, you get little dots at the bottom of the screen above the Dock icons, indicating which of the Home screens you're on.

Application icons

The Dock

Figure 2-4: Icons for various apps live in the Dock or on the Desktop.

4. **To experience the rotating screen feature, while holding the iPad firmly, turn it sideways.**

   The screen flips to a horizontal orientation.

5. **To flip the screen back, just turn the device so it's oriented like a pad of paper again.**

6. **Tap iPod in the Dock.**

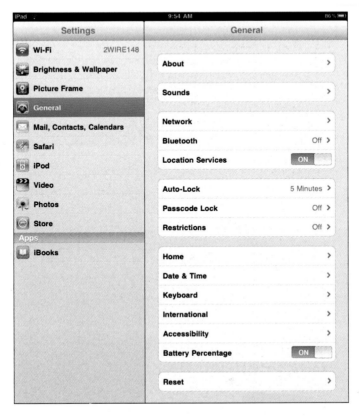

Figure 2-5: Settings is your control center for all things iPad.

7. **Practice the multitasking feature by double-tapping the Home button.**

   All apps appear in a bar along the bottom of the screen.

8. **Swipe to scroll through the apps and tap on one to jump to it without going back to the Home screen.**

You can customize the Home screen by changing the wallpaper and brightness. Read about making these changes in Book I, Chapter 7.

Goodbye click-and-drag, hello tap-and-swipe

If you're like me, you'll fall in love with the touchscreen interface that iPad sports. It's just so intuitive using your finger as a pointing device — something you're probably already doing on your iPhone or other mobile device.

There are several methods you can use for getting around and getting things done in iPad using its Multi-Touch screen, including:

🖙 **Tap once.** To open an application on the Home screen, choose a field such as a search box, select an item in a list, select a backward arrow to move back one screen, or follow an online link, tap the item once with your finger.

🖙 **Tap twice.** Use this method to enlarge or reduce the display of a Web page (see Book I, Chapter 5 for more about using the Safari Web browser) or zoom in or out in the Maps app.

🖙 **Pinch.** As an alternative to the tap-twice method, you can pinch your fingers together or move them apart on the screen (see Figure 2-6) when you're looking at photos, maps, Web pages, or e-mail messages to quickly reduce or enlarge them, respectively.

Figure 2-6: Pinch to zoom in or out on a page.

TIP

You can use a three-finger tap to zoom your screen to be even larger. This is handy if you have vision challenges. Go to Book I, Chapter 7 to discover how to turn this feature on using Accessibility features.

✔ **Drag to scroll (also referred to as *swiping*).** When you press your finger to the screen and drag to the right, left, up, or down, you move around the screen. (See Figure 2-7.) Swiping to the right on the Home screen moves you to the *Spotlight screen,* Apple's term for the iPad search screen. Swiping down while reading an online newspaper moves you down the page, while swiping up moves you back up the page.

✔ **Flick.** To scroll more quickly on a page, quickly flick your finger on the screen in the direction you want to move.

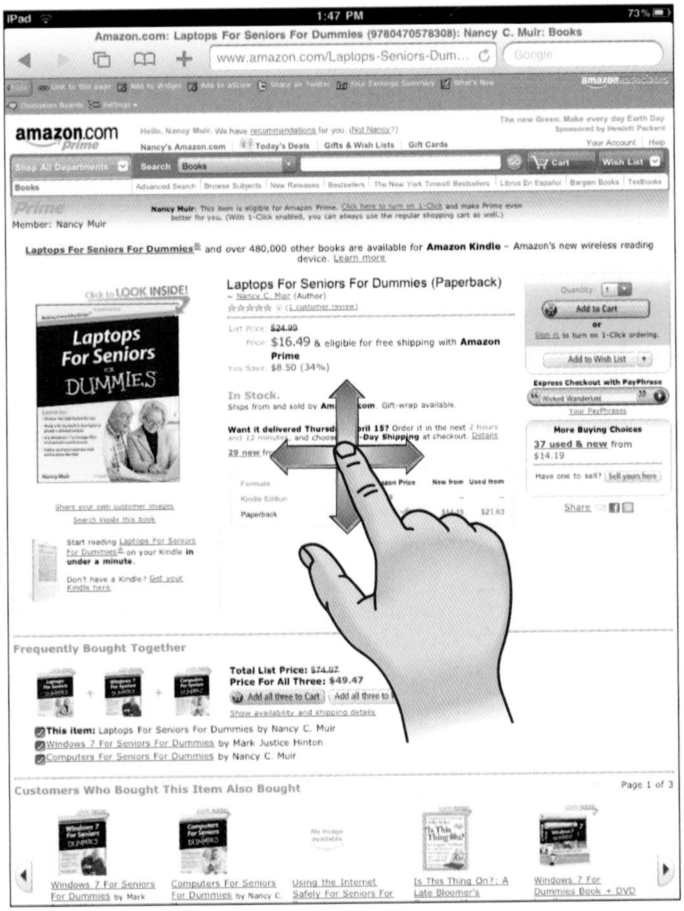

Figure 2-7: Swiping gets you around a screen quickly.

⊬ **Tap the Status bar.** To move quickly to the top of a list, Web page, or e-mail message, tap the Status bar at the top of the iPad screen.

⊬ **Press and hold.** If you're in any application where selecting text would be an option, such as Notes or Mail, or if you're on a Web page, pressing and holding near text will select a word and bring up editing tools that allow you to select, cut, or copy text. You can also use this method to reposition the insertion point under the magnifying glass icon that appears.

If you feel like a practice session, try out these actions by following these steps:

1. **Tap the Safari button to display the Web browser. (You may be asked to enter your Wi-Fi network password to access the network to go online.)**

2. **Tap a link to move to another page.**

3. **Double-tap the page to enlarge it; then double-tap again to reduce its size.**

4. **Drag one finger around the page to scroll.**

5. **Flick your finger quickly on the page to scroll more quickly.**

6. **Press and hold your finger down on text that isn't a link. A magnifying glass icon appears.**

   Release your finger and the item is selected, and a Copy tool is displayed, as shown in Figure 2-8.

7. **Press and hold your finger on a link or an image.**

   A menu appears with commands that allow you to open the link or picture, open it in a new page, or copy it. The image menu also offers a Save Image command.

8. **Put your fingers slightly apart on the screen, and then pinch your fingers together to reduce the page; with your fingers already pinched together, place them on the screen, and then move them apart to enlarge the page.**

9. **Press the Home button to go back to the Home screen.**

The Copy tool

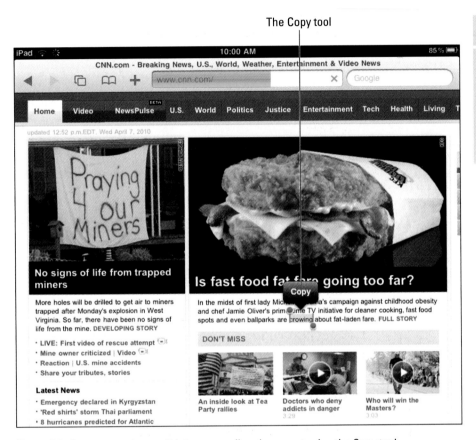

Figure 2-8: Copy text and paste it into an e-mail or document using the Copy tool.

Displaying and using the onscreen keyboard

Part of the beauty of iPad is that it's highly portable, but that portability
comes at a price: a physical keyboard. There is the Keyboard Dock accessory, but for short text entry, you don't really need it. That's where the
onscreen keyboard comes in handy, allowing you to enter text as you may
have done on a touchscreen mobile phone screen.

iPad has a built-in keyboard that appears whenever you're in a text-entry location, such as a Search field or e-mail message. Follow these steps to practice using the onscreen keyboard:

1. **Tap the Notes icon on the Home screen to open this easy-to-use notepad.**

2. **Tap the note.**

   The onscreen keyboard appears.

3. **Type a few words using the keyboard.**

   To get the widest keyboard display possible, rotate your iPad to be in landscape (horizontal) orientation. (See Figure 2-9.)

4. **If you make a mistake (and you may when you first use it), use the Delete key (the key in the top-right corner with a little *x* on it) to delete text to the left of the insertion point.**

5. **To move to a new paragraph, press the Return key, just as you would on a regular computer keyboard.**

6. **To type numbers and some symbols, press one of the number keys (labeled .?123) located on either side of the spacebar. (Refer to Figure 2-9.)**

   Characters on the keyboard change. To return to the letter keyboard at any time, simply tap one of the letter keys (labeled ABC) on either side of the spacebar.

   If you type a number in the number/symbol keyboard and then tap the spacebar, the keyboard automatically returns to the letter keyboard.

7. **Use the Shift buttons just as you would on a regular keyboard to type uppercase letters or alternate characters.**

8. **Double-tap the Shift key to turn the Caps Lock feature on; tap the Shift key again to turn it off.**

   (You can control whether this feature is available in iPad Settings).

9. **To type a variation on a symbol (for example, to get alternate currency symbols when you press the dollar sign on the number keyboard), press the key and drag slightly; a set of alternate symbols appears. (See Figure 2-10.)**

   Note that displaying variations on symbols works only on some symbols.

Tap in the note...

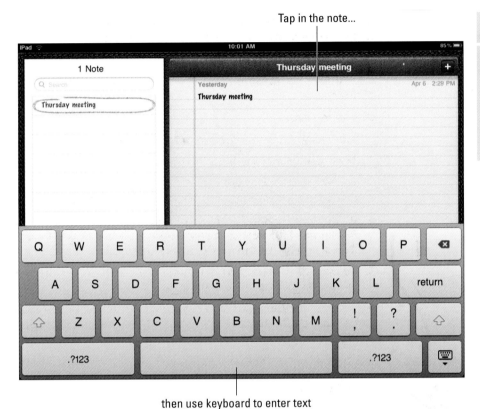

then use keyboard to enter text

Figure 2-9: The onscreen keyboard is handiest to use in landscape orientation.

10. **To hide the keyboard, press the Keyboard key in the bottom-right corner.**

11. **Tap the Home button to close Notes.**

To type a period and space, just double-tap the spacebar.

To type a number and automatically be returned to the alpha keys, press a .?123 key and slide your finger to the number you want to enter. When you release the key, you're back to the alpha keyboard.

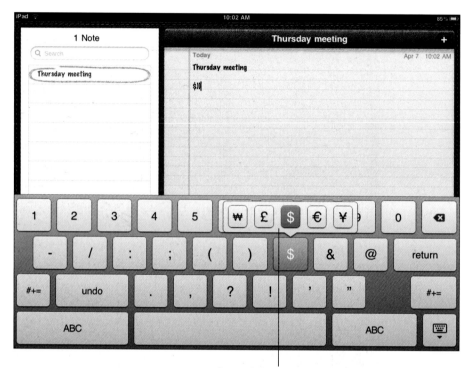

A set of alternate symbols

Figure 2-10: Only some symbols offer alternatives when you press and drag them.

Flicking to search

Can't find that song you downloaded or an e-mail from your boss? You'll be relieved to know that a search feature in iPad called Spotlight helps you find photos, music, e-mails, contacts, movies, and more. This search feature can be found on the screen to the left of the default Home screen.

Follow these steps to access and use Spotlight:

1. **Press and drag from left to right on the Home screen to display the Spotlight screen.**

   You can also, from the primary Home screen, tap the left side of the Home button to move one screen to the left.

2. **Tap in the Search iPad field.**

   The keyboard appears. (See Figure 2-11.)

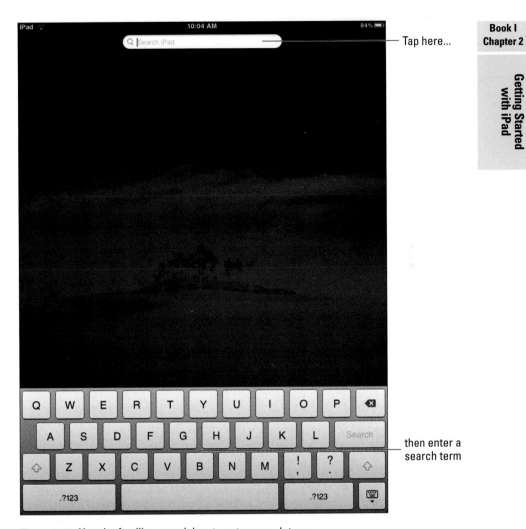

Tap here...

then enter a
search term

Figure 2-11: Use the familiar search box to enter search terms.

3. Begin entering a search term.

In the example in Figure 2-12, I typed the letter *S* and came up with a
contact, a couple of built-in apps, and some music I had downloaded, as
well as a few e-mail messages. As you continue to type a search term,
the results are narrowed down to match.

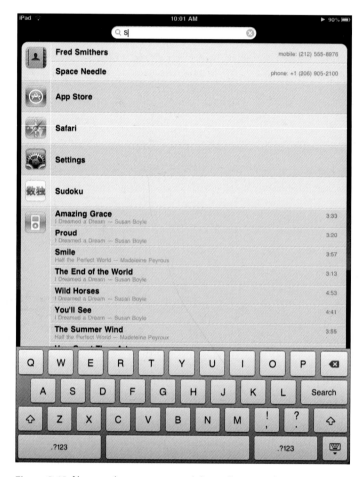

Figure 2-12: Narrow down your search by typing more letters.

4. Tap an item in the search results to open it in the associated app.

To close the app and go back to the search screen, tap the Home button and then tap the left side of the Home button to display the search screen again.

5. To enter a different search term, tap in the search box and tap the Delete key on the keyboard to delete the current term and then enter another.

You can use some standard search techniques to narrow your search. For example, if you want only the e-mails that include both Bob Smith and Jane Jones, enter **"Smith, Jones" or "Bob, Jane"** as your search term. To change the search language, tap the key on the onscreen keyboard that looks like a little globe to cycle through available languages.

Exploring the Status Bar

Across the top of your iPad screen is a Status bar. (See Figure 2-13.) Little icons in this area can provide some useful information, such as the time, your battery charge, or the status of your wireless connection. Table 2-1 lists some of the most common items you'll find in the Status bar:

iPad ☐ ☐   3:30 PM   ☐ ▶ 79% ☐

Figure 2-13: The Status bar provides some handy info about your iPad.

Table 2-1		Common Status Bar Icons
Icon	*Item*	*What It Indicates*
	Wi-Fi	You're connected to a Wi-Fi network.
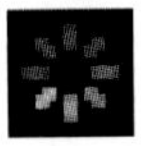	Activity	Something's in progress, such as a Web page loading.
 3:30 PM	Time	You guessed it: the time.
	Screen Rotation Lock	The screen is locked and will not rotate when you turn the iPad.
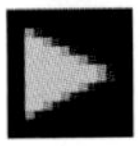	Play	Media is playing.
 79% ☐	Battery Life	The percentage of charge your battery has left. (It changes to a lightning bolt when battery is charging.)

If you have GPS, 3G, Bluetooth devices, or a connection to a virtual private network (VPN), symbols appear on the Status bar when these are active. The 3G icon will appear only with 3G-enabled iPad models. If you have a 3G model but no 3G available, you may see an icon for Edge. If you're out of range of both 3G and Edge, you see GPRS. Essentially iPad tries for the best connection and then jumps to a lesser connection if the best isn't available. Note that 3G is the only one of the three that allows both voice and data transmission.

Putting iPad to Sleep, Waking It Up, and Turning It Off

You've seen how simple it is to turn the power on for your iPad earlier in this chapter. Now it's time to put it to *sleep* (the iPad screen goes black, but iPad can be quickly awakened again) or turn the power off to give the darn thing a rest. Here are the procedures you can use:

- ✔ **Press the Sleep/Wake button.** iPad goes to sleep, the screen goes black, and it's locked.

- ✔ **Press the Home button or slide the Sleep/Wake slider.** This wakes up iPad. Swipe the onscreen arrow on the Slide to Unlock bar (see Figure 2-14) to unlock the iPad.

- ✔ **Press and hold the Sleep/Wake button until the Slide to Power Off bar appears at the top of the screen, and then swipe the bar.** You've just turned off your iPad.

iPad automatically goes into sleep mode after a few minutes of inactivity. You can change the time interval at which it sleeps by adjusting the Auto-Lock feature in Settings. (I tell you how to do that in Book I, Chapter 7.)

Wondering about that little flower symbol in the lower-right corner of a sleeping iPad's screen? That's the slideshow button. Tap it if you'd like a cool slideshow of the images in Photos displayed on the sleep screen. The Slide to Unlock area disappears, but you can get it back by clicking the Home button on your iPad. See Book II, Chapter 4, for more about working with Photos.

Figure 2-14: Use the Slide to Unlock area to wake iPad up.

Chapter 3: Overview of Bundled Apps

In This Chapter

✓ Getting the most of the Internet with Safari and Mail

✓ Organizing your photos

✓ Getting organized with Calendar, Contacts, Notes, and Maps

✓ Using built-in apps for playing music and videos

✓ Shopping for content at iTunes and apps at the App Store

*i*Pad comes with certain functionality and applications (which you probably know as *apps,* for short) already installed. When you look at your
Home screen (one of eleven possible Home screens you can fill up with
other apps), you'll see twelve icons for apps, plus one for accessing iPad
settings. Four icons are displayed across the bottom in iPad's Dock, including Safari, Mail, Photos, and iPod. The other eight (Calendar, Contacts,
Notes, Maps, Videos, YouTube, iTunes, App Store, and Settings) are nearer
the top of your screen and include apps for organizing your time and contacts, playing videos, and shopping for content and yet more
apps. The Dock icons will appear on every Home screen, but
the others you can access on only the first Home screen
unless you move them elsewhere.

This chapter gives you a quick overview of what
each bundled app does. You'll find out more about
every one of them as you move through the chapters in this book.

Settings isn't exactly an app, but it's an icon you
should know about: It's the central location in iPad
where you can adjust settings for various functions,
change settings for how apps function, and do admin-
istrative tasks like setting up e-mail accounts or a password. Read more about using Settings in Book I, Chapter 7.
There is also advice about using settings for various apps in
Books II, III, and V, and information about e-mail settings in Book I,
Chapter 6.

Getting Online with iPad

iPad would kind of be an expensive calendar, address book, and music player if you couldn't go online to browse, buy things, get e-mail, stream video and audio, and more. Two bundled apps, Safari and Mail, open iPad up to the whole world of the Internet.

Going on Safari

Safari is Apple's Web browser. If you've owned a Mac computer or iPhone, you've already used Safari (see Figure 3-1) to navigate around the Internet, create and save bookmarks of favorite sites, and add Web clips to your Home screen so you can quickly visit favorite sites from there.

If you've been a Windows user in the past, you may also have used Safari, or you may be more familiar with browsers such as Internet Explorer or Firefox. If you haven't used Safari, don't worry: the browser should be pretty easy for you to get the hang of with its familiar address field, Search field, navigation buttons, and bookmarks.

Using a browser on iPad is a lot of fun because of the touchscreen functionality and the ability to zoom in or out on a page by flicking two fingers inward or outward. The thumbnail views let you see all open pages at once. You can read more about using Safari in Book I, Chapter 5.

Getting Mail

iPad lets you get all your mail in one place through the Mail app. Mail is the program you use to access e-mail accounts you set up in iPad. You can set up accounts you have with popular e-mail providers such as Gmail, Yahoo!, AOL, and Windows Live. You can also access accounts through Apple's paid MobileMe service or Microsoft Exchange. (Your work e-mail account might use Microsoft Exchange, for example.) Most any IMAP- or POP3-type account (the two most common mail protocols out there) is also supported. You can also arrange to access the e-mail accounts you have with your Internet Service Provider (ISP).

Once you set up an account, when you press the Mail icon, your e-mail will display without you having to browse to the site or sign in. Then you can use tools to move among a few preset mail folders, read and reply to mail, and download attached photos to iPad. You can also use the Print feature in Mail to print your e-mail messages to a wireless printer. You can read more about setting up and using e-mail accounts in Book I, Chapter 6.

In portrait orientation, e-mails are displayed full screen, and you can use a drop-down menu to view your inbox. In landscape orientation, the inbox stays put on the left side of your screen.

Figure 3-1: Find what you need on the Web with Safari.

Playing with Photos

Photos isn't exactly Photoshop or any other sophisticated photo-imaging program — it's just a pretty simple app for organizing and viewing photos. Still, though it doesn't do much, what it does, it does in a very cool way.

Photos (see Figure 3-2) allows you to organize pictures in folders, e-mail photos to others, use a photo as your iPad wallpaper, or upload someone's picture to a contact record. You can also run slideshows of your photos. You can open albums, pinch or unpinch to shrink or expand photos, and scroll through photos with a swipe.

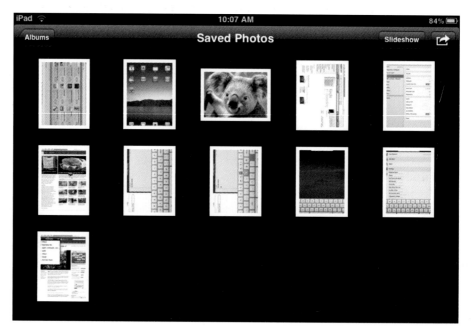

Figure 3-2: A simple but fun way to view your photos.

The sexy part of Photos is the way you interact with the photos with your fingers on the touchscreen. You can also use Photos to convert iPad into a digital photo frame while you have it docked or charging, and you can run slideshows of your photo albums, as well. If Photos sounds like fun (and it is), you should read more about how it works in Book II, Chapter 4.

Note that from iOS 4.2 on, iPads have native print capability. In Photos that means that you can select a photo or photos, tap to display the main menu, tap the Print option, select your printer and print. You have to have a printer that supports wireless printing to use this method. See Book V, Chapter 1 for more about printing.

Using Apps to Stay Organized

Scheduling your time, tracking contacts, jotting down notes — they're all a part of keeping organized in today's hectic world. iPad offers three apps to help you do just that: Calendar, Contacts, and Notes.

Staying on schedule with Calendar

What would any computing device today be without a calendar feature, given our hectic lives? If the calendar features on your computer and mobile phone don't already keep you on track, try iPad's Calendar. This app provides a handy onscreen daybook you can use to set up appointments (shown in Figure 3-3) and send alerts to remind you about them.

Figure 3-3: Calendar features various views for daily, weekly, or monthly appointments.

You can also sync Calendar with your computer or iPhone, so you don't have to make duplicate entries. See Book I, Chapter 4 for more about syncing and Book V, Chapter 3 for details on using Calendar.

Keeping in touch with Contacts

Today, it's all about who you know and staying in touch. Contacts is the built-in address book feature (see Figure 3-4) for iPad that lets you do just that. You can use Contacts to enter contact information (including photos, if you like, from your Photos app), and share contact information via e-mail. You can also use a search feature to find contacts easily.

Contacts is another app you can sync with your iPhone or computer to save you tedious reentry of information. Read more about this in Book V, Chapter 4.

Want to find your contact in the real world? Tap that person's address in Contacts and the iPad Maps app shows you how to get there!

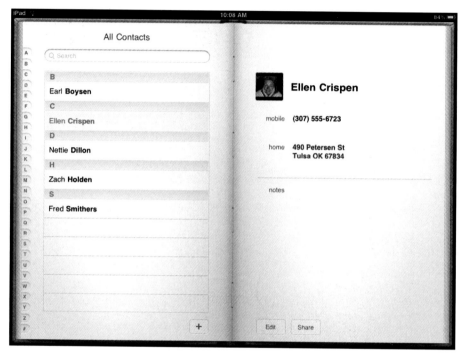

Figure 3-4: Keep the basics about all your contacts in this handy app.

Making Notes

Notes is a simple notepad app where you can enter text or cut and paste text from a Web site or e-mails. You can't do much except save your notes or e-mail them — there are no features for formatting text or inserting objects. But for simple notes on-the-fly, it's useful.

Figure 3-5 shows the familiar yellow pad interface that Notes sports. The font has a casual handwritten look and the icons along the bottom are pretty straightforward. You can move to the previous note, e-mail a note, trash a note, or move to the next note.

If this simple note-keeper appeals to you, read more about the Notes app in Book V, Chapter 2.

You enter info into Notes using the onscreen keyboard. If you are a heavy note taker, consider buying the add-on keyboard dock from Apple. You can slot your iPad onto it, and type away on the small but very usable physical keyboard.

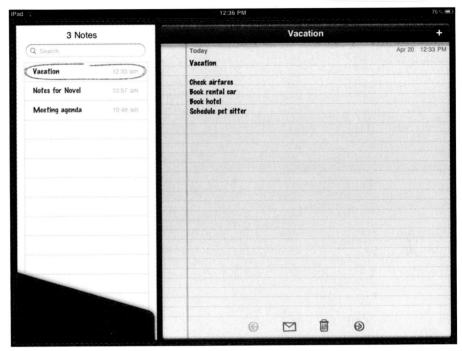

Figure 3-5: In landscape orientation, Notes includes the notepad and an index of notes.

Going Places with Maps

This app is a very cool iPad version of Google Earth. You can view classic maps (see Figure 3-6) or aerial views of addresses, get directions from one place to another by car, foot, or public transportation, and even view an address as if you were standing in front of the building at street level.

If you own a Wi-Fi iPad, a less sophisticated system than 3G can identify your current location and help you find directions from there to other places. 3G iPad owners enjoy a much more targeted location system, but all models can take advantage of the ability to bookmark or share locations, or add a location address to Contacts.

See Book III, Chapter 2 for step-by-step procedures for using the Maps app.

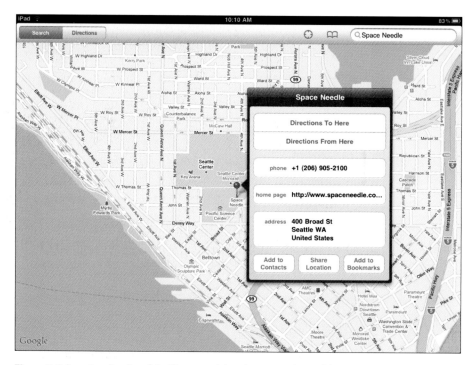

Figure 3-6: Locate a landmark in Maps, and the phone number, address, and Web address appears.

Being Entertained by iPad

One of the joys of iPad is its use as a media consumption tool. Playing music and watching videos is a very entertaining use of iPad, indeed. The bundled iPod and Videos apps make playing media easy to do.

Playing music with iPod

Unless you've been living in a cave without 3G or satellite TV for the last several years, you know perfectly well what iPod is. On your iPad, the iPod app is your media player with a heavy emphasis on music. (See Figure 3-7.) You can use iPod to play movies, music, podcasts, audiobooks, or TV shows that you've downloaded or transferred from your computer to your iPad (though I much prefer Videos for playing back TV shows or movies).

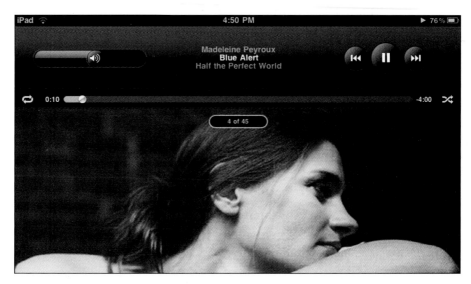

Figure 3-7: While playing music, the iPod app displays an album's cover image.

One of the nicest things about iPod on iPad is the fact that iPad comes with a very nifty sound system and speakers, so the experience of listening with or without headphones will be a pleasing experience to all of you who have become addicted to MP3 listening devices. You can also browse your music by a variety of criteria, such as artist, album, song, or genre.

You can also use the Videos app to play TV or movies, and it offers a few more features for controlling video playback.

Watching videos and browsing YouTube

The Videos app is a media player like iPod, but it specializes in playing videos and offers a few more features, such as chapter breakdowns and information about movie plots and cast for media you got from iTunes. You can move between wide-screen and full-screen display, and it shines at showing high-definition content. See Book II, Chapter 3 for more on the Videos app.

YouTube is the app you should use to access all those videos, good and bad, that people upload to this popular video sharing site. Tap the YouTube icon on your iPad Home screen, and you're taken to the YouTube site. (See Figure 3-8.) Here you can watch videos people have posted, comment on them, share them with others, and so on.

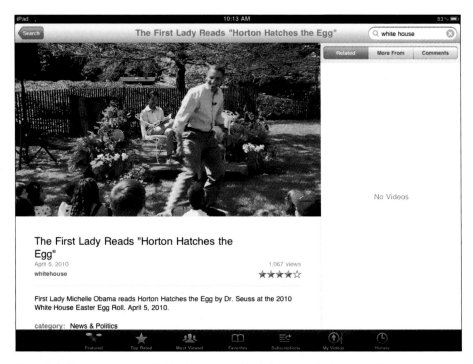

Figure 3-8: Pretty much everybody shows up on YouTube, even the Easter rabbit.

Going Shopping at iTunes and the App Store

The iTunes app takes you to the iTunes Store, where you can shop till you drop (or your iPad battery runs out of juice) for music, movies, TV shows, audiobooks, and podcasts and download them directly to your iPad. You can also preview content before you download it. See Book I, Chapter 4, for more about how to buy apps, and Book VI for a listing of some of the very best apps out there.

Ready for more shopping? Tapping the App Store icon takes you directly to an Apple online store, where you can buy and download apps that do everything from enabling you to play games to building business presentations. At last count, there were over 150,000 apps available for iPad, with more being added all the time. Some were created for iPod and run on iPad; some were created especially for the iPad.

iBooks is an eReader application that isn't built in to iPad out of the box. It's free (like many other apps out there), but you'll have to download it from the App Store. Because iPad has been touted as a great *eReader,* you should definitely consider getting this app or another eReader, such as Kindle or Stanza, as soon as possible. For more about downloading applications for your iPad, see Book II, Chapter 1, and to work with the iBooks' eReader application itself, go to Book II, Chapter 5.

Playing with Game Center

Apple's iOS 4.2, released in November 2010, added the Game Center app to the iPad mix. Game Center is a way to essentially browse game apps in the App Store by bestselling titles. Tap Game Center on your Home Screen, tap one of the sets of colorful icons that appears on the Game Center screen, and you're taken to the app store with information about a game displayed.

From then on it's about obtaining the game (either free or for a price through your itTunes account) and playing it. You can add friends to build your gaming social network and play and track scores for interactive games. See Book I, Chapter 4 for more about buying apps, and Book II, Chapter 6 for more about gaming with your iPad.

Multitasking with iPad

Version 4.2 of the iOS for iPad made multitasking available. That means that you don't have to return to the Home screen every time you want to open another app.

As on the iPhone, multitasking is dead simple. With one app open, just double-tap the Home button and a vertical bar with app icons appears along the bottom of the screen. Scroll to find the one you want, tap it, and it opens.

Chapter 4: Setting Up iTunes to Sync and Buy Apps

In This Chapter

- ✔ Getting connected to the Internet
- ✔ Downloading iTunes and creating an account
- ✔ Making iPad settings in iTunes
- ✔ Syncing iPad to your computer
- ✔ Purchasing apps from the App Store

A pple made its iTunes service the default way for you to manage settings for how your iPad *syncs* with your computer so you can share information and content like calendar events, pictures, music, movies, and contacts. Before you can use iTunes to sync, you have to download the software and if you want to make purchases from the store, open an iTunes account, both of which I cover in this chapter.

Some apps, such as Contacts and Videos, come pre-installed on your iPad. But, as you know if you're an iPhone user, there's a world of other apps out there, including many that you can get for your iPad. Once you've set up iTunes, you can buy apps (or download free ones) in the iPad App Store using your iTunes account. Some are free, such as iBooks, and some you can get for a price (typically from 99 cents to about $10, though a few go up to $50 or more).

In this chapter, I tell you how to set iTunes to sync your iPad with your computer and how you can acquire apps for your iPad through the App Store.

Once you have an iTunes account, you can also shop iTunes for music, videos, audiobooks, and more. See Book II, Chapter 1, for more about shopping for multimedia content.

Connecting to the Internet

In order to browse the Web, access Mail, and shop online, you have to first be connected to the Internet, so I'm putting this information right up front. How you connect to the Internet depends on which iPad model you own:

✔ The Wi-Fi–only iPad connects to the Internet via a Wi-Fi network. You may already have set up such a network in your own home using your computer and some equipment from your Internet provider. You can also connect through public Wi-Fi networks *(Hotspots)*. You probably have already noticed how many Hotspots your town or city has: Look for Internet cafes, coffee shops, hotels, libraries, transportation centers such as airports or bus stations, and so on. In fact, once you start looking, you'll notice lots of signs alerting you to free Wi-Fi — they're everywhere.

✔ If you own a Wi-Fi and 3G-enabled iPad, you can still use a Wi-Fi connection, but you can also use a paid data network through AT&T to connect from just about anywhere via their cellular network, just as you connect with your mobile phone.

See Book I, Chapter 1, for more about the capabilities of different iPad models and the costs associated with 3G.

When you're in range of a Hotspot, if access to several nearby networks is available you may see a message asking you to tap one to select it. After you select one (or if only one network is available), you will see a message similar to the one shown in Figure 4-1 if a password is required. Enter a network password, and then tap the Join button.

Enter the network password...

then tap Join

Figure 4-1: Joining a Wi-Fi network.

Free public Wi-Fi networks typically don't require a password. However, that means they're *unsecured,* so it's possible for someone else to track your online activities over the network. No matter how much you might be tempted, try to avoid accessing financial accounts or sending sensitive e-mails when connected to a public Hotspot.

Setting Up iTunes

Think of iTunes as Apple's version of the Mall of America. It's both the place from which you can manage your iPad settings for syncing content, and a great big online store where you can buy content and apps for your MacBook, iPod, iPhone, and iPad. It's also the place where you can make settings for several of these devices to control how they download and share content. Even if you find some other sources of apps or content for your iPad, it's worth having an iTunes account, if only to use the settings it provides.

You actually have to have access to an iTunes account to register your iPad when you first buy it before you can use it. In my case and perhaps in yours, the nice man at the Apple Store activated my iPad before I left the store with it, so I set up my own iTunes account the first time I needed to buy a hot movie title.

Downloading iTunes to your computer

Your first step in connecting to iTunes is simply to download the software. You should do this on your old-fashioned computer or laptop. As of this writing, iTunes 10.0 is the latest version of this software. iTunes 10.0 requires that you have Windows XP Service Pack 2 or later on your PC, or Mac OS X version 10.4.11 or later on your Apple computer. You'll also need a broadband Internet connection, 512MB of RAM (1GB for playing HD video), and at least a 1024 x 768 screen resolution for viewing content.

You can probably handle this one yourself and if you're a Mac user, you've probably already got iTunes, but just in case, here are the steps involved in downloading iTunes:

1. **On your computer, go to www.apple.com/itunes using your browser of choice.**

2. **Click the iTunes Free Download link shown in Figure 4-2 and in the screen that follows, click the Download Now button.**

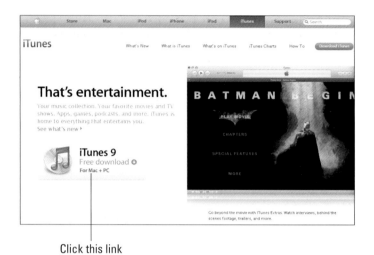

Click this link

Figure 4-2: Get the free iTunes download.

3. **In the dialog that appears (see Figure 4-3), click Run. The iTunes application downloads.**

4. **When the download is complete, another dialog appears, asking if you want to run the software; click Run.**

   The iTunes Installer appears. (See Figure 4-4.)

Click Run

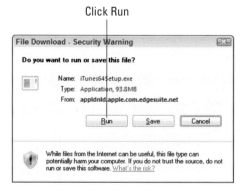

Figure 4-3: Your garden-variety download dialog.

5. **Click Next.**

6. **Select the I Accept the Terms of the License Agreement check box in the following dialog and click Next.**

7. **Review the installation options and click to deselect ones you don't want to use, and then click the Install button shown in Figure 4-5.**

   A dialog appears, showing the installation progress.

8. **When a dialog appears telling you the installation is complete, take it at its word and click Finish.**

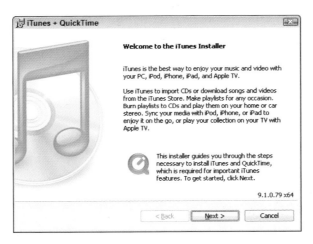

Figure 4-4: The iTunes Installer gets you set up quickly.

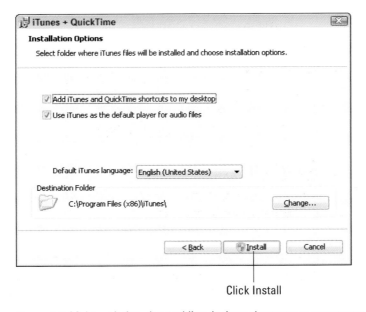

Click Install

Figure 4-5: Make a choice about adding desktop shortcuts on your computer here.

You've probably already guessed that you'll have to restart your computer if it's a Windows machine for the configuration settings made during the installation to take effect. Once your computer restarts, you can use the iTunes desktop shortcut (if you decided to create one) to open iTunes.

Apple updates things all the time, so occasionally on your computer click Help, Check for Updates from iTunes to get any updated version. Also, when you connect your iPad to your computer and open iTunes, it will alert you if there is an update to your iPad operating system and if you choose to update, will download the update and sync it to your iPad.

Getting an iTunes account

To be able to buy and download items from the Apple Store (even free apps and content) on your iPad, you have to open an iTunes account. (Don't worry. It's free, though you'll have to provide a credit card.)

Follow these steps to get your iTunes account:

1. **First, open iTunes.**

   This is the application you downloaded to your computer in the preceding section. If you didn't create a desktop shortcut, you can open iTunes from your computer's Start menu in Windows or by clicking the iTunes item in the Mac Dock.

2. **Choose the Store menu and select Create Account from the menu that appears. (See Figure 4-6.)**

3. **In the Welcome to the iTunes Store screen that appears, click Continue.**

4. **In the following screen (see Figure 4-7), click to select the I Have Read and Agree to the iTunes Terms and Conditions check box and then click the Continue button.**

5. **In the Create iTunes Store Account (Apple ID) screen that follows (see Figure 4-8), fill in the information fields, click the last two check boxes to deselect them if you don't want to get e-mail from the Apple Store, and click the Continue button.**

6. **In the Provide a Payment Method screen that appears (see Figure 4-9), enter your payment information and then click the Continue button.**

7. **The screen shown in Figure 4-10 appears, confirming that your account has been opened. Click the Done button to return to the iTunes store.**

Select this option

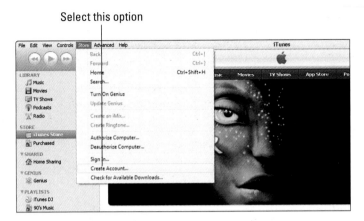

Figure 4-6: Start the process to create an account.

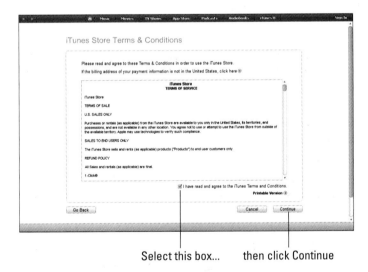

Select this box...   then click Continue

Figure 4-7: Click the usual check box for agreeing to terms, and proceed!

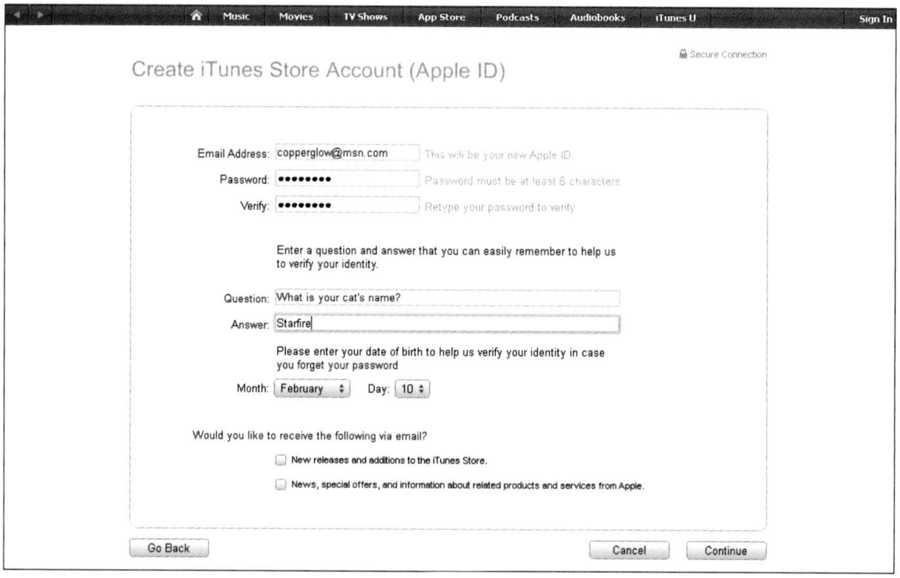

Figure 4-8: Choose any question and fill in the answer you want (cats optional).

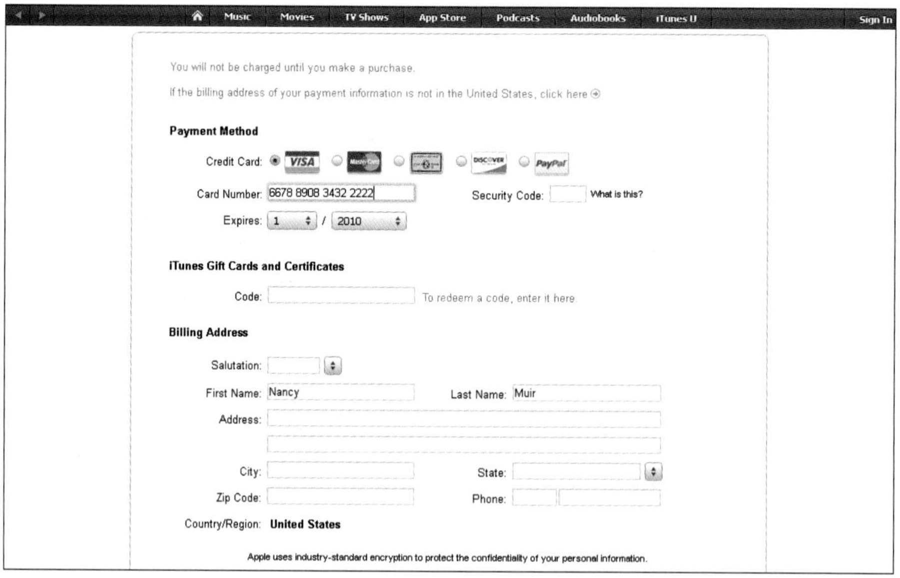

Figure 4-9: Okay, you know the routine: fill in your payment information. . . .

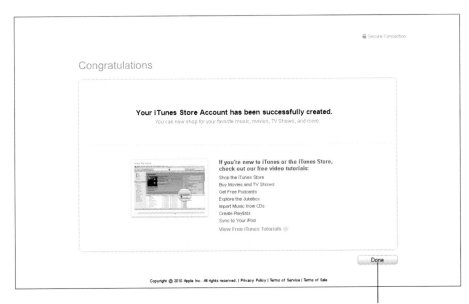

Click Done to return to the store

Figure 4-10: Success — you are an official iTunes person.

Making Settings and Syncing

Remember that cute photo of your promotion party you have on your hard drive? How do you get that onto iPad so you can show it off at the next family reunion? Or how about that audiobook on career success you bought and downloaded to your laptop on your last business trip? It would sure be handy to get that sucker onto your iPad. Never fear: By making a few easy settings and syncing with your computer, you can bring all that content over in a (you should pardon the term, Steve Jobs) flash.

Making iPad settings using iTunes

When you plug your Dock Connector to USB Cable into your iPad and computer and then open iTunes, you'll find a whole group of settings becomes available. These help you determine how content will sync between the two devices.

Here's how to use the iTunes settings for your iPad:

1. **Connect your iPad to your computer using the Dock Connector to USB Cable.**

   Plug the data connection cord into your iPad (using the wider connector) and plug the other end of the cord into a USB port on your computer.

2. **Open your iTunes software.**

   (On a Windows computer, choose Start⇨All Programs⇨iTunes; on a Mac, click the iTunes icon in the Dock.)

   iTunes opens, and your iPad is listed in the Devices section of the left pane.

3. **Click the name of your iPad in the Devices section, and a series of tabs displays, as shown in Figure 4-11.**

   The tabs offer information about your iPad and settings for items such as how to download music, movies, or podcasts. (You can see the simple choices on the Music tab in Figure 4-12.) The settings relate to what kind of content you want to download, and whether you want to download it automatically when you sync or do it manually. See Table 4-1 for an overview of the settings that are available on each tab. Make all settings for the types of content you plan to obtain on your computer and sync to your iPad, and then click the Sync button in the bottom-right corner to sync files with the iPad.

Click on your iPad...   to display this series of tabs

Figure 4-11: The various tabs you can use to control iPad from iTunes.

Figure 4-12: Settings to control how music syncs to your iPad.

Table 4-1	iPad Settings in iTunes
Tab	**Description**
Summary	Perform updates to iPad software and set general sync options.
Info	Choose what information to sync: contacts, calendars, e-mail, bookmarks, notes.
Apps	Sync apps you've downloaded to your computer to iPad.
Music	Choose what music to download to your iPad when you sync.
Movies	Select the option to automatically download movies or not.
TV Shows	Choose which shows and episodes to automatically sync.
Podcasts	Choose which podcasts and episodes to automatically sync.
iTunes U	Select the course collections and items to sync to iPad.
Books	Choose to sync all or selected audio and electronic books to iPad.
Photos	Choose the folders from which you want to download photos.

Be alert to warnings when you sync your iPad and computer because, depending on your settings, you may overwrite or erase content you've downloaded when you sync. You may want to copy content you've downloaded to your iPad directly to your iTunes library before syncing so your computer doesn't erase what you've downloaded during the sync.

Syncing iPad to your computer

Now that you've made settings for what content to download in iTunes (see the preceding section), you can use the data connection cord to connect your iPad and computer to sync info like contacts and calendar settings.

With iTunes installed on your computer and an iTunes account set up, follow these simple steps to sync to your iPad:

1. **Plug the data connection cord into your iPad.**

2. **Plug the other end of the data connection cord into your computer.**

   iTunes opens and shows an item in the left pane for your iPad and an icon indicating that it's syncing. (See Figure 4-13.) Your iPad screen shows the words "Sync in Progress."

Icon indicating the iPad is syncing

Figure 4-13: Syncing connects your computer and iPad so you can share data.

When the syncing is complete, your Home screen returns on the iPad, and iTunes shows the message in Figure 4-14 indicating that the iPad sync is complete and that it's okay for you disconnect the cable. Any media you chose in your iTunes settings to have transferred, and any new photos in the folder on your computer containing pictures, have been transferred to your iPad.

3. **After syncing, unplug the data connection cord from your iPad and your computer.**

iTunes lets you know when syncing is complete

Figure 4-14: You're done. Syncing is complete.

If you're into social networking, you might try tapping the Ping button at the bottom of the iTunes screen to check out Apple's new entry in the social networking world. It's described as a great way to follow your favorite artists or friends and keep tuned to the music everybody's listening to. As of this writing it's not a very robust service, but as with all things social on the Internet, it could grow very fast!

Buying or Downloading Free Apps

Apps are the technology equivalent of all the sports paraphernalia (caps, t-shirts, beer can cooler sleeves, and so on) that you might buy to support your favorite team. However, apps also provide all kinds of functionality, from the ability to plan travel, manage finances, and find local restaurants and gas stations to hard-core business productivity and serious gaming fun.

Most iPhone apps will work on your iPad, so if you own the pricey mobile phone and have favorite apps on it, you might want to use them on your iPad! Also, for more about my recommended apps, see Book VI.

Searching the App Store

Apple is not one to miss a profit opportunity, so naturally, one of the iPad built-in apps is the App Store. This is the apps portal that will get you to thousands of great apps for everything from games to bean counting.

If you want to get non-Apple apps, such as Google Voice, you can join the estimated 4 million people who have done what's called *jailbreaking* to liberate their iPhones or iPads from the tyranny of getting apps solely through iTunes. Check out this article for details about jailbreaking, but be forewarned that jailbreaking voids your iPad warranty: http://gizmodo.com/5530906/jailbreaking-your-ipad-how-you-can-and-why-you-should.

Here's your quick introduction to using the App Store to obtain whatever apps your heart desires (including Stethoscope Expert, to monitor your heart):

1. **Tap the App Store icon on your iPad Home screen.**

   The site shown in Figure 4-15 appears.

2. **At this point, you have several options for finding apps:**

   - Tap in the Search field, enter a search term, and tap the Search button on the onscreen keyboard to see results.

   - Tap the Previous or Next arrow to see more selections, or tap the See All link to display all selections.

   - Tap one of the images of an app in the Spotlight area at the top of the screen to see more details about it.

- Tap the New or What's Hot tab at the top of the screen to see those categories of apps.

- Tap the Top Charts button on the bottom of the screen to see what free and paid apps other people are downloading most.

- Tap the Categories button to search by types of apps, as shown in Figure 4-16.

Figure 4-15: Welcome to the App Store!

Figure 4-16: Find the apps that fit your needs.

Getting apps from the App Store

Buying apps requires that you have an iTunes account, which I cover earlier in this chapter. Once you have an account, you can use the saved payment information there to buy apps with a few simple steps, or download free apps. I strongly recommend you install the free iBooks app, so I walk you through the steps for getting it here.

1. **With the App Store open, tap the Search field and enter** iBooks.

2. **Tap the Price button (which in this case reads "Free") for iBooks in the results that appear, as shown in Figure 4-17.**

   Note that, to get a paid app, you'd tap on the Price button which would display the cost of the app at this point.

3. **The Price button changes to read Install App (or in the case of a paid app, the button changes to read Buy App). Tap that button.**

   You may be asked to enter your iTunes password and tap the OK button to proceed.

   The app downloads; if you purchase an app that isn't free, at this point your credit card is charged for the purchase price.

Only pre-installed apps are located on the first Home screen of your iPad by default. Apps you download are placed on additional Home screens, and you have to scroll to view and use them unless you move them to a different Home screen. See the next task for help in finding your newly downloaded apps using multiple Home screens.

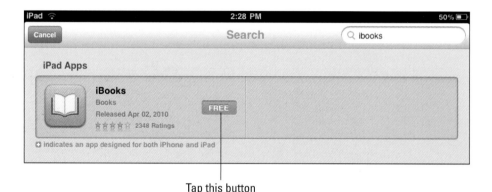

Tap this button

Figure 4-17: Tap the app you need.

If you're a road warrior, you'll be glad to hear that the travel industry is all over apps to help you get around, as the iPad is such a logical travel companion. Lonely Planet has released country guides for the iPad, and iPhone apps for travellers are being re-created for iPad. See Book III, Chapter 3, if you're someone who hits the road on a regular basis and want to make the most of your iPad.

Organizing your apps

iPad can display up to 11 Home screens. By default, the first contains pre-installed apps; other screens are created to contain any apps you download or sync to your iPad. At the bottom of the original iPad Home screen (just above the Dock), a magnifying glass icon represents the Search screen to the left of the primary Home screen; dots that appear indicate how many screens there are and which Home screen you are on at the moment, as shown in Figure 4-18.

Here's some advice on how to organize your apps:

1. **Tap the Home button to open the last displayed Home screen.**

2. **Flick your finger from right to left to move to the next Home screen.**

   Note that the dots near the bottom of the screen indicate which Home screen you're on.

3. **To reorganize apps on a Home screen, press and hold any app on that page.**

   The app icons begin to jiggle. (See Figure 4-19.)

4. **Press, hold, and drag an app icon to another location on the screen to move it.**

5. **Tap the Home button to stop all those icons from jiggling!**

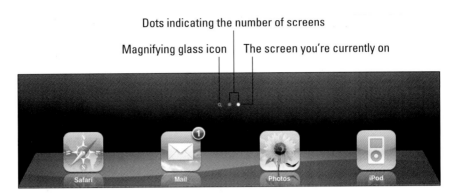

Dots indicating the number of screens

Magnifying glass icon | The screen you're currently on

Figure 4-18: Finding apps on the various iPad Home screens.

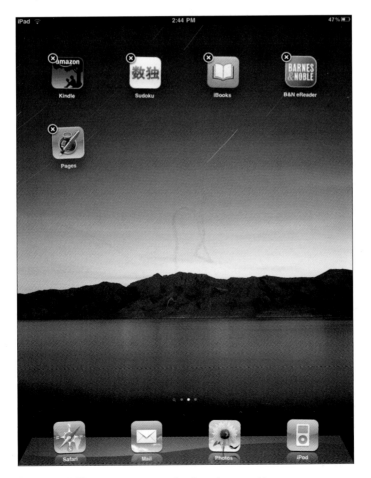

Figure 4-19: Move an app to another location on a Home screen.

To move an app from one page to another, while things are jiggling, you can tap and drag an app to the left or right to move it to the next home screen.

Organizing apps in folders

As with iPhone, iPad lets you organize apps in folders (if you have iOS version 4.2 or later). The process is simple:

1. **Tap and hold an app till all apps do their jiggle dance.**

2. **Drag an app on top of another app.**

   A bar appears across the screen showing the two apps and a file with a placeholder name (see Figure 4-20).

Figure 4-20: Collect apps in logical folders to help you save Home screen space.

3. **To change the name, tap in the field at the end of the placeholder name, and the keyboard appears.**

4. **Press the Back key to delete the name and type one of your own.**

5. **Tap anywhere outside of the bar to save the name.**

6. **Tap the Home key to stop all that jiggling!**

Deleting apps you no longer need

Not all apps are endlessly entertaining or useful. When you no longer need an app that you have installed, it's time to get rid of it to save some space on your iPad. (Note, however, that you can't delete apps that come built into the iPad.)

To send an app on its way, do this:

1. **Display the Home screen that contains the app you want to delete.**
2. **Press and hold the app until all apps begin to jiggle.**
3. **Tap the Delete button for the app you want to delete. (See Figure 4-21.)**

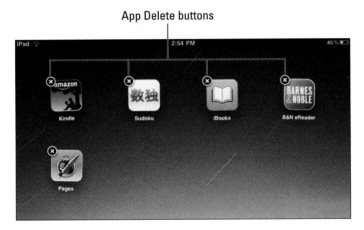

App Delete buttons

Figure 4-21: Tap Delete on the jiggling app.

4. **In the confirmation dialog shown in Figure 4-22, tap Delete to proceed with the deletion.**

   A dialog asking you to rate an app before deleting it appears.
5. **You can tap the Rate button to rate the app or No Thanks to opt out of the survey.**

Figure 4-22: Cancel if you have regrets; otherwise, tap Delete to send the app on its way.

Chapter 5: Browsing the Web

*G*etting on the Internet with your iPad is easy, using its Wi-Fi or 3G capabilities. Once you're online, the built-in browser, Safari, can take you all around the Web. Safari will be familiar to you if you've used an Apple device before or used the browser on your PC. On iPad, you're actually using the mobile version of Safari, which should also be familiar to iPhone users.

If you've never used Safari, this chapter helps you get up to speed quickly. In this chapter, you discover how to connect your iPad to the Internet and navigate among Web pages. Along the way, you learn how to place a bookmark for a favorite site or Web clip on your Home screen. You can also view your browsing history, save online images to your Photo library, and e-mail a hotlink to a friend.

Getting on the Internet

How you connect to the Internet depends on which iPad model you own:

✔ The Wi-Fi–only iPad obviously connects to the Internet via a Wi-Fi network. You may have set up such a network in your own home using your computer and some equipment from your Internet provider. You can also connect through public *Hotspots* (locations that provide wireless access to an Internet connection) in Internet cafes, coffee shops, hotels, libraries, transportation centers such as airports or bus stations, and so on.

✔ If you own a 3G-enabled iPad, you can still use a Wi-Fi connection, but you can also use a paid data network through AT&T to connect from just about anywhere via their cellular network.

When you're in range of a Hotspot or available Wi-Fi network, if access to several nearby networks is available you may see a message asking you to tap one to select it. After you select one (or if only one network is available), you will see a message similar to the one shown in Figure 5-1. If it's required, just enter a network password, and then tap the Join button and you'll be connected.

Enter the network password...

then tap Join

Figure 5-1: The network sign in dialog.

See Book I, Chapter 1, for more about the capabilities of different iPad models and the costs associated with 3G.

Free public Wi-Fi networks typically don't require a password, which is cool because it means your connection is free. However, that also means they're *unsecured,* so it's possible for someone else to track your online activities over the network. Bottom line: avoid accessing financial accounts or sending sensitive e-mails when your iPad is connected to a public Hotspot.

Exploring Safari

Just in case you've never used Safari, here's a quick rundown of how it works on your iPad. It offers all the typical browser tools, but an important iPad twist is how you can use gestures on the touchscreen to manipulate pages and navigate the Web.

Though Safari is a fine browser, you aren't limited to it. You can download other browsers to iPad, such as Atomic Web Browser and Duo Browser. Check out the App Store for the latest available browsers.

Try the following steps to get practice using Safari:

1. **After you're connected to a network, tap the Safari button on the Home screen.**

   Safari opens, probably displaying the Apple iPad home page the first time you go online using it. (See Figure 5-2.)

Figure 5-2: These tools will be familiar to you from almost any browser you may have used.

2. **Double-tap the screen with a single finger to enlarge it, as shown in Figure 5-3.**

   Double-tap again to return to the default screen size.

3. **Put your finger on the screen and drag upward to scroll down the page.**

4. **To return to the top of the Web page, put your finger on the screen and drag downward, or tap the Status bar at the top of the screen.**

You can also use the pinch method (see Book I, Chapter 2) to enlarge or reduce the size of a Web page on your screen. Using this method, you can enlarge or reduce the screen to various sizes, giving you more flexibility than with the double-tap your finger method described in Step 2.

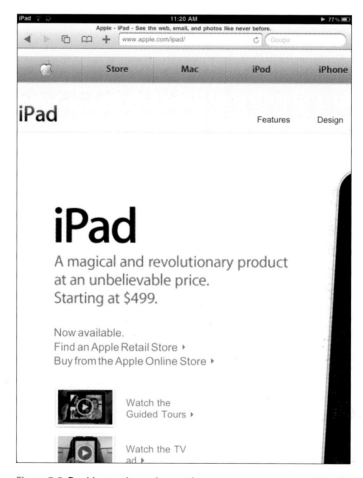

Figure 5-3: Double-tapping enlarges the screen so you can read the fine print.

When you enlarge the screen, you get more control using two fingers to drag left to right or top to bottom on the page. In a reduced screen, one finger works fine for these gestures.

Navigating among Web pages

I expect that most of you have entered URLs and used the Next and Previous buttons to navigate around the Web. However, getting used to the iPad's onscreen keyboard differs slightly from a standard keyboard, and it might help you to run through how you navigate with the mobile version of Safari.

Follow these steps for a bit of navigating practice:

1. **Tap in the Address field.**

   The onscreen keyboard appears, as shown in Figure 5-4.

 2. **Enter a Web address, using the .com key to make entry faster.**

   Note: By holding down the .com key, you get access to options like `.edu`, `.gov`, and `.net`.

3. **Tap the Go key on the keyboard. (Refer to Figure 5-4.)**

   The Web site appears.

    • If, for some reason, a page doesn't display, tap the Reload icon on the right side of the Address field.

    • If Safari is loading a Web page and you change your mind, you can tap the Cancel icon (the X) that appears on the right side of the Address field during this process to stop loading the page.

 4. **Tap the Previous arrow to go backward to the first page.**

 5. **Tap the Next arrow to go forward to the second page you displayed.**

6. **To follow a link to another Web page, tap the link with your finger.**

   If you would like to view the destination Web address of the link before you tap it, just touch and hold the link, and a menu appears that displays the address at the top, as shown in Figure 5-5.

 By default, AutoFill is turned on in iPad, causing entries you make in fields such as the Address field to automatically display possible matching entries. You can turn AutoFill off using iPad Settings.

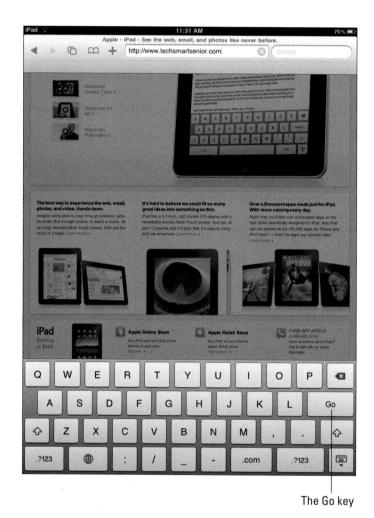

The Go key

Figure 5-4: This keyboard requires you do a few unique things to use numbers and symbols.

Unless you live in a cave, you know by now that Apple doesn't support Flash, the technology that *lots* of sites use to play videos. That's because Steve Jobs considers that Flash is a poor technology. Whatever the justification, you have a couple of options. There are some sites posting non-Flash versions of content, so you can search these out using the keywords *non-flash movies*. Or you can convert a Flash file to AVI or MPG movie format. To do this, you can download a free tool, such as one of these:

✔ **swf>>avi:** www.avi-swf-convert.com

✔ **SWF to Video Scout:** http://tinyurl.com/28a4g7f

The link's Web address

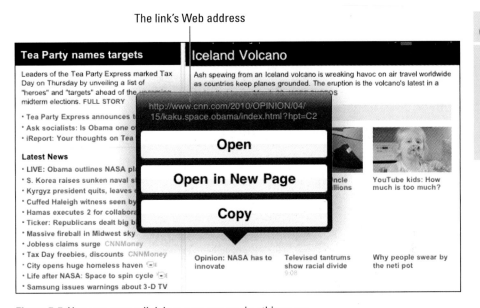

Figure 5-5: You can open a link in a new page using this menu.

If you like tabbed browsing as found on other browsers such as Internet Explorer, the desktop version of Safari, and Opera, consider downloading the Atomic Web Browser app from the App Store. The app provides more than tabs: You can enlarge the browser to full screen and get a few more search tools and some finger-swipe shortcuts.

Viewing browsing history

As you know, when you move around the Web your browser keeps a record of your browsing history. This can be handy when you visit a site that you want to view again but you forget its address. (We've all done it.) On your iPad, you use the Bookmarks menu to get to your history.

Follow these steps to browse your browsing history:

1. **With Safari open, tap the Bookmarks icon.**

2. **In the menu shown in Figure 5-6, tap History.**

3. **In the History list that appears (see Figure 5-7), tap a site to navigate to it.**

Tap this option

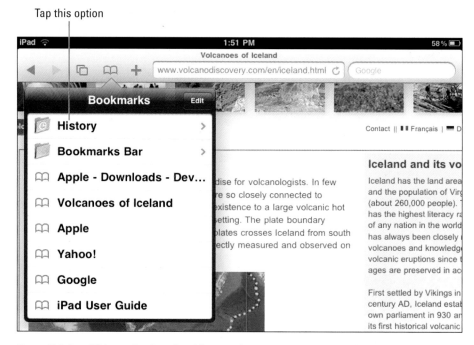

Figure 5-6: In addition to bookmarks, this menu is your gateway to your browsing history.

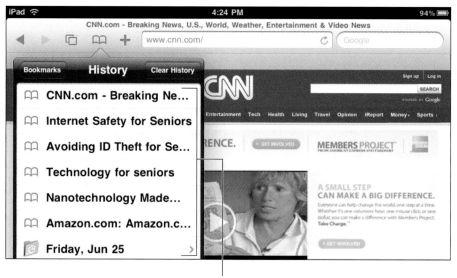

Tap a site to view it

Figure 5-7: Use your finger to scroll down to view more of this list.

To clear the history, tap the Clear History button. (Refer to Figure 5-7.) This is useful when you don't want your spouse or children seeing where you've been browsing for birthday or holiday presents!

Displaying Web pages as thumbnails

Another great way to access your favorite Web sites is to open multiple pages in a thumbnail display. You can display up to nine pages in this multiple-page view and tap any open page to go there.

 1. **With Safari open, tap the Multiple Pages icon in the Status bar.**

Recently visited pages are displayed as thumbnails, as shown in Figure 5-8.

Tap to delete

New Page thumbnail

Figure 5-8: Add or delete pages from this view for quick access to your favorites.

2. **In this view, you can do several things:**

- To delete a page from this view, tap the Delete icon in a Web site's upper-left corner (the circle with an X in it).

- To go to a new page, tap the New Page thumbnail and then tap in the Address field and enter a Web address.

- To go to a full view of any of the pages shown, tap or pinch it.

The Multiple Pages feature isn't the same as the History feature, which automatically keeps a record of recently visited sites. You set up multiple pages yourself. Consequently, clearing your history won't clear the multiple pages view of sites you have set up there. To remove sites from this view, you have to delete them one by one.

Searching the Web

If you don't know the address of the site you want to visit (or you want to research a topic or find something you need online), you need to get acquainted with Safari's search feature on iPad. By default, Safari uses the Google search engine.

1. **With Safari open, tap in the Search field. (It's to the right of the Address field; refer to Figure 5-2.)**

   The onscreen keyboard appears. (See Figure 5-9.)

2. **Enter a search word or phrase and then tap the Search key on your keyboard.**

3. **In the search results that are displayed, tap a link to a site to visit it.**

You can change your default search engine from Google to Bing or Yahoo! In iPad Settings, tap Safari, and then tap Search Engine. Tap Yahoo!, and your default browser changes.

You can browse for specific items such as images, videos, or maps by tapping any of the links at the top of the Google screen. Also, tap the Advanced Search link to the right of Google's Search button to specify more search details and narrow your search. If you'd like more tips about searching the Web efficiently, go to www.google.com/help/features.html or http://help.yahoo.com/us/yahoo/search/basics.

**Book I
Chapter 5**

Browsing the Web

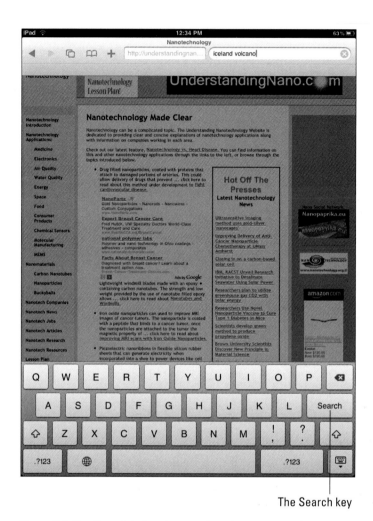

The Search key

Figure 5-9: Use Search to locate a word or phrase on any site.

Adding and Using Bookmarks

Bookmarks, which you have probably used in other browsers, are a way to save favorite sites so you can easily visit them again. Follow these steps to add bookmarks:

1. **With a site you want to bookmark displayed, tap the Add icon.**

2. **In the menu that appears (see Figure 5-10), tap Add Bookmark.**

3. **In the Add Bookmark dialog shown in Figure 5-11, edit the name of the bookmark (if you wish) by tapping the name of the site and using the onscreen keyboard to edit its name.**

4. **Tap the Save button.**

 5. **To go to the bookmark, tap the Bookmarks icon.**

6. **In the menu that appears (see Figure 5-12), tap the bookmarked site you want to visit.**

Tap this option

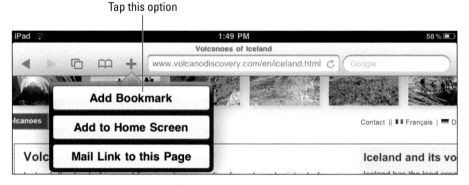

Figure 5-10: Choose to add a bookmark in this menu.

Edit the name here

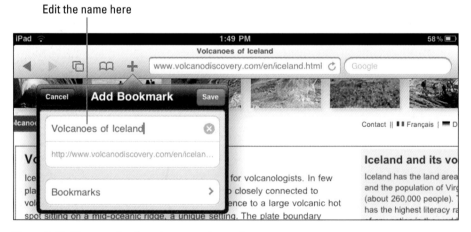

Figure 5-11: Give your bookmark a name that makes sense to you.

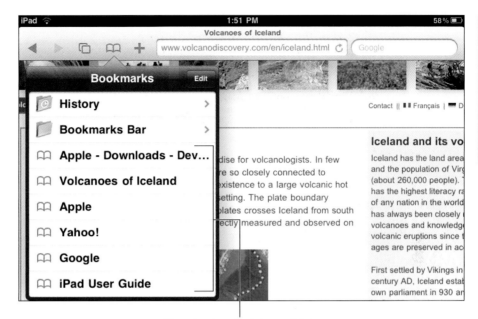

Tap a bookmarked site to visit it

Figure 5-12: Tap to go to a favorite bookmark.

If you want to sync your bookmarks on your iPad browser to your computer or using your MobileMe account, connect your iPad to your computer and make sure the setting on the Info tab of iTunes has Sync Safari Bookmarks activated.

When you tap the Bookmarks button, you can use the Bookmarks Bar option to create folders to organize your bookmarks. First, turn on the Bookmarks Bar Display in iPad Settings. When you next add a bookmark, you can then choose to add the new bookmark to any folder by clicking the Bookmarks button in the dialog that appears.

Adding Web Clips to the Home Screen

Web Clips is a feature that allows you to save a Web site as an icon on your Home screen so you can go to it at any time with one tap. You can then reorganize those icons just as you can reorganize apps icons. (See the preceding chapter for information on organizing apps on Home screens.)

Here are the steps for adding Web Clips:

1. **With Safari open and the site you want to add displayed, tap the Add icon.**
2. **In the menu that appears (see Figure 5-13), tap Add to Home Screen.**
3. **In the Add to Home dialog that appears (see Figure 5-14), you can edit the name of the site to be more descriptive (if you like) by tapping the name of the site and using the onscreen keyboard to edit its name.**
4. **Tap the Add button.**

   The shortcut to the site is added to your Home screen.

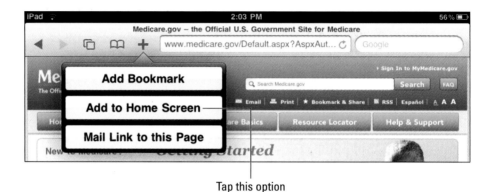

Tap this option

Figure 5-13: Set up a Web Clip to go to a favorite site from your Home screen.

Edit the name here

Figure 5-14: Give your Web Clip a descriptive name or use the site's URL.

You can have up to 11 Home screens on your iPad, so all the Web Clips and apps you download have room to spread out. If you want to delete an item from your Home screen for any reason, press and hold the icon on the Home screen until all the items on the screen start to jiggle and Delete badges appear on every item except pre-installed apps. Tap the Delete button on the item you want to delete, and it's gone. (To get rid of the jiggle, tap the Home button.)

Saving an Image to Your Photo Library

Have you found a photo you like online? Maybe your BF's Facebook image, or a picture of your upcoming vacation spot? You can easily save images you find online to the iPad Photos app library. Here's how:

1. **Display a Web page that contains an image you want to copy.**

2. **Press and hold the image.**

   The menu in Figure 5-15 appears.

Tap this option

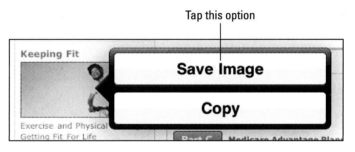

Figure 5-15: Quickly saving an online image into Photos.

3. **Tap Save Image.**

   The image is saved to your Photos library.

Be careful about copying images from the Internet and using them for business or promotional activities. Most images are copyrighted in some fashion, and you may violate that copyright if you use an image in a brochure for your association or a flyer for your community group. Note that some search engines, through their advanced search settings, offer the option of browsing only for images that aren't copyrighted.

E-Mailing a Link

If you find a great site that you want to share, you can do so easily by sending a link in an e-mail. Follow these steps to do so:

1. **With Safari open and the site you want to share displayed, tap the Add icon.**

2. **In the menu shown in Figure 5-16, tap Mail Link to This Page.**

3. **In the message form that appears (see Figure 5-17), enter a recipient's e-mail address, subject, and your message.**

4. **Tap Send, and the e-mail goes on its way.**

The e-mail is sent from the default e-mail account you have set up on iPad. For more about setting up an e-mail account, see the next chapter.

When entering text in any online form, such as an e-mail message or search box, you can take advantage of Safari's AutoFill feature. Turn this on in the Safari area of iPad's Settings. Safari can then use information from iPad's Contacts app and remember names and passwords you've entered before to offer options for completing text entries as you type.

Tap this option

Figure 5-16: Found something worth sharing? E-mail it using this menu.

Figure 5-17: Use this simple e-mail form to send an image and message.

Chapter 6: Working with E-Mail in Mail

In This Chapter

✓ **Adding a Gmail, Yahoo!, or AOL account**

✓ **Setting up a POP3 e-mail account**

✓ **Opening Mail and reading messages**

✓ **Searching e-mail**

✓ **Deleting an e-mail**

✓ **Organizing e-mail**

*W*hat use would an iPad be if you couldn't stay in touch with your friends online? You can access an existing e-mail account using the handy Mail app supplied with your iPad, or if the mail service has a Web-based interface, you can sign in using the Safari browser. Using Mail involves adding an e-mail account. Then you can use Mail to write, retrieve, and forward messages.

Mail offers a small set of folders for organizing your messages, and a handy search feature. In this chapter, you find out about Mail and its various features.

 If you're wondering about IM (instant messaging) and iPad, there's no built-in app for it in the first version. You'll need to get an app for that, like BeejiveIM for iPad, AIM for iPad, or IM+ from the App Store.

Adding a Gmail, Yahoo!, or AOL Account

To use the Mail app to access e-mail on iPad, you first have to set up an existing e-mail account on your iPad. You can add one or more e-mail accounts using iPad Settings. If you set up multiple accounts, you can then switch between accounts by tapping an account name in the upper-left corner of the displayed inbox, and then tapping Accounts and choosing which account to display. Or, you can use the consolidated inbox and check your mail from all active accounts on one page.

If you have a Gmail, Yahoo!, or AOL account, iPad pretty much automates the setup. Here are the steps to get you going with any of these e-mail providers:

1. **Tap the Settings icon on the Home screen.**

2. **In the Settings dialog, tap Mail, Contacts, Calendars.**

   The settings shown in Figure 6-1 appear.

3. **Tap Add Account.**

   The options shown in Figure 6-2 appear.

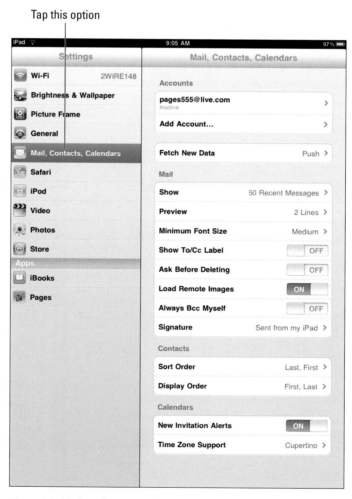

Figure 6-1: Mail settings allow you to set up multiple e-mail accounts.

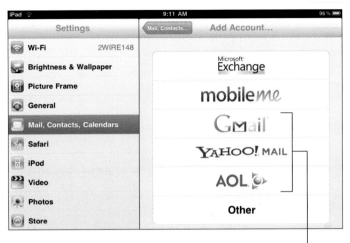

Tap on your e-mail provider

Figure 6-2: Choosing built-in e-mail providers is a quick way to get set up, if you have an account with one.

4. **Tap Gmail, Yahoo! Mail, or AOL and then enter your account information in the form that appears. (See Figure 6-3.)**

5. **After iPad takes a moment to verify your account information, tap Save.**

   The account is saved, and you can now open it using Mail.

If you have a Microsoft Exchange or MobileMe account, you can sync to your computer to exchange contact and calendar information as well as e-mail. See the iPad User Guide for more about these options. See Book III, Chapter 1, for more about working with Microsoft Exchange accounts.

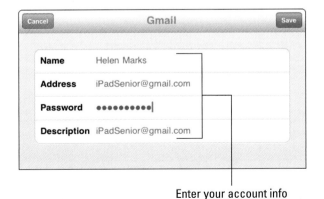

Enter your account info

Figure 6-3: Enter your name, e-mail address, and password, and iPad finds your settings for you.

Setting Up a POP3 E-Mail Account

You can also set up most e-mail accounts, such as those from Windows Live, Comcast, or Earthlink, by obtaining the host name from the provider. To set up an existing account for an account with a provider other than Gmail, Yahoo!, or AOL, you may need to enter the account settings yourself.

Follow these steps to set up an IMAP or POP3 account:

1. **First, tap the Settings icon on the Home screen.**

2. **In Settings, tap Mail, Contacts, Calendars, and then tap Add Account.**

3. **In the screen that appears (refer to Figure 6-2), tap Other.**

   The form in Figure 6-4 appears.

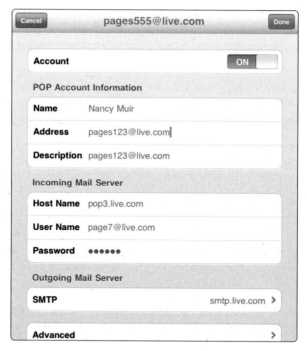

Figure 6-4: Contact your provider for setting info if iPad doesn't automatically fill in settings.

4. **Enter your name, the account address, the incoming server (which you can get from your provider), and your password.**

iPad will probably add the outgoing mail server information for you, but if it doesn't, tap SMTP and enter this information.

5. **Make sure the Account field is set to On, and then tap Done to save the account, which you can now access through Mail.**

You can have more than one account set to On in Settings. When you do, you can then open different accounts to view their inboxes from within the Mail app. If you don't want a particular account's e-mails to be downloaded, you can turn any e-mail account on or off by opening it in Settings and tapping the On/Off button.

Opening Mail and Reading Messages

The whole point of e-mail is to send and receive messages. Mail offers a pretty simple interface for reading your e-mail. It displays an open message and a pane that you can use to show inbox contents or change to a different folder. In landscape orientation, the Mailboxes/Inbox pane is always displayed, but in portrait orientation, you display it by tapping the Inbox button.

When you tap the Mail app to open it, it automatically heads out and checks for any new e-mail. (If you use Microsoft Exchange or MobileMe, you can turn on push settings to have your e-mail host send messages to your iPad automatically.)

To follow a link in a message, you simply tap it. Note that tapping on Web links opens them up in Safari and tapping on address links opens the Maps apps with a map to that address displayed. To open an attachment, simply tap it, and it downloads and opens in iPad. iPad supports many common file types — including those that run on multiple platforms, such as PDF and text; those available on Macs, including iWork Pages and Numbers; those familiar to Windows users, including Microsoft Word and PowerPoint; as well as most common graphics and audio file formats. To open a meeting invitation, tap the meeting icon.

When your iPad gets an e-mail, it alerts you with a chime. If those e-mail-received alerts are driving you nuts, you can go to the Settings and under General, Sounds, use the slider to turn off the chimes.

These steps take you through the simple process of using Mail to open and read e-mails if you have a single e-mail account set up on iPad:

1. **Tap the Mail app icon located in the Dock on the Home screen (see Figure 6-5), which displays the number of unread e-mails in your inbox in a red circle.**

2. **Tap a message to read it.**

The message opens, as shown in Figure 6-6.

3. **If you need to scroll to see the entire message, just place your finger on the screen and flick upward to scroll down.**

Tap this icon

Figure 6-5: Without having to open Mail, you can see how many unread messages you have.

Figure 6-6: Open your e-mail and read it.

If you have multiple e-mail accounts set up, you can choose which inbox to display. From the inbox that appears when you open Mail, tap Mailboxes to go to the list shown in Figure 6-7.

With several accounts set up, in addition to each account listed on the Mailboxes screen, there's an All Inboxes item listed. Tapping this takes you to a consolidated Inbox containing all messages from all accounts in one place.

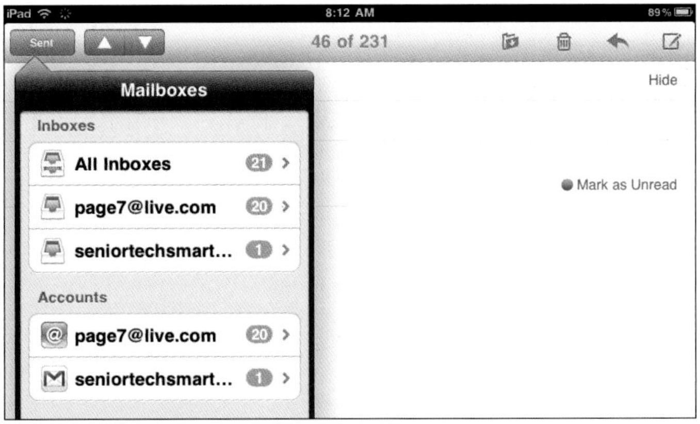

Figure 6-7: Mailboxes for various accounts and the consolidated Inbox are listed here.

You can tap the Hide button to hide the address details (the To field) so more of the message appears on your screen. To reveal the field again, tap the Details button (which becomes the Hide button when details are displayed).

E-mail messages you haven't read are marked with a blue circle in your inbox. After you read a message, the blue circle disappears. If you'd like, you can mark a read message as unread. This can help remind you to read it again later. With a message open, tap the Mark as Unread link on the right side.

You can use gestures such as double-tapping and pinching to reduce or enlarge an open e-mail.

Replying to or forwarding e-mail

Replying to or forwarding e-mails is pretty darn easy with iPad, as well. In fact, there's a handy button for replying or forwarding (on iPads with iOS version 4.2 or later, there's also a Print command on this menu).

One thing you need to know right now: You can't attach anything to e-mail messages when you create, reply to, or forward them. Instead, you can use features in apps such as Photos, Contacts, Notes, iWork Pages, and Maps to share individual documents via e-mail.

Here's how to use the simple Reply/Forward functions in iPad:

1. **With an e-mail message open (see the previous section), tap the Reply/Forward/Print button shown in Figure 6-8.**

Tap the Reply/Forward/Print button

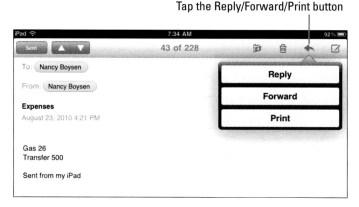

Figure 6-8: The Reply/Forward button sports a left-pointing arrow.

2. **Now for the simple part. Do one of the following:**

   • *Tap Reply to respond to the message sender.* The reply message form shown in Figure 6-9 appears. Tap in the message body and jot down your inspired thoughts.

   • *Tap Forward to send the message to somebody else.* If the e-mail has an attachment, you can choose Include or Don't Include in the dialog that appears. The form in Figure 6-10 then appears. Enter a recipient in the To field, and then tap in the message body and enter a message.

3. **Tap Send.**

   The message goes on its way.

Tap here to enter a reply

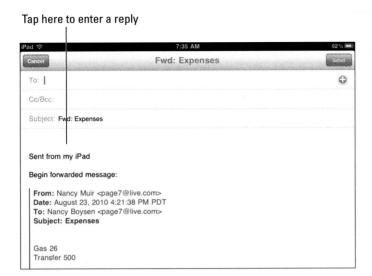

Figure 6-9: What you reply is up to you!

Tap here to enter a message

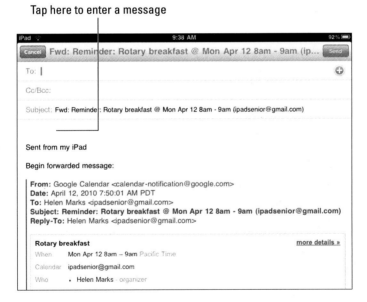

Figure 6-10: When you forward a message, all previous contents are included.

Although you can include whether to keep original attachments when *forwarding* an e-mail, any attachments to the original e-mail can't be included in a *reply*.

Creating and sending a new message

You're probably an old pro at creating and sending e-mail messages, but it's worth a quick trip through iPad's Mail feature and its approach to writing an e-mail using the onscreen keyboard.

Note that, by default, your e-mails have a signature that says, "Sent from my iPad." This will definitely impress your geekiest friends, but if you want to change it to something a little more useful, just go to Settings. In the Mail settings, choose Contacts and Calendars, and then Signature. You can then enter any signature text you want.

Follow these steps to create and send e-mail:

1. **With Mail open, tap the New Message icon.**

   A blank message form (see Figure 6-11) appears.

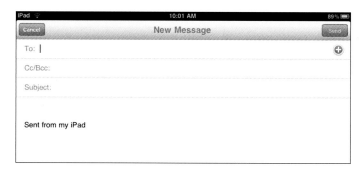

Figure 6-11: A very basic e-mail message form.

2. **Enter a recipient's address in the To field.**

   If you have saved addresses in Contacts, tap the plus symbol in an address field to choose an addressee from the Contacts list.

3. **If you want to copy other people on the message, enter other addresses in the Cc/Bcc field.**

   When you tap the Cc/Bcc field, both cc and bcc fields are displayed.

4. **Enter a subject for the message in the Subject field.**

5. **Tap in the message body and type your message.**

6. **Tap (you guessed it) Send.**

Mail keeps a copy of all sent messages. To view sent messages, tap the Inbox button and then tap Mailboxes. Tap the Sent button, and the folder containing all sent messages opens. Tap a message to review it.

Want to shout at somebody in an e-mail (not, of course, a practice I advocate)? You can activate Caps Lock when using the onscreen keyboard in your iPad by double-tapping either Shift key. To turn Caps Lock off, tap either Shift key once. To use this functionality, first be sure to use the General, Keyboard settings to enable Caps Lock.

Searching E-Mail

I'm sure you've never mislaid an e-mail, but most of the rest of us do it all the time. Say you want to find all messages from a certain person or with a certain word in the Subject field. You can use Mail's handy Search feature to find that e-mail. You can search To, From, and Subject fields.

Follow these steps to practice using Mail's Search feature:

1. **With Mail open, tap the Inbox button.**

2. **In the Inbox, shown in Figure 6-12, tap in the Search Inbox field.**

   The onscreen keyboard appears.

3. **Enter a search term or name.**

4. **Tap the From, To, or Subject tab to view messages that contain the search term in one of those fields, or tap the All tab to see messages in which any of these three fields contains the term.**

   Matching e-mails are listed in the results, as shown in Figure 6-13.

Tap in the Search field

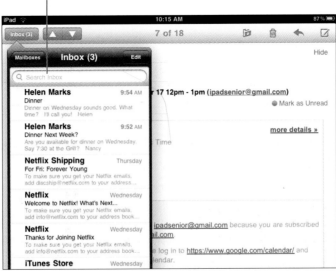

Figure 6-12: Tapping in the Search Inbox field opens the onscreen keyboard.

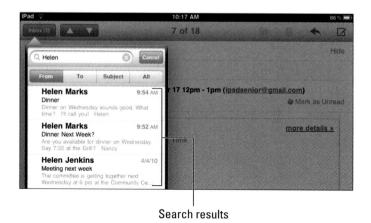

Search results

Figure 6-13: Any e-mail that contains your search term in the To, From, or Subject field is listed.

 To start a new search or go back to the full inbox, tap the Delete key in the upper-right corner of the onscreen keyboard to delete the term, or tap the Cancel button.

Printing E-mails

As of iOS version 4.2, iPad has native printing capabilities that can be used by certain apps, including Mail. You need a wireless printer setup to use this feature. For more about printing from your iPad, see Book V, Chapter 1.

With an e-mail message open, follow these steps to print:

1. **Tap the Reply/Forward/Print button and then tap Print.**

2. **In the Printer Options dialog that appears (if you haven't used this feature with your printer before), tap Select Printer.**

   iPad searches for any available wireless printers; tap yours to select it.

3. **Tap Printer Options to return to the Printer Options dialog and use the + or – buttons in the Copies field to adjust the number of copies.**

4. **Tap Print and your print job is on its way.**

Deleting an E-Mail

I have friends who never delete e-mails, but that, frankly, drives me nuts. When you no longer want an e-mail cluttering up your inbox, you can delete it. When you delete an e-mail on your iPad, it's gone from your inbox, including the inbox you access through your mobile phone or computer e-mail setup. However, for a time, you can retrieve it from the Trash folder of your e-mail account (get to that folder by tapping the name of your e-mail account in the upper-left corner of the Inbox pane).

Here's how to delete those e-mails you no longer want:

1. **With the inbox displayed, tap the Edit button.**

   Circular check boxes are displayed to the left of each message. (See Figure 6-14.)

Tap here to select a message

Check marks indicate selected messages

	10:28 AM	84%
iPad		
Inbox (3)	Select messages to delete or move.	

Inbox (3) Cancel

Search Inbox

Hide

Helen Marks 9:54 AM
Dinner
Dinner on Wednesday sounds good.
What time? I'll call you! Helen

Helen Marks 9:52 AM
Dinner Next Week?
Are you available for dinner on
Wednesday. Say 7:30 at the Grill? ...

emails, add info@netflix.com to your address
book.

Netflix Shipping Thursday
For Fri: Forever Young
To make sure you get your Netflix
emails, add discship@netflix.com to...

Browse | Queue | Help

Netflix Wednesday
Welcome to Netflix! What's Next...
To make sure you get your Netflix
emails, add info@netflix.com to your...

● Mark as Unread

There's no check out.
Simply add movies & TV
shows to your Queue.

Figure 6-14: Delete several messages at once using the Delete feature.

2. **Tap the circle next to the message you want to delete.**

   You can tap multiple items if you have several e-mails to delete. Messages marked for deletion show a check mark displayed in the circular check box. (Refer to Figure 6-14.)

3. **Tap the Delete button.**

   The message(s) is moved to the Trash folder.

If you delete a message and then want to view it again, go to the list of deleted e-mails in the Trash folder. If you want to retrieve one, you can move it back into the inbox, using the procedure in the next section.

You can also delete an open e-mail by tapping the trashcan icon in the toolbar that runs across the top.

Organizing E-Mail

I won't kid you: the message-management features in Mail aren't super robust. You can't create your own folders, though I'm hoping that will be a feature added to the next version of iPad. Here's what you can do: You can move messages into any of a few predefined folders in Mail. With the folder containing the message you want to move (for example, the Trash or Inbox) displayed, tap the Edit button. Circular check boxes are displayed to the left of each message. (Refer to Figure 6-14.)

Now follow these steps to move any message into another folder:

1. **Tap the circle next to the message you want to move.**
2. **Tap the Move button.**
3. **In the Mailboxes list that appears (see Figure 6-15), tap the folder where you'd like to store the message.**

   The message is moved.

If you get a junk e-mail, you might want to move it to the Spam folder. Once you do, any future mail from that same sender is automatically placed in the Spam folder.

If you have an e-mail open, you can move it to a folder by tapping the Folder icon on the toolbar that runs along the top. The Mailboxes list displays; tap a folder to move the message.

Figure 6-15: There aren't many folders here, but you'll probably make do.

Chapter 7: Managing iPad Settings

In This Chapter

⟶ **Setting brightness and changing the wallpaper**

⟶ **Managing Picture Frame settings**

⟶ **Controlling general settings**

⟶ **Handling accessibility features**

⟶ **Getting an overview of apps settings**

*i*Pad Settings is a control center for the device, offering settings that let you adjust things like the screen brightness and wallpaper, sound volume, and security features. In addition, there are settings for accessibility that can help if you have vision or hearing challenges. You can also set up e-mail accounts (which I tell you about in the preceding chapter) and control how the Calendar and Contacts apps manage their respective details. Finally, there are settings for each of the individual built-in apps, as well as any apps designed for the iPad that you've downloaded to your device.

In this chapter, you get some highlights of the settings you're likely to need most often, and advice for how to use them.

If you've installed an app that uses the Apple Push Notification Service to push alerts at you, you'll see a Notifications item in Settings. This lets you control the alerts sent to you. You can turn alerts on and off, for example, which can save you battery life.

Making Brightness and Wallpaper Settings

You might as well set up the visual side of iPad first so your interaction with the device is easy on the eyes and battery power. There are two such settings that fall together as one category in the Settings window: Brightness & Wallpaper.

Setting brightness

Especially when using iPad as an e-book reader, you may find a little less brightness in the display reduces strain on your eyes. Also, reducing the brightness can save a little on your iPad's battery life.

To modify the brightness setting, follow these steps:

1. **To begin, tap the Settings icon on the Home screen.**

2. **In the Settings dialog shown in Figure 7-1, tap Brightness & Wallpaper.**

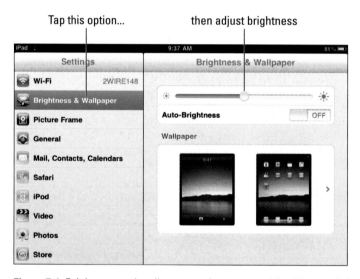

Figure 7-1: Brightness and wallpaper settings are combined in one dialog.

3. **To control brightness manually, tap the Auto-Brightness On/Off button (refer to Figure 7-1) to turn it off.**

4. **Tap and drag the Brightness slider to the right to make the screen brighter, or to the left to make it dimmer.**

5. **Tap the Home button to close the Settings dialog.**

If glare from the screen is a problem for you, consider getting a screen protector. This thin film not only protects your screen from damage, but can also reduce glare. These are available from a wide variety of sources (just search for *iPad screen protector*) and cost about $2 each.

Changing the wallpaper

Just as your desktop computer or laptop has the ability to display a pretty picture or pattern as a desktop background called a *wallpaper,* your iPad can display an image on the Home screen that displays when your iPad is locked.

The picture of a mountain lake that's the default iPad image may be pretty, but it's also pretty dark. Choosing different wallpaper may help you to see all the icons on your Home screen, or just allow you to display an image that appeals to your artistic sensibilities.

To change the wallpaper, do this:

1. **Tap the Settings icon on the Home screen, and then, in the Settings dialog, tap Brightness & Wallpaper.**

2. **In the Brightness & Wallpaper settings that appear, tap the arrow to the right of the Wallpaper section. (See Figure 7-2.)**

Tap this arrow

Figure 7-2: Tap to reveal Wallpaper settings.

3. **When options shown in Figure 7-3 appear, tap Wallpaper to display all the built-in wallpaper images.**

4. **Tap a wallpaper selection in the Wallpaper dialog (see Figure 7-4) to set it.**

   A preview of it appears onscreen.

Tap this option

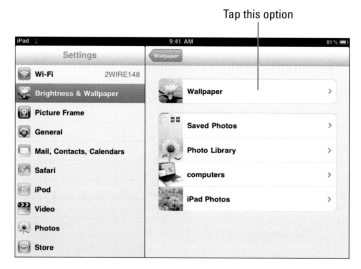

Figure 7-3: Access all the built-in wallpapers by tapping the Wallpaper option.

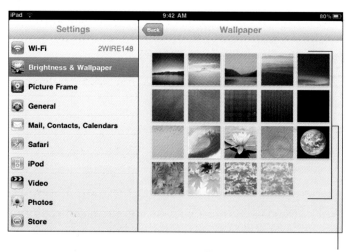

Tap on a wallpaper selection

Figure 7-4: Choose from various built-in wallpapers.

5. **Tap the Set Home Screen button. (See Figure 7-5.)**

   Alternatively, you can tap Set Lock Screen to use the image only when the
   screen is locked, or you can tap Set Both to use the image for both
   the wallpaper and when the screen is locked. If you want to go back to
   the other wallpapers, tap Cancel.

Tap this button

Figure 7-5: Choose whether you want this wallpaper for the Home screen, Lock screen, or both.

6. **Tap the Home button and you return to your Home screen with the new wallpaper set as the background.**

You can also use your own picture for your wallpaper. In Step 3, instead of choosing Wallpaper, tap Saved Photos or choose a photo library to browse your saved photos, select the picture you want to assign, and then resume with Step 5 above to apply that screen to your iPad.

Controlling the Picture Frame

The *Picture Frame* is a feature of iPad that allows you to play a slideshow of images from the Lock screen. When the Lock screen is displayed, you just tap the little flower-like icon in the bottom-right corner to start the show. It's a great way to show a presentation to a customer, or dazzle somebody with the pictures from your latest vacation.

To turn on Picture Frame and select the images it displays, follow these steps:

1. **Tap the Settings icon on the Home screen.**

2. **From the Settings dialog, tap Picture Frame.**

   The settings shown in Figure 7-6 appear.

3. **Tap either Dissolve or Origami to choose a transition style.**

   • *Dissolve:* Has one picture fade away, and another replaces it.

   • *Origami:* Displays several pictures on the screen and folds them together in an interesting way to change the picture display.

4. **Tap the Zoom in on Faces feature to have iPad zoom in on faces that appear in images.**

   This mode allows iPad to work with images on which you have used your computer's photo imaging software facial recognition feature.

5. **Tap Shuffle to move randomly among the pictures in your library.**

   Without shuffle, Picture Frame moves through the pictures in sequence.

6. **Tap either All Photos or Albums to choose which photos to display.**

e-mail arrives or whatever? iPad also makes sounds when certain events occur, if you want it to. You can turn on and off the following system sounds:

- New Mail
- Sent Mail
- Calendar Alerts
- Lock Sounds
- Keyboard Clicks

To turn any of these off or on, from the Settings dialog, tap General, then tap Sounds and use the sliders for each setting to turn it on or off.

Making network and Bluetooth settings

There are a few settings you can make for your networks and Bluetooth under the General settings: ones for virtual private networks, ones for Wi-Fi networks, and finally, settings for 3G networks.

Another setting you can make in the Network area of General settings is to turn Location Services on or off. Turning this on lets apps like Maps find your current physical location. If you turn this feature off and an app needs Location Services to function, it will prompt you to turn it on.

Setting up a VPN

A *virtual private network* (VPN) allows you to access a private network, such as one at your office, over the Internet. A VPN lets you make such a connection securely, and your iPad allows you to make settings for activating your connection.

In Settings you can do two things: turn VPN on or off, and configure a VPN network. In this chapter I'll handle the on/off task only, as configuring a VPN network is covered elsewhere.

For more about connecting to your company network remotely and configuring a VPN, see Book III, Chapter 1.

To turn VPN on, follow these steps:

1. **Tap the Settings icon on the Home screen.**

2. **Tap General and then tap Network.**

3. **Tap VPN and in the following dialog (see Figure 7-8) tap the Off button and slide it to the left till it reads On.**

   Note that if you haven't yet configured your VPN, an Add Configuration dialog appears. See Book III, Chapter 1, for more about configuring a VPN connection.

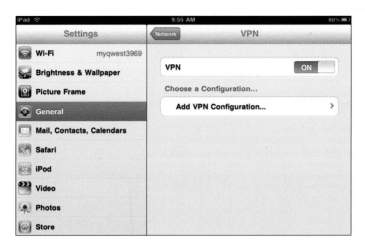

Figure 7-8: Turn your VPN connection on from this dialog.

Making Wi-Fi settings

The Wi-Fi settings include simply turning Wi-Fi on or off, choosing which network to connect to, and activating a feature that joins recognized networks automatically.

To make Wi-Fi settings, follow these steps:

1. **Tap the Settings icon on the Home screen.**

2. **Tap General and then tap Network.**

3. **Tap Wi-Fi and you see the settings shown in Figure 7-9.**

   Here you can do the following:

   - *Tap the Off button and slide it to turn Wi-Fi on or off.*

   - *Tap the arrow on a listed network to see its details, as shown in Figure 7-10.* Because you are connecting with a network set up on another device, you can't edit this information from your iPad.

   - *Tap the Ask to Join Networks button and slide it to turn this feature on or off.* If you turn it off, iPad won't join available networks automatically.

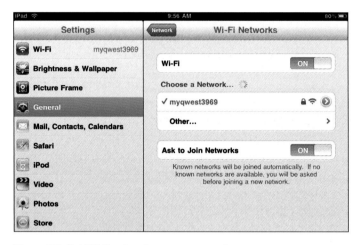

Figure 7-9: Get Wi-Fi set up for easy connections.

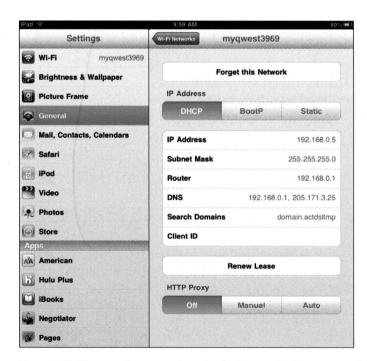

Figure 7-10: These settings come from the device on which your network has been set up.

If you have the Ask to Join Networks feature turned on and there are no known networks out there, iPad will ask you whether you want to join any new networks that surface.

Going 3G

Let's not forget 3G. If you have a 3G iPad, you can make some settings for your 3G connections through the General settings, including:

- ✓ **Turning a data network on or off:** If you don't want to connect to your data provider, turn this setting off.

- ✓ **Turning data roaming on or off:** If you don't want to allow your iPad to use roaming signals, which might cost you more, turn this one off.

- ✓ **Viewing your account information:** You can both view and change your 3G account information from your iPad.

- ✓ **Adding a SIM PIN:** To protect the data on your iPad's micro-SIM card, you might want to add a PIN to it. If somebody doesn't have the PIN, the SIM card stays locked so nobody can hack it to get data like your Contacts information.

Note that if you have a Wi-Fi + 3G model of iPad, you can also use Airplane mode settings to turn your Wi-Fi and Bluetooth signals off when in flight, and quickly turn them back on again later. On a Wi-Fi–only device, you won't see the Airplane mode feature under Settings.

Handling security

Because you are likely to take your iPad on the road on a regular basis, it's a good idea to consider a few security features. Some save battery life and protect your data or access to certain apps.

Security settings involve three features which you access through the General settings:

- ✓ **Auto-Lock:** Turns your display off to save battery power. You can set the amount of time you'd like to expire before Auto-Lock locks your iPad.

- ✓ **Passcode Lock:** Assigns a password to the Lock screen. You can set a passcode, turn it on or off, change the passcode, and set the time interval at which your passcode is required. This is useful if you don't want to bother with a passcode for only brief periods of locking your iPad. Finally, you can use the Erase Data After Ten Failed Passcode Attempts setting so that multiple failed attempts to access your device results in your iPad erasing all data on it. This could protect, for example, your contacts' information or map data that shows your location from prying eyes.

- ✓ **Restrictions:** Allows you to restrict access to certain apps and content using a passcode. (See Figure 7-11.) This is useful if you don't want your kids to access a particularly adult app or simply don't want them browsing with Safari or buying things with iTunes, for example.

Figure 7-11: Choose the apps or content you want to restrict in this dialog.

If you forget a passcode, the only thing to do is restore iPad software, which can be a headache. The big advice here: don't forget your passcode!

Setting the date and time

By default, your iPad is set to Cupertino time — Cupertino, California, that is, home to Apple Computer. If you have occasion to reset the time zone or date and time, either because you live somewhere other than Apple head-quarters or you travel around with your iPad, here's how you control time with your iPad.

1. **Tap the Settings icon on the Home screen.**

2. **Tap General.**

3. **Tap Date & Time.**

   The settings in Figure 7-12 appear. Do any of the following:

   • *Tap the Off button and slide it to the left to turn 24-hour time on.* This is military time, so that 2 p.m. is 14:00, and so on.

- *Tap Time Zone, and a text entry field displays along with your onscreen keyboard.* Press the Delete key to delete Cupertino, and type your location. (If you type a major city near you, it will come up on a list as you type, and you can just tap to select it.)

- *Tap Set Date & Time, and the Date & Time dialog shown in Figure 7-12 appears.* Here you can tap the date and use a spinner to choose a different date; or tap the time and flick the spinner to change the time.

Figure 7-12: Use these settings to let iPad know what time (and date) it is.

Controlling keyboard settings

Your keyboard is one of the most important ways you interact with iPad, so it's helpful if you have all the onscreen keyboard settings just the way you want them. You can access these under the Keyboard option in the General settings (see Figure 7-13), and they include the following:

✓ **Auto-Correction** and **Auto Capitalization:** Allows iPad to help you avoid mistakes by automatically suggesting corrections to what it perceives as spelling errors, based on a built-in dictionary, or correcting capitalization mistakes you make after you finish entering a sentence.

✔ **Enable Caps Lock:** Activates a feature that lets you double-tap the Shift key to activate Caps Lock. Note that when Caps Lock is activated, the Shift key on the onscreen keyboard is blue. This setting is turned off by default.

✔ **"." Shortcut:** Turning this on activates a shortcut that allows you to enter a period by double-tapping the spacebar.

✔ **International Keyboards:** Gives you access to the choice of two built-in keyboards: French and English. If you tap Add New Keyboard in this dialog, you are offered nine more language options, including German, Italian, Russian, Spanish, and my personal favorite, Flemish.

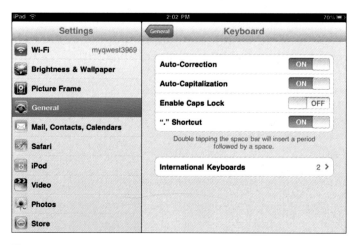

Figure 7-13: Set up your keyboard to work the way you want it to.

Accessibility and Ease of Use

iPad users are all different, and some face vision or hearing challenges. If you're one of those folks, you'll be glad to hear that iPad offers some handy accessibility features.

To help you read your screen more easily, there's a Zoom feature that lets you enlarge the screen even more than the standard Zoom feature does. There's even a White on Black screen option, which offers a black background with white lettering that some people find easier to read. You can also set up a feature called VoiceOver to read onscreen commands out loud.

If hearing is your challenge, there's a setting for Mono Audio that's useful when you're wearing headphones. Finally, Speak Auto-text is a feature that iPad uses to tell you when any autocorrections or capitalizations are made to text that you enter in any iPad application.

Turning on Zoom

Normally, you can increase the size of things on your screen by double-tapping with two fingers. However, the Zoom feature enlarges the contents displayed on the iPad screen even more when you double-tap the screen with three fingers.

To turn the Zoom feature on, follow these steps:

1. **Tap the Settings icon on the Home screen and then tap General.**

2. **In General settings, tap Accessibility.**

   The Accessibility dialog shown in Figure 7-14 appears.

Figure 7-14: The Accessibility dialog.

3. Tap Zoom.

4. In the Zoom dialog shown in Figure 7-15, tap the Zoom On/Off button to turn the feature on.

5. Now go to a Web site (www.wiley.com, for example) and double-tap the screen using three fingers; it enlarges. (See Figure 7-16.)

6. Press three fingers on the screen and drag to move around it.

7. Double-tap with three fingers again to go back to regular magnification.

8. Tap the Home button to close Settings.

This Zoom feature works pretty much everywhere in iPad: in Photos, on Web pages, in your Mail, in iPod and Videos — give it a try!

Turning on White on Black

White on Black is an accessibility setting that reverses colors on your screen so backgrounds are black and text is white. This can help people with particular vision challenges to read text more easily.

Tap to turn on Zoom

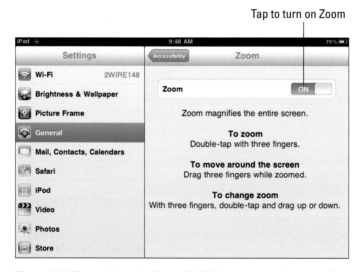

Figure 7-15: Tap and drag the Zoom On/Off button to turn it on or off.

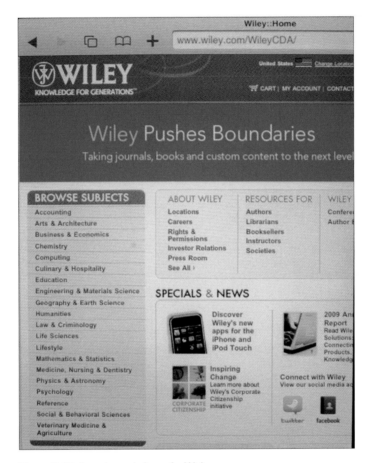

Figure 7-16: An enlarged view of a Web page.

To turn this feature on:

1. **Tap the Settings icon on the Home screen and then tap General.**

2. **Tap Accessibility.**

3. **In the Accessibility dialog shown in Figure 7-17, tap the White on Black On/Off button to turn it on.**

   The colors on the screen reverse, as shown in Figure 7-18.

Tap to turn on White on Black

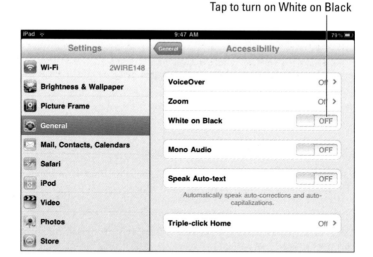

Figure 7-17: Turning on the White on Black setting can help you read text more easily.

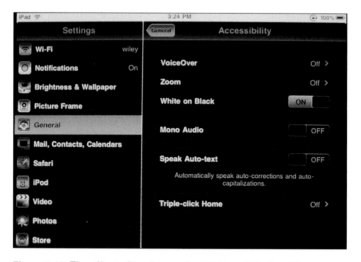

Figure 7-18: The effect of turning on the White on Black setting.

The White on Black feature works great in some places and not so well in others. For example, in the Photos application, pictures appear almost as photo negatives. Your Home screen image will likewise look a bit strange. And don't even think of playing a video with this feature turned on! However, if you need help reading text, it can be very useful in several applications.

Setting up VoiceOver

VoiceOver reads the names of screen elements and settings to you, but it also changes the way you provide input to iPad. In Notes, for example, you can have VoiceOver read the name of the Notes button to you, and when you enter Notes, read any words or characters you've entered, and tell you if features such as AutoCorrect are on.

To turn the feature on:

1. **Tap the Settings icon on the Home screen and then tap General.**

2. **Tap Accessibility.**

3. **In the Accessibility dialog shown in Figure 7-19, tap the VoiceOver button.**

4. **In the VoiceOver dialog shown in Figure 7-20, tap the VoiceOver On/ Off button to turn it on.**

   The first time you turn on the feature, you'll see a dialog noting that turning on VoiceOver changes gestures used to interact with iPad. Tap OK to proceed.

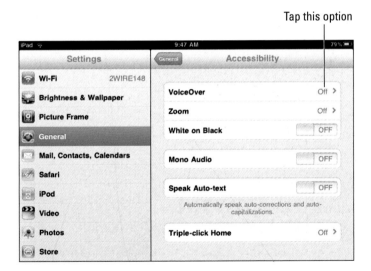

Figure 7-19: VoiceOver reads onscreen elements to you.

Tap to turn on VoiceOver

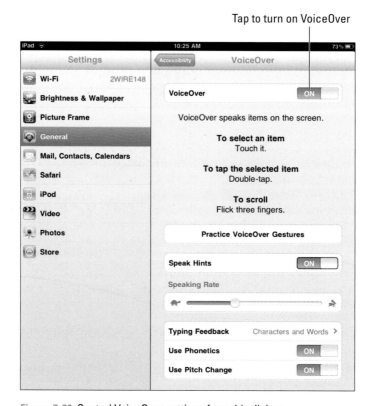

Figure 7-20: Control VoiceOver settings from this dialog.

5. **Tap the Practice VoiceOver Gestures button to select it, and then double-tap to open it. (This is the new method of tapping that VoiceOver activates.)**

   It's important that you first single-tap to select an item such as a button, which causes VoiceOver to read the name of the button to you. Then double-tap the button to activate its function. (VoiceOver reminds you to do this if you turn on Speak Hints, which is a help when you first use VoiceOver but gets annoying after a short time.)

6. **Tap the Speaking Rate field, and VoiceOver speaks the name of the item.**

   If you find the rate of the voice too slow or fast, double-tap the slider and move the slider to the left to slow it down or the right to speed it up.

7. **If you'd like VoiceOver to read words or characters to you (for example, in the Notes app), double-tap Typing Feedback.**

8. **In the Typing Feedback dialog, tap to select the option you prefer.**

   The Words option will read words, but not characters such as dollar sign. The Characters and Words option reads both.

Be sure to review the next section to find out how to navigate your iPad now that you have turned VoiceOver on.

You can change the language that VoiceOver speaks. In General settings, choose International, then Language, and select another language. This will, however, also change the language used for labels on Home icons and various settings and fields in iPad.

You can use the Set Triple-Click Home setting to help you more quickly turn the VoiceOver and White on Black features on and off. In the Accessibility dialog, tap Triple-Click Home. In the dialog that appears, choose what you want a Home button triple-click to do: toggle VoiceOver on or off; toggle White on Black on or off; or display a menu of options using the Ask choice. Now a triple-click with a single finger on the Home button provides you with the options you selected wherever you go in iPad.

Using VoiceOver

Now that VoiceOver is turned on, you need to know how to use it. I won't kid you; it's hard at first, but you'll get the hang of it! Here are the main onscreen gestures you should know:

- **Tap an item to select it, and VoiceOver speaks its name.**
- **Double-tap a selected item to activate it.**
- **Flick three fingers to scroll.**

Table 7-1 provides additional gestures that will help you use VoiceOver. I suggest that, if you want to use this feature often, you read the section of the iPad online User Guide, which goes into a great deal of detail about the ins and outs of using VoiceOver.

Table 7-1	VoiceOver Gestures
Gesture	*Effect*
Flick right or left.	Select next or preceding item.
Tap with two fingers.	Stop speaking current item.
Flick two fingers up.	Read everything from the top of the screen.
Flick two fingers down.	Read everything from the current position.
Flick up or down with three fingers.	Scroll one page at a time.
Flick right or left with three fingers.	Go to next or preceding page.
Tap three fingers.	Speak the scroll status (for example, line 20 of 100).
Flick four fingers up or down.	Go to first or last element on a page.
Flick four fingers right or left.	Go to next or preceding section (as on a Web page).

Using Mono Audio

Stereo used in headphones breaks up sounds so that you hear a portion in one ear and a portion in the other to simulate the way we actually hear sounds. However, if you're hard of hearing or deaf in one ear, you're getting only a portion of a sound in your hearing ear, which can be difficult. Turn on Mono Audio, and iPad plays all sounds in each ear.

Follow these steps to turn Mono Audio on:

1. **Tap the Settings icon on the Home screen and then tap General.**

2. **In the General settings dialog, tap Accessibility.**

3. **In the Accessibility dialog shown in Figure 7-21, tap the Mono Audio On/Off button to turn it on.**

Tap to turn on Mono Audio

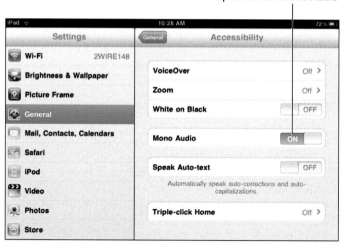

Figure 7-21: Mono audio helps people who hear better in one ear than the other.

If you have hearing challenges, another good feature that iPad provides is support for closed-captioning. In the Videos player, you can use a closed-captioning feature to provide onscreen text for dialogs and actions in a movie as it plays. For more about playing videos, see Book II, Chapter 3.

Utilizing iPad's Speak Auto-text

Speak Auto-text is a feature that speaks autocorrections and autocapitalizations (two features that you can turn on with Keyboard settings). When you enter text in an application such as Word or Mail and then make either type of change, Speak Auto-text lets you know.

To turn Speak Auto-text on, follow these steps:

1. **Tap the Settings icon on the Home screen and then tap General.**

2. **In the General settings dialog, tap Accessibility.**

3. **In the Accessibility dialog shown in Figure 7-22, tap the Speak Auto-text On/Off button to turn the feature on.**

Tap to turn on Speak Auto-Text

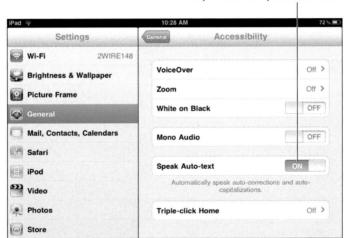

Figure 7-22: Let iPad speak to you.

Why would you want iPad to tell you when an autocorrection has been made? If you have vision challenges and you know you typed "ain't" when writing dialog for a character in your novel, but iPad corrected it to "isn't," you would want to know, right? Similarly, if you typed the poet's name e.e. Cummings and autocapitalization corrected it (incorrectly), you need to know immediately so you can change it back again!

Working with the Reset feature

If only life had a reset button to put some things back the way they were. Well, it doesn't, but iPad does. The last item under General settings is Reset. When you click it, you get options for resetting the following:

- **Reset All Settings:** Every one of the preferences and settings are reset, though information you've added to apps like Calendar and Contacts doesn't change at all.

- **Erase All Content and Settings:** This one both resets your settings and erases information you've added to apps like Calendar and Contacts. This is useful if you plan to sell your iPad.

- **Reset Network Settings:** By choosing this, any networks you've set up are removed. iPad will also turn off Wi-Fi, and then turn it on again, which disconnects you from any network you're connected to. Note that the Ask to Join Networks setting stays on.

- **Reset Keyboard Dictionary:** When you turn down iPad suggestions of words as you type, you can add words to the keyboard dictionary. You do this by tapping a suggested word, which rejects it but adds the current spelling of the word to the dictionary. If you don't want to keep all those added words, use this reset option.

- **Reset Home Screen Layout:** If you want to get back to the original home screen you saw when you took iPad out of its box, choose this reset option.

- **Reset Location Warnings:** When you use an app like Maps that checks your location, it asks you if it's okay to do that. When you tap OK to let it proceed two times, it stops asking. If you want it to start asking again, tap this reset option.

Settings for Individual Apps

Each built-in app has a corresponding group of settings in iPad. Rather than bore you by taking you through each and every one, I provide Table 7-2, which gives you an overview of the types of settings you can control. If there's a particular app you like to work with often, it's worth your while to explore the settings for it to see if there's one that might make your life with that app a bit easier.

Table 7-2	Built-in Apps Settings Overview
App	*Types of Settings*
Mail	Set Up Accounts, Fetch New Data Frequency, Display Settings (how many messages to show, font size, and so on)
Contacts	Display Settings (sort order, display order)
Calendars	Turn on Alerts, Time Zone, Default Calendar
Safari	Search Engine, Turn AutoFill On/Off, Show Bookmarks Bar, Security and History
iPod	Sounds and Volume Settings, Display Lyrics and Podcast Information
Videos	Where to Resume Playing; Closed Captioning, Widescreen On/Off, Type of TV Signal
Photos	Slideshow Settings

Also note that apps that you download, which have been designed for iPad, will appear in your Settings under the heading of Apps. Non-iPad apps (for example, iPhone apps) don't seem to appear. The settings vary based on the app, so go exploring and see what you find!

What happened to my Screen Rotation Lock button?

Having your screen orientation flip depending on how you hold your iPad can be handy, or it can be annoying if you're, say, reading in bed and every time you turn over on your side the screen flips. That's why it's useful to be able to lock the orientation. If you bought a first generation iPad and upgraded the iOS to version 4.2 or later, you may have noticed that the little switch on the top right of the device that you used to click to lock your screen rotation feature now mutes and unmutes your speakers. This feature change was made when you installed the new iOS, but the ability to lock the screen rotation hasn't gone away. To lock the orientation to the current display, you use the new multitasking bar that also came with your new iOS. Double-tap the Home button to display the multitasking bar. Flick to scroll to the left until you see the Screen Rotation Lock button, which displays a circle with an arrow on it. Tap this button, and the screen is locked in its current orientation. Tap again to unlock the orientation.

Chapter 8: Maintaining and Troubleshooting

In This Chapter

✔ **Taking care of your iPad**

✔ **Solving common iPad problems**

✔ **Finding technical support**

*i*Pads don't grow on trees — they cost a pretty penny. That's why it's important that you know how to take care of your iPad and troubleshoot any problems that might come up so you get the most out of it.

In this chapter, I provide some advice about care and maintenance of your iPad, as well as some tips about how to solve common problems, update iPad system software, and even reset iPad should something go seriously wrong.

Maintaining Your iPad

You've got a great gadget and an investment to protect in your iPad. A few simple precautions can keep it damage-free — at least until you rush out and buy the next version.

It's wise to keep the screen clean and safe from damage, as well as maximize your battery use. The following sections tell you how.

Keeping the iPad screen clean

If you've been playing with your iPad at all, you know, despite Apple's claim that iPads have fingerprint-resistant screens, that iPads are fingerprint magnets. They are covered with an oil-resistant coating, but that definitely doesn't mean they are smudge-proof.

Here are some tips about how to clean your iPad screen:

- You can get most fingerprints off with a dry, soft cloth such as the one you use to clean your eyeglasses or a cleaning tissue that is lint- and chemical-free.

- If you want to get the surface even cleaner, you can use a soft cloth that has been slightly dampened. Again, make sure whatever cloth material you use is free of lint.

This may go without saying, but I'll say it anyway: If you don't want a fried iPad, turn it off and unplug any cables from it before cleaning the screen with a moistened cloth.

- Avoid getting too much moisture around the edges of the screen where it could seep into the unit.

- Never use any household cleaners on your iPad screen. They can degrade the coating that keeps the screen from absorbing oil from your fingers.

It definitely *isn't* wise to use premoistened lens cleaning tissues to clean your screen. Most of these wipes contain alcohol, which can damage the coating.

Protecting your gadget with a case

Your screen isn't the only thing on the iPad that can be damaged, so it isn't a bad idea to get a case for it so you can carry it around the house or around town safely. Besides providing a bit of padding if you should drop the device, a case makes the iPad less slippery in your hands, offering a better grip when working with it.

Several cases came out pretty much the day iPad shipped, and more are showing up all the time. You can choose from the neoprene one offered by Apple at around $39, and those from other manufacturers such as I-inique's Tuff-Luv model (www.i-nique.com) and MiniSuit Case Manufacturers (www.globalsources.com/manufacturers/Mini-Suit-Case.html) that come in materials ranging from leather (see Figure 8-1) to silicone. (See Figure 8-2.)

Figure 8-1: A lovely leather case, with a built-in stand mechanism for better viewing.

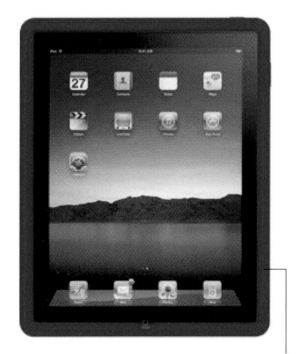

A silicone "skin" case

Figure 8-2: A less-expensive option is a silicon skin.

Cases range in price from a few dollars to $70 or more for leather. Some provide a cover (refer to Figure 8-1), and others protect only the back and sides. (Refer to Figure 8-2.) If you carry your iPad around much at all, consider a case with a cover to provide better protection for the screen or use a screen overlay such as the one from Zagg (www.zagg.com).

Getting battery charging tips

iPad's much-touted, 10-hour battery life is a wonderful feature, but there are things you can do to extend that battery life even further. You can judge how much battery life you have left by looking at the Battery icon in the far-right corner of the Status bar at the top of your screen. Here are a few tips to help that little icon stay full up:

- ✔ **Use a wall outlet to charge.** Hmm . . . I wonder why, but when connected to a Mac computer, iPad can slowly charge; however, some PC connections slowly drain the battery. Even so, the most effective way to charge your iPad is to plug it into the wall outlet using the Dock Connector to USB Cable and the 10W USB Power Adapter that came with your iPad. (See Figure 8-3.)

- ✔ **Turn the iPad off.** The fastest way to charge the iPad is to turn it off while charging it.

- ✔ **Avoid USB ports on keyboards.** Your battery may lose some power if you leave it connected to the USB port on a keyboard.

- ✔ **Use a dock device.** You can use a dock device available from Apple to charge the iPad while it rests in the dock through the connector on the dock itself. (See Figure 8-4.)

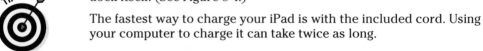

The fastest way to charge your iPad is with the included cord. Using your computer to charge it can take twice as long.

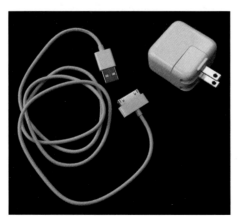

Figure 8-3: The provided cord and power adapter.

Figure 8-4: A dock can be used for charging as well as for propping iPad up.

> ✓ **Limit the screen's impact on the battery:** Turn the screen off when not in use, as the display eats up power. Also, reduce the screen brightness in Settings to save power.

> ✓ **Turn off Wi-Fi:** If you're not using Wi-Fi, turn it off under Settings. Constantly maintaining a Wi-Fi connection or searching for a signal can use up a bit of power.

Your iPad battery is sealed in the unit, so you can't replace it as you can with a laptop or cellphone battery. If it's out of warranty, you'll have to fork over the money, possibly more than $100, to get a new battery. See the "Getting Support" section, later in this chapter, to find out where to get a replacement battery.

Troubleshooting Your iPad

Though we'd all like to think that our iPads are perfect machines, unburdened with the vagaries of crashing Windows PCs and system software bugs, that's not always the case.

Here are some common issues that can come up with iPad, and ways around them.

Dealing with a nonresponsive iPad

If iPad goes dead on you, it's most likely a power issue, so the first thing to do is to plug the Dock Connector to USB Cable into the 10W USB Power Adapter, plug the 10W USB Power Adapter into a wall outlet, plug the other end of the Dock Connector to USB Cable into your iPad, and charge the battery.

Another thing to try — especially if you think an app is hanging up the iPad — is to press the Sleep/Wake button for a little bit. Next, press and hold the Home key. The app you were using should close.

There's always the old reboot procedure, which in the case of an iPad means pressing the Sleep/Wake button on the top until the red slider is displayed. Drag the slider to turn your iPad off. After a few moments, press the Sleep/Wake button to boot the little guy up again.

If things seem drastic and none of these ideas works, try to reset your iPad. To do this, press the Sleep/Wake button and the Home button together until the Apple logo appears onscreen.

Making the keyboard reappear

When you're using a Bluetooth keyboard or Apple's iPad Keyboard Dock, your onscreen keyboard won't appear. The physical keyboards have, in essence, co-opted keyboard control of your device. Here's what you can do to make the onscreen keyboard reappear:

- **iPad Keyboard Dock:** If you're using the iPad Keyboard Dock and want the onscreen keyboard to show up, press the Keyboard button in the set of function buttons that run across the top of the iPad Keyboard Dock. The onscreen keyboard appears.

- **Bluetooth keyboard:** To use your onscreen keyboard with a Bluetooth keyboard connected, you have a few options: You can turn the Bluetooth keyboard off, turn off Bluetooth in iPad's General settings, or move the keyboard out of range. Your onscreen keyboard should reappear.

Are you accidentally tapping extra keys on the onscreen keyboard as you type? Wearing a wrist support can keep you from hitting extra characters with your wrists. Also, it's much easier to use the onscreen keyboard in landscape mode where it's just plain wider.

Updating software

Just as software manufacturers provide updates for your main computer, Apple occasionally updates iPad system software to fix problems or offer enhanced features. It's a good idea to occasionally check for an updated version (say, every month).

Follow these steps to update the iPad system software:

1. **Start by connecting your iPad to your computer.**

2. **On your computer, open the iTunes software you installed. (See Book I, Chapter 4 for more about this.)**

3. **Click your iPad's name in the iTunes source list on the left.**

4. **Click the Summary tab shown in Figure 8-5.**

Click on your iPad...

then click the Summary tab

Figure 8-5: Get system updates for iPad through your iTunes account.

5. **Click the Check for Update button.**

   iTunes displays a message telling you if a new update is available.

6. **Click the Update button to install the newest version.**

If you're having problems with iPad, it's possible to use the Update feature to restore the current version of the software on it as a possible fix. Follow the steps above, and then click the Restore button instead of the Update button in Step 6. Typically restoring an OS to another version does run the risk of going back to original settings, so be aware of that going in.

Getting sound back on

Coincidentally, the very morning I wrote this chapter, my husband was puttering with our iPad. Suddenly, the sound stopped. We gave ourselves a quick course in recovering sound, so now I can share these tips with you:

- ✓ If you're using the iPad Keyboard Dock, check to see that you haven't touched the volume control keys on the right side of the top row and inadvertently muted the sound. (See Figure 8-6.)

- ✓ Make sure you haven't covered up the speaker in a way that muffles the sound.

- ✓ Do you have a headset plugged in? Sound won't play through the speaker and headset at the same time.

- ✓ There is a volume limit you can set up in Settings for the iPod app that will control how loudly iPod can play (useful if your partner's into loud Rap music). Tap the Settings icon on the Home screen, then on the left side of the screen that displays, tap iPod and use the Volume Limit controls (see Figure 8-7) to make sure Volume Limit is set to Off.

- ✓ If all else fails, reboot. That's what worked for us — just press the Sleep/Wake button until the red slider appears. Press and drag the slider to the right. After iPad turns off, press the Sleep/Wake button until the Apple logo appears, and you may find yourself back in business sound-wise.

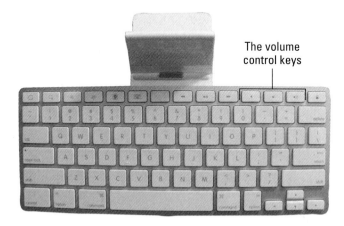

The volume control keys

Figure 8-6: Did you lower the volume or hit Mute?

Make sure this is set to Off

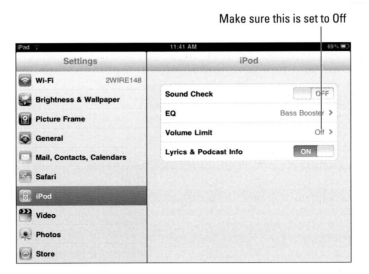

Figure 8-7: Volume Limit lets your iPad get only so loud.

Getting Support

As you may already know if you own another Apple device, Apple is known for its great customer support, so if you're stuck, I definitely recommend you try them out. Here are a few options you can explore for getting help:

✔ Go to your local Apple Store if one is handy and see what the folks there might know about your problem.

✔ Visit the Apple support Web site at `www.apple.com/support/ipad`. (See Figure 8-8.) Here you'll find online manuals, discussion forums, downloads, and the Apple Expert feature, which enables you to contact a live expert over the phone.

✔ Visit the iPad User Guide at `http://manuals.info.apple.com/en_ US/iPad_User_Guide.pdf`. This is a more robust version of the User Guide that came with your iPad. You can open it using the bookmarked manual on the Safari browser.

✔ Finally, if you need repair or service for your battery, visit the battery replacement service at `www.apple.com/batteries/replacements. html`.

Figure 8-8: Don't forget to check out the manuals and discussions for help.

Note that Apple recommends that the iPad battery should be replaced only by an Apple Authorized Service Provider.

Finally, here are a few useful non-Apple discussion forums that may help provide some answers:

🖙 MacRumors at `http://forums.macrumors.com/forumdisplay.php?f=137`

🖙 The iPad Guide discussions at `www.theipadguide.com/forum`

🖙 iPad.org provides several useful threads at `http://ipad.org/forum`

Finding a Missing iPad

Staring with iOS 4.2, you can take advantage of the FindMyiPad feature to pinpoint the location of your iPad using your computer. This is a very handy feature if you forget where you left your iPad or it is stolen. FindMyiPad not only lets you track down the critter, it lets you wipe off the data contained in it if you have no way to get the iPad back.

Follow these steps to get this feature set up:

1. **Tap Settings.**

2. **Tap Mail, Contacts, Calendars.**

3. **Tap Add Account.**

4. **Tap MobileMe.**

5. **In the MobileMe dialog that appears, enter your Apple ID and password.**

   At this point MobileMe might have to verify your ID, which it does by sending an email to your ID e-mail account. Go open the message and click the verify link.

6. **Back in the MobileMe dialog, tap and drag to turn the FindMyiPad feature on (see Figure 8-9).**

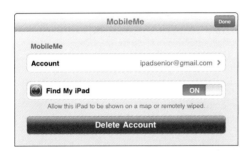

Figure 8-9: Turn the feature on or off to locate your iPad from your computer

7. **Tap Save.**

8. **Now go to** `http://me.com` **and enter your ID and password.**

9. **The Find My iPhone screen appears with your iPad's location noted on a map.**

10. **To wipe information on the iPad, tap the arrow on the information bar for the iPad and tap Wipe (see Figure 8-10).**

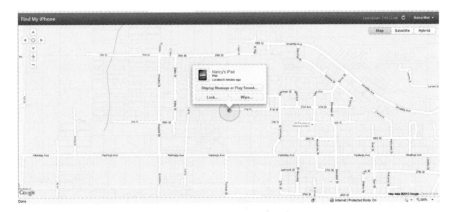

Figure 8-10: To protect data on your iPad, as a last resort you can wipe it clean

You can also tap Lock to lock out anybody who doesn't have a password, or tap Display a Message or Play a Sound to send whoever has your iPad a note about how to get it back to you or a note that the police are on their way if it's been stolen! If you choose to play a sound, it plays for two minutes, helping you track down anybody who is holding your iPad and within earshot.

Book II
Just for Fun

The music, videos, photos, and eBooks you can view on iPad are a big part of its fun factor. In fact, iPad is considered by many to be mainly a content consuming machine, so here's where you discover how to gobble up all that great content using iPad's easy-to-use media apps.

And then there's games: There are some absolutely awesome games out there that you may have played on your phone, but that really come to life on iPad's larger screen.

Chapter 1: Buying Content at iTunes and Beyond

*i*Pad is set up with an iTunes app that makes it easy to shop for music, movies, TV shows, audiobooks, podcasts, and even online classes at Apple's iTunes Store.

In this chapter, you find out how to use your iPad to open an iTunes account and find content on the iTunes Web site. That content can be downloaded directly to your iPad, or to your computer and then synced to your iPad. In addition, I cover a few options for buying content from other online stores.

Note that I cover opening an iTunes account and downloading iTunes software to your computer in Book I, Chapter 4. If you need to, go back and handle those two tasks before digging into this chapter.

Exploring the iTunes Store

Like it or not, the iTunes Store is set up to be your most convenient source for content on your iPad at the moment. Sure, you can get content from other places, but the iTunes app comes pre-installed on your iPad and Apple makes it easy to access from its devices.

TIP

If you want to use the Genius playlist feature, which recommends additional purchases based on your previous purchases, turn this feature on in iTunes on your computer, and then on your iPad, tap the Genius tab. Song and album recommendations appear.

Figure 1-3: Detailed information may include the genre, release date, and song list.

Finding a selection

There are several ways to look for a selection in the iTunes Store. You can use the Search feature, search by genres or categories, or view artists' pages. Here's how these work:

- Tap in the Search field shown in Figure 1-4 and enter a search term using the onscreen keyboard. Tap the Search button on the keyboard or, if one of the suggestions given appeals to you, just go ahead and tap it. Search results will be divided into categories such as Music and Podcasts. Flick down to scroll through them and find what you need.

- Tap the Genre button (in some content types, such as Audiobooks, this is called the Categories button). A list of genres/categories like the one shown in Figure 1-5 appears.

- In a description page that appears when you tap a selection, you can find more offerings by the people involved. For example, for a music selection, tap the Artist's Page link to see all of that artist's selections. For a movie, tap the name of someone in the movie credits to see more of that person's work, as shown for Kate Winslet in Figure 1-6.

Enter a search term here

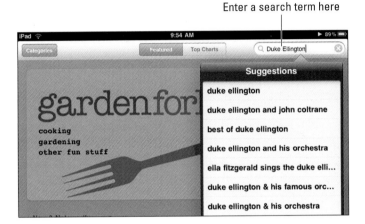

Figure 1-4: Search by composer, artist, or album title.

If you find a selection you like, tap the Tell a Friend link on its description page to share your discovery with a friend via e-mail. A message appears with a link to the selection. Enter an address in the To field and tap Send. Your friend is now in-the-know.

Tap here to view the list

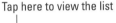

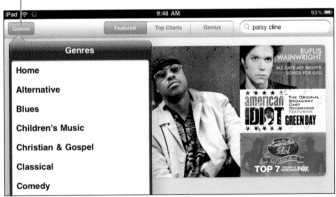

Figure 1-5: Find a genre of music to help you narrow down your search.

Want to see every option? Tap the See All link to see additional selections in a category or by a particular artist.

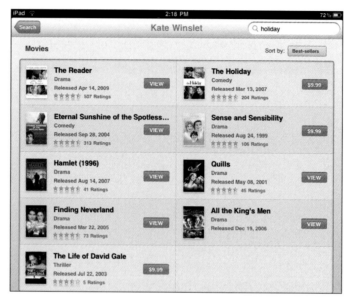

Figure 1-6: If you have an artist you favor, search for him or her.

Sorting movie selections

When you're out to find a movie to watch or music to listen to on your iPad some Tuesday or Saturday night and you don't know what you want to experience, using a sort feature can help you find something that might appeal to you. You can sort movie selections by best-sellers, name, or release date.

With iTunes open, tap the Sort By field. In the menu shown in Figure 1-7, tap the criteria you want to sort by.

Selections are sorted by the criteria you chose (for example, alphabetically if you chose Name or with the latest release first if you chose Release Date). Find the item that interests you and click on it for more info, or tap the price button to buy it.

Figure 1-7: Choose search criteria from this menu.

Previewing music, a movie, or an audiobook

Because you've already set up an iTunes account (if you haven't done so yet, refer to Book 1, Chapter 4), when you choose to buy an item, it's automatically charged to the credit card you have on record.

However, you might just want to preview an item before you buy it to be sure it's a good fit. If you like it, buying and downloading are then easy and quick.

Follow these steps to preview your content:

1. **Open iTunes and locate a selection you might want to buy using any of the methods I outline in earlier sections.**

2. **Tap the item to see detailed information about it, as shown in Figure 1-8.**

3. **If you're looking at a music selection, tap the track number or name of a selection (refer to Figure 1-8) to play a preview. For a movie or audiobook selection, tap the Preview button shown in Figure 1-9.**

Tap a track number or name to listen to a preview

Patsy Cline
Patsy Cline's Greatest Hits
(Remastered)

Artist Page >

Tell a Friend >

Genre: Country
Released: 1967
12 Songs
★★★★★ 61 Ratings
$9.99

iTunes Review

Considering her legendary status, it's amazing that Patsy Cline only recorded 104 tracks over a span of eight years. Her ability to convey romantic torment without ever losing her grace or dignity remains unmatched, and for those looking for the essence of Cline's music, *Greatest* ... More ▼

Tap to Preview

	Name	Time	Popularity	Price
1	**Walkin' After Midnight (1961 Remake)**	1:59		$1.29
2	**Sweet Dreams (Single Version)**	2:33		$0.99
3	**Crazy (Single Version)**	2:41		$1.29

Figure 1-8: Why not preview before you buy?

If you like what you hear or see, you're ready to buy. Which brings you to the next section.

The iTunes Store offers several free selections, especially in the Podcast and iTunes U content categories. If you see one you want to try out, download it by tapping the button labeled Free and then tapping the Get Episode or similar button that appears.

Tap here to preview the selection

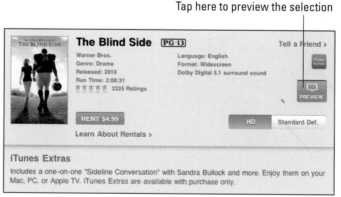

The Blind Side PG-13

Tell a Friend >

Warner Bros.
Genre: Drama
Released: 2010
Run Time: 2:08:31
★★★★★ 2325 Ratings

Language: English
Format: Widescreen
Dolby Digital 5.1 surround sound

PREVIEW

RENT $4.99

HD   Standard Def.

Learn About Rentals >

iTunes Extras

Includes a one-on-one "Sideline Conversation" with Sandra Bullock and more. Enjoy them on your Mac, PC, or Apple TV. iTunes Extras are available with purchase only.

Figure 1-9: You can also preview movies before you rent or buy.

Buying a selection

For all but movie selections which you can often rent, other types of content require that you buy what you want to consume. Buying involves authorizing the purchase and downloading the content to your iPad (which is done automatically once the purchase part is complete).

When you find an item you want to buy, here's how to make your purchase:

1. **Tap the button that shows either the price (if it's a selection available for purchase; see Figure 1-10) or the word Free (if it's a selection available for free).**

   The button label changes to Buy X, where X is the particular content you're buying (refer to Figure 1-10).

Tap a price button to make a selection...

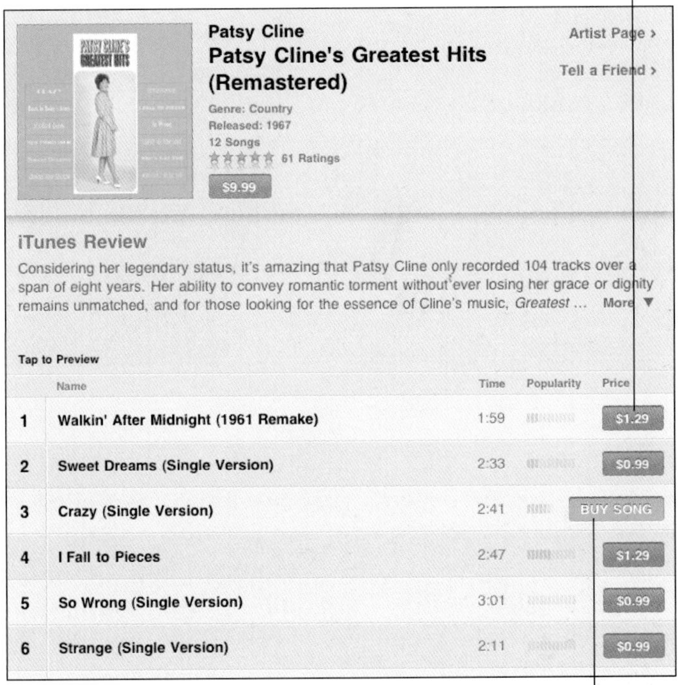

	Name	Time	Popularity	Price
1	Walkin' After Midnight (1961 Remake)	1:59		$1.29
2	Sweet Dreams (Single Version)	2:33		$0.99
3	Crazy (Single Version)	2:41		BUY SONG
4	I Fall to Pieces	2:47		$1.29
5	So Wrong (Single Version)	3:01		$0.99
6	Strange (Single Version)	2:11		$0.99

then tap Buy Song when the button's name
changes to purchase the selection

Figure 1-10: Buy the content you want using these buttons.

2. **Tap the Buy X button.**

   The iTunes Password dialog appears (refer to Figure 1-1).

3. **Enter your password and tap OK.**

   The item begins downloading (see Figure 1-11) and is automatically charged to your credit card. When the download finishes, you can view the content using the iPod or Videos app, depending on the type of content you bought.

If you want to buy music, you can open the description page for an album and buy individual songs rather than the entire album. Tap the price for a song, and then proceed to purchase it.

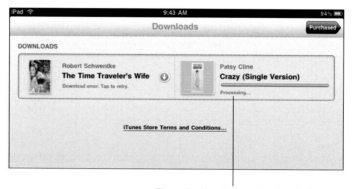

The selection being downloaded

Figure 1-11: iTunes shows you the progress of your download.

Note the Redeem button on many iTunes screens. Tap this button to redeem any iTunes gift certificates you might get from your generous friends, or from yourself.

Renting movies

In the case of movies, you can either rent or buy content. If you rent, which is less expensive, you have 30 days from the time you rent the item to begin to watch it. Once you have begun to watch it, you have 24 hours from that time left to watch it as many times as you like.

1. **With iTunes open, tap the Movies button.**

2. **Locate the movie you want to rent and tap the View button shown in Figure 1-12.**

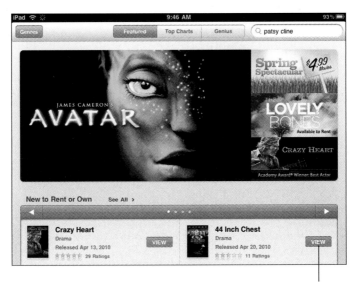

Tap this button

Figure 1-12: To rent, start by viewing details about the content.

3. **In the detailed description of the movie that appears, tap the Rent button shown in Figure 1-13.**

   The gray Rent button changes to a green Rent Movie button; tap it to confirm the rental. The movie begins to download to your iPad immediately and the credit card associated with your account is charged the rental fee.

4. **To check the status of your download, tap the Downloads button.**

   The progress of your download is displayed. Once the download is complete, you can use either the iPod or Videos app to watch it. (See Chapters 2 and 3 in this book to read about how these apps work).

Some movies are offered in high-definition versions. These HD movies look great on that crisp, colorful iPad screen.

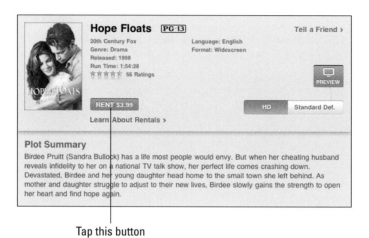

Tap this button

Figure 1-13: If you only want to watch it once, rent and save money.

You can also download content to your computer and sync it to your iPad. Refer to Book 1, Chapter 4 for more about this process.

Listening to Podcasts

Podcasts are audio broadcasts you can listen to on your iPad. Most of these are free (at least I haven't found any that aren't, yet!) and feature a wide variety of topics. They're usually informative rather than strictly entertaining, and great for listening to on that long drive to your friend's cabin in the woods.

It's simple to find podcasts. With iTunes open, tap the Podcast button in the row of buttons at the bottom of the screen. Tap a podcast selection and a detailed listing of podcasts like the one shown in Figure 1-14 appears.

Now you can tap the name or number of a podcast for a preview, or simply tap the Free button, and then tap the Get Episode button (refer to Figure 1-14) to download the podcast. After it downloads, you can play it using the iPod app.

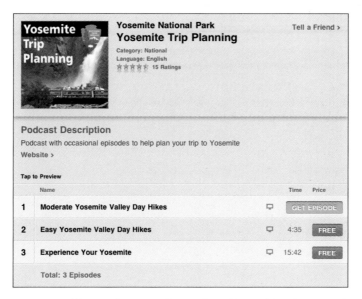

Figure 1-14: Many podcasts are free and provide useful and entertaining information.

Going to School at iTunes U

Feel like you could use a little more learning? Who couldn't? One very cool feature of iTunes is *iTunes U,* a compilation of free online courses from universities and other providers. This is a great way to fill in the blanks in your knowledge. The quality and sources may vary, but some content is outstanding, so it's worth a look.

To explore what's available on the iTunes U campus:

1. **Tap the iTunes U button in the row of buttons at the bottom of the screen to display selections.**

2. **Tap one of the three tabs shown in Figure 1-15: Universities & Colleges, Beyond Campus, or K-12.**

3. **On the list that appears, tap an item to select the source for a course.**

   That provider's page appears.

Tap one of these buttons

Figure 1-15: Choose the educational category that's of interest to you.

4. **Tap the Next or Previous button to scroll through offerings. When you find a topic of interest, tap a selection and it opens, displaying a list of segments of the course, as shown in Figure 1-16.**

5. **Tap the Free button next to a course, and then tap the green Download button that appears.** The course begins downloading.

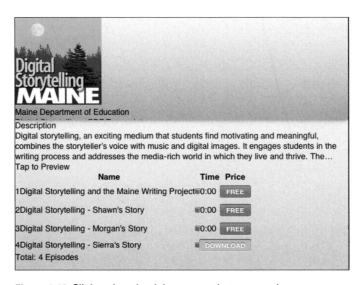

Figure 1-16: Click to download the course that you need.

Once you're on a provider's page, to return to iTunes U, just tap the back button labeled iTunes U (located in the upper-left corner of the screen) and you return to the page with the three provider tabs (refer to Figure 1-15).

Shopping Anywhere Else

As mentioned earlier in this chapter, one feature that's missing from iPad is support for Flash, a format of video playback that many online video-on-demand services use. However, many content stores are hurriedly adding iPad-friendly videos to their collections, so you do have alternatives to iTunes for your choice of movies or TV shows.

You can open accounts at these stores by using your computer or your iPad's Safari browser and then following a store's instructions for purchasing and downloading content. Keep in mind that costs will vary. For example, one such provider is Hulu.com (see Figure 1-17). To get iPad-friendly content from Hulu, you have to sign up for their Hulu Plus service and pay $9.99 a month. Then, download their app directly from Hulu.com and start watching content.

Figure 1-17: Hulu has jumped on the iPad wagon through its paid Hulu Plus service.

Here are some of the other online stores that are looking at offering iPad-compatible content, with more coming all the time:

- Clicker.com is planning to provide its online television and movie content to iPad.

- UStream.com has a mobile app for streaming sports and entertainment programs to mobile devices.

↙ ABC and CBS news will soon stream live TV programming to the iPad.

↙ Netflix.com will soon make non-flash movies available.

Also keep an eye out for Verizon's iPad app, called "What's Hot" at the time of this writing. It will allow for live streaming television from your iPad via the subscription based FiOS service. This service involves a home Wi-Fi network, and a set top box, meaning you'll only be able to stream video to your iPad in your home. If your home computer is a Mac, you can use EyeTV from Elgato to do the same thing.

Additionally, if you can get Flash-based content onto your Mac or Windows machine, you can stream it to your iPad using Air Video and Air Video Server and it will do an on-the-fly conversion.

Chapter 2: Playing Music with the iPod App

In This Chapter

- Sorting by songs, artists, and more
- Searching for audio
- Playing music and other audio
- Shuffling music

Almost everybody on Earth has heard of the iPod — that small, portable, music-playing device from Apple that's seemingly glued into the ears of many kids and teens. iPad includes an iPod app that allows you to take advantage of its pretty amazing little sound system to play your own style of music or podcasts and audiobooks. You can also play movies with the iPod app (though the Videos app provides a few more features, so you might prefer it to iPod, whose specialty is music).

Whether you own an iPod or not, in this chapter, you can get acquainted with the iPod app and its features that enable you to sort and find music and control playback from your iPad.

Looking over Your Library of Music

In the previous chapter I guided you through the process of getting content onto your iPad. After you have some audio content in the form of music, podcasts, or audiobooks, you can find it organized into collections and find that content by categories such as artist or genre with predefined category buttons along the bottom of the iPod app screen.

Viewing the Library Contents

You can easily view the contents of your library collections, which you may have synced from your computer or downloaded directly using iPad's Wi-Fi capability (see the previous chapter for details).

Take a tour of your iPod library collections by following these simple steps:

1. **Tap the iPod app icon located in the Dock on the Home screen.**

   The iPod Library appears (see Figure 2-1).

Figure 2-1: The iPod Library showing your downloaded music.

2. **Tap the Music, Podcasts, or Audiobooks button in the left pane of the Library to open one of these collections (see Figure 2-2).**

3. **Tap the Purchased button in the Library to view all the items you've purchased, including videos, podcasts, music, and audiobooks.**

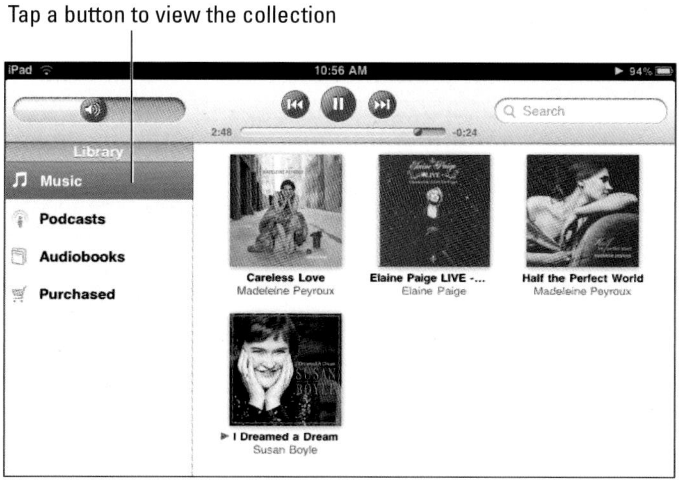

Tap a button to view the collection

Figure 2-2: View various collections in the Library.

iTunes has several free items you can download and use to play around with the features in iPod, including music, podcasts, and audiobooks. You can also sync content stored on your computer to your iPad and play it using iPod. See Book I, Chapter 4 for more about syncing.

You can use the iTunes Summary tab to make a setting to download music at 128 Kbps. Doing this saves space on your iPad if you're an avid music downloader. You can also make a setting for downloading album covers or not in iTunes.

Sorting by songs, artists, and more

With the iPod app open, you can easily view music by a variety of criteria by tapping the buttons along the bottom of the screen to sort music by these self-explanatory categories:

- Songs
- Artists
- Albums
- Genres (see Figure 2-3)
- Composers

Tap a category button to sort the collection

Figure 2-3: Choose various categories to sort your collection by.

Want to know how many songs you have by a certain artist? When you display the Artists category, it includes a column that lists the number of albums and songs in your collection by that artist.

It's kind of fun to tap the Composers tab and see who wrote the music you seem to prefer. With the Composers pane displayed, tap an album/song link to connect the composer with the songs he or she wrote. You might be surprised who wrote your favorite songs!

Creating playlists

Everybody loves playlists. They let you compile your very own music mix to match your mood or the occasion. You can easily create your own playlists with the iPod app to put tracks from various sources into collections of your choosing.

With iPod open, follow these steps to create your own playlists:

1. **Tap the plus sign in the bottom-left corner of the iPad screen, and enter a name for the playlist in the New Playlist dialog that appears.**

2. **Tap Save, and then in the list of selections that appears, tap the plus sign next to each item you'd like to include (see Figure 2-4).**

   Selected items turn gray.

3. **Tap the Done button.**

4. **Tap Done again on the list that appears.**

   Your playlist appears in the Library list and you can now play it by tapping the list name and then the Play button.

You can use the Genius Playlist feature in iTunes to set up playlists of recommended content in your iPad Library. Based on items you've purchased, iTunes suggests other purchases that would go well with your collection. Okay, it's a way to get you to buy more music, but if you are building your music collection, it might be worth a try! Visit the iTunes site at www.apple.com/itunes for more information.

After Hours	Rickie Lee Jones	Rickie Lee Jones	2:13	⊕
Amazing Grace	Susan Boyle	I Dreamed a Dream	3:33	⊕
Argentina Introduction	Elaine Paige	Elaine Paige LIVE - Celebratin...	0:56	⊕
As If I Never Said Good...	Elaine Paige	Elaine Paige LIVE - Celebratin...	6:47	⊕
Blue Alert	Madeleine Peyroux	Half the Perfect World	4:10	⊕
Broadway Baby	Elaine Paige	Elaine Paige LIVE - Celebratin...	5:08	⊕
By The Sea	Elaine Paige	Elaine Paige LIVE - Celebratin...	4:48	⊕
California Rain	Madeleine Peyroux	Half the Perfect World	2:57	⊕
Chuck E's in Love	Rickie Lee Jones	Rickie Lee Jones	3:31	⊕
Come Dance With Me	Diana Krall	From This Moment On (Bonus...	4:21	⊕
Company	Rickie Lee Jones	Rickie Lee Jones	4:54	⊕
Coolsville	Rickie Lee Jones	Rickie Lee Jones	3:52	⊕

Figure 2-4: Choose items to include in your playlist.

Searching for audio

If you can't find what you want by going through collections or categories, you can search for an item in your iPod Library using the Search feature. You can enter an artist's name, author's/composer's name, or a word from the item's title in the Search field to find what you're looking for.

With iPod open, tap in the Search field. The onscreen keyboard opens, as shown in Figure 2-5.

Tap here to search for audio

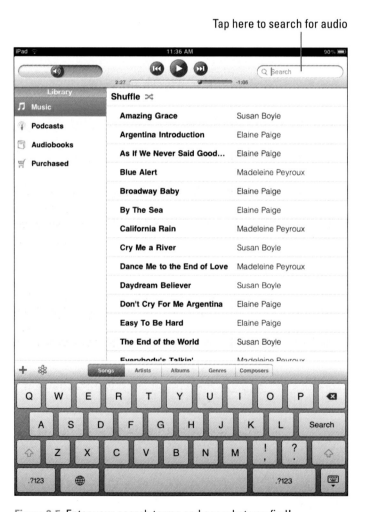

Figure 2-5: Enter your search terms and see what you find!

Enter a search term in the Search field. Results are displayed, narrowing down as you type, as shown in Figure 2-6. Now just tap any item in the Search results to play it.

Results display as you type

Figure 2-6: iPod search results.

Playing Music and Other Audio

You got all that music and other audio content to listen to, and beyond downloading and organizing your selections, that's what iPod is mainly for. You'll find the typical playback tools in the iPod app, but in case you want a refresher, here's the quick rundown on how to use the iPod as a player.

Playing your tunes

Playing an audio file is simple and you'll be glad to hear iPod can continue to play in the background while you go use other apps. If you're browsing in Safari, for example, with music playing in iPod you can double-tap the Home button and a mini toolbar opens where you can control playback without leaving the browser.

The procedure for playing music is to basically find what you want to play, and then use the playback tools. Here's how:

1. **Locate the album, podcast, or audiobook you want to play using the methods I describe in previous sections.**

2. **Tap the album, podcast, or audiobook that contains the audio you want to play.**

    It begins playing back. If you are displaying the Songs tab or the Purchased library, you need only tap a song to play it without first starting the album.

3. **If you want to go a specific item, such as a song in the album that's playing, tap the item you want to play from the list that appears (see Figure 2-7); it begins to play.**

Tap an item to play it

Figure 2-7: Tap a tune to get it going.

4. **Use the Previous and Next buttons at the top of the screen shown in Figure 2-8 to navigate the audio file that's playing.**

   The Previous button actually takes you back to the beginning of the item that's currently playing; the Next button takes you to the next item.

5. **Tap the Pause button to pause playback.**

6. **Tap and drag the circle that indicates the current playback location on the Progress bar left or right to "scrub" to another location in the song.**

7. **Don't like what's playing? Tap the Back to Library arrow in the bottom-left corner to return to the Library view, or tap the Album List button in the bottom-right corner to show other selections in the currently playing album and make another selection.**

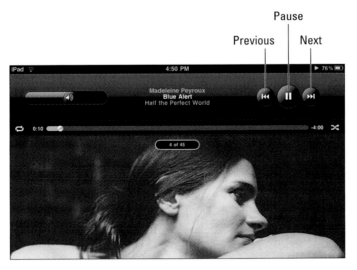

Figure 2-8: Your typical playback tools displayed in the iPod app.

If you love album covers, just tap the cover of the album labeled Now Playing in the lower-left corner (refer to Figure 2-3) and it is displayed full screen. Tap in the middle of the album cover and it flips, revealing the individual songs list along with playback controls.

Shuffling music

If you'd like to play a random selection of the music you've purchased or synced from your computer, you can do that using the Shuffle feature. With iPod open, tap either the Music or Purchased button in the Library pane on the left and then tap the Songs button on the bottom of the screen.

Tap the Shuffle button (see Figure 2-9). Your content plays in random order.

In the Purchased collection of your library, all media is displayed. If you shuffle, you might find TV shows, movies, and podcasts playing here and there. If you just want music, tap the Music collection before tapping Shuffle.

Adjusting the volume

iPod offers its own volume control that you can adjust during playback. With iPod open, tap a piece of music, podcast, or audiobook to play it. In the controls that display (see Figure 2-10), press and drag the button on the Volume slider to the right for more volume or to the left for less volume. To mute iPad's speaker at any time, press the Mute button or press and hold down the iPad volume rocker.

Tap this button

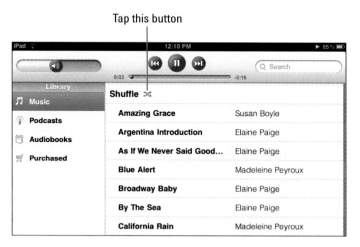

Figure 2-9: Shuffle your music for a varied musical experience.

If you've got volume set at high and you're still having trouble hearing, consider getting a headset. These devices cut out extraneous noises and may improve the sound quality of what you're listening to. You need a 3.5-mm stereo headphone; insert it in the headphone jack on the top of your iPad. You can also use Apple's iPod or iPhone earbuds, which work just fine with iPad. The iPhone buds include a microphone, as well.

Use the Volume slider to adjust the volume

Figure 2-10: Louder or softer, just use the slider to get the effect you want.

Chapter 3: Watching Videos and YouTube

In This Chapter

✔ **Playing movies, podcasts, or TV shows with Videos**

✔ **Going to a movie chapter**

✔ **Deleting an item from iPad**

✔ **Finding videos on YouTube**

You have two built-in applications on your iPad that focus on viewing videos. The Videos app is a player with which you can watch downloaded movies or TV shows or media you've synced from your Mac or PC. The YouTube app takes you online to the popular video-sharing site. As you probably know, videos here range from professional music videos to clips from news or entertainment shows and personal videos of cats dancing and news-making events as they happen.

In this chapter, I explain how to use controls in both apps to play programs and how to use some of the YouTube features to rate, share, and save favorite videos. You might want to refer to Book II, Chapter 1 first to purchase or download one of many free TV shows or movies you can practice with.

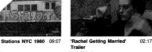

Getting Visual with Videos

Note that you can get video content through iTunes, and some third party companies that support iPad like Netflix and ABC TV. You can also use an app like Air Video to send content from your Mac or PC to your iPad via a wireless connection, or use the EyeTV app from your Mac to send live TV or recordings. Some of the content you find online is free, and some shows or movies will cost you a few bucks.

This chapter focuses mainly on the built-in Videos and YouTube apps, but you should also note that more and more online content providers are making it possible to view videos on their sites. For example, you can go to Flickr and use their HTML 5 player for video playback.

See Book II, Chapter 1, for more about buying or renting movies or TV shows using the iTunes Store.

Playing movies, podcast, or TV shows with Videos

Did you realize your iPad is a mini home entertainment center? The built-in Videos app can play TV shows, movies, and podcasts that you find online and download to your iPad.

Use the steps in Book II, Chapter 1, to download video content to your iPad. After you have downloaded content, use these steps to work with pretty familiar playback tools to play it:

1. **Tap the Videos app icon on the Home screen to open the application.**

2. **In the screen like the one shown in Figure 3-1, tap the Movies, Podcast, or TV Shows tab, depending on which you want to watch.**

Tap the Movies or TV Show tab

Figure 3-1: Choose the type of content you want to view.

3. **Tap an item to open it.**

   A description appears, as shown in Figure 3-2.

The Play button

Figure 3-2: You can get information about the media on this opening screen.

4. **Tap the Play button.**

   The movie, podcast, or TV show opens and begins playing. The progress of the playback is displayed on the top of the screen, showing how many minutes you've viewed and how many remain (see Figure 3-3). If you don't see this information, tap the screen once and it will display briefly along with a set of playback tools at the bottom of the screen.

5. **With the playback tools displayed, take any of the following familiar actions:**

   • Tap the Pause button to pause playback.

   • Tap Go to Previous Chapter or Go to Next Chapter to move to a different location in the video playback.

   • Tap the circular button on the Volume slider and drag it left or right to decrease or increase the volume, respectively.

6. **To stop the video and return to the information screen, tap the Done button.**

TIP

You can set up widescreen viewing options in the Videos section of iPad Settings. For more about using Settings, see Book I, Chapter 7.

Done button   Progress bar

Audio and Subtitles button   Go to Next Chapter button

Go to Previous Chapter button | Volume slider

Pause button

Figure 3-3: Use the standard playback controls to play your content.

Watching non-iTunes videos

Are you limited to iTunes video content on your iPad or viewing all your downloaded content on the smaller screen? Not at all. You can connect iPad to your television, so you can watch videos on the more vision-friendly larger screen. To do this, you have to buy either an Apple iPad Dock or a VGA connector cable at the Apple Store. You also need any other appropriate cables for your TV to complete the connection.

Note that iPad only supports the following video formats: H.264 video up to 720p, 30 frames per second; MPEG-4 video, up to 2.5 Mbps, 640 by 480 pixels, 30 frames per second; and Motion JPEG (M-JPEG) up to 35 Mbps, 1280 by 720 pixels, 30 frames per second. If you want to play AVI videos, you use conversion

software like Mac AVI to iPad Video Converter to be able to convert, edit, and play AVI movies on your iPad. You can also stream with Air Video Live Conversion, or use the free Handbrake app to convert to an iPad-friendly format.

In addition you can rip Blu-ray video disc content to an iPad-compatible format and then transfer the content by syncing to your computer using iTunes. You can use the free Blu-ray to iPad Ripper at www.softdiggs. com/blu-ray-ripper.php to handle the transfer.

Finally, check out an app called Air Video from In Method. Using this app you can stream content to your iPad, convert content, or save content to iTunes which you can then sync to your iPad.

TIP Note that if you've watched a video before and stopped partway through, the next time you open the video in iPad it opens at the last spot you were viewing by default. To start a video from the beginning, just as with most players, you simply tap and drag the circular button on the Progress bar all the way to the left. You can also change the default setting to start where you left off to starting from the beginning in iPad's Settings under Video.

Turning on closed captioning

If you have hearing challenges, or are a fan of foreign flicks, you'll be glad to hear that iPad offers support for closed captioning and subtitles. This feature requires that you have content that supports closed captioning (not all shows or movies do) and that you use iPad Settings to turn on the feature.

Turn on the feature in iPad Settings by following these steps:

1. **Tap the Settings icon on the Home screen.**

2. **On the screen that appears (see Figure 3-4), tap Video in the Settings section on the left side of the screen.**

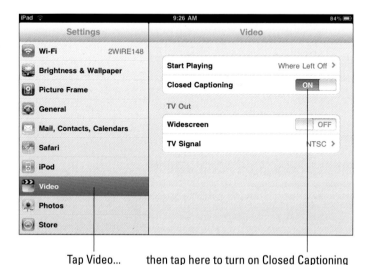

Tap Video...   then tap here to turn on Closed Captioning

Figure 3-4: Use the Settings icon on your Home screen to access video settings.

3. **In the menu that displays on the right-hand side of the screen (refer to Figure 3-4), tap the Closed Captioning On/Off button to turn on the feature.**

Now when you play a movie with closed captioning, you can click the Audio and Subtitles button to the left of the playback controls to manage these features.

Going to a movie chapter

You know that movies you view on a DVD or online are divided into chapters, so you can jump from one part to another quickly. Jumping to another chapter using the Videos app is a pretty simple procedure.

1. **Tap the Videos app icon on the Home screen.**

2. **Tap the Movies tab if it isn't already displayed.**

3. **Tap the movie you want to watch.**

   Information about the movie is displayed, as shown in Figure 3-5.

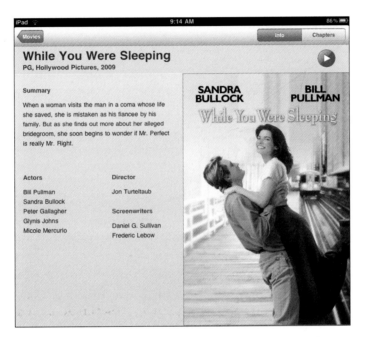

Figure 3-5: The default Info screen is informative, but doesn't allow you to jump among chapters.

4. **Tap the Chapters tab.**

   A list of chapters is displayed, as shown in Figure 3-6.

5. **Tap a chapter to play it.**

You can also use the playback tools to go back one chapter or forward one chapter. See the "Playing movies, podcast, or TV shows with Videos" section, earlier in this chapter, for more information.

Tap this tab...

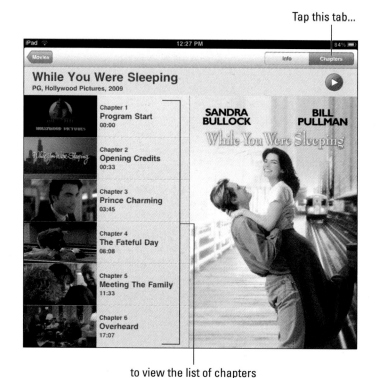

to view the list of chapters

Figure 3-6: Click a chapter in this list to go to it.

Deleting an item from iPad

Media files can, as we all know, take up lots of space in a computing device. Even if you bought the iPad model with the largest amount of memory, its memory can fill up fast. When you've bought content on iTunes, you can always download it again, so if you're not planning on watching an item again soon, it's a good idea to delete it on your iPad and free up some space.

To delete items, start by tapping the Videos app icon on the Home screen. Locate the item you want to delete on the Movies, Podcasts, or TV Shows tab and then press and hold the item; a Delete button appears, as shown in Figure 3-7. Tap the Delete button, and the item is deleted.

The Delete button

Figure 3-7: Click Delete and your video is gone.

TIP

If you buy a video using iTunes, download it to your iPad, and then delete it from iPad, you'll find it saved in your iTunes library. You can sync your computer and iPad again to download it once more. However, rented movies, once deleted, are gone with the wind.

YouTube the iPad Way

How did we ever survive before YouTube? What would most of us do without all that free content, from new tech gadget demos by a 14-year-old kid or a CNET reviewer, to TV show clips and dancing pets? Love it or not, YouTube, the popular video sharing site, has become part of most of our lives.

So, you may be glad to hear that the built-in YouTube app on your iPad makes it easy to view, subscribe to, and save favorites from the site.

Finding videos on YouTube

Although you can go to YouTube and use all its features using iPad's Safari browser, it's easier using the dedicated YouTube app that's included on the iPad. This version features buttons you can tap to display different content and features using the touchscreen.

Start by opening the app and finding videos you want to view:

1. **Tap the YouTube app icon on the Home screen to open it.**

2. **Tap the Featured button at the bottom of the screen if it's not already selected (see Figure 3-8).**

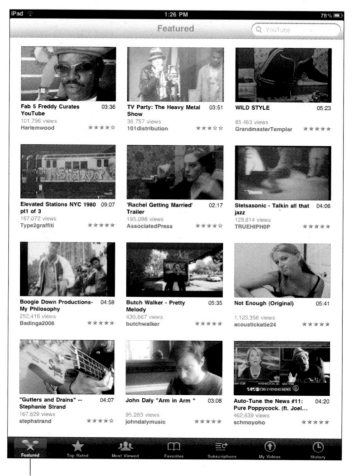

Tap this button

Figure 3-8: Buttons along the bottom help organize content.

3. **To find videos you want to watch, tap in the Search field.**

   The onscreen keyboard opens, as shown in Figure 3-9.

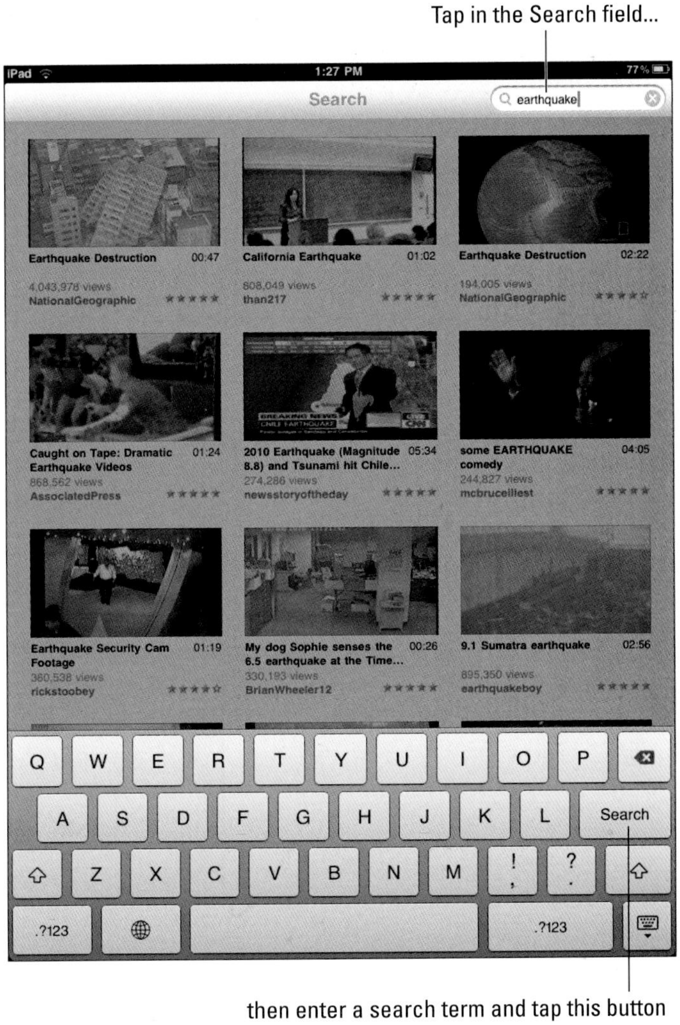

Tap in the Search field...

then enter a search term and tap this button

Figure 3-9: Using the onscreen keyboard to enter a search term.

4. **Type a search term and tap the Search button on the keyboard (refer to Figure 3-9).**

5. **Use your finger to scroll down the screen to see additional results.**

6. **To display the top-rated or most-viewed videos, tap the Top Rated or Most Viewed button on the bottom of the screen.**

7. When you find a video you want to view, tap it to display it.

The video begins loading (see Figure 3-10). See the next section for details of how to control the playback.

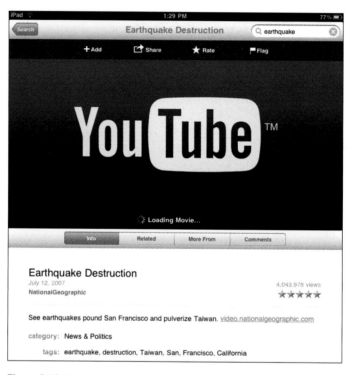

Figure 3-10: Watch your video in this window.

When you load a video, you can use the Related and More From tabs in the playback window (refer to Figure 3-10) to find additional content related to the topic, or more videos posted on YouTube by the same source. If you find a video you like, tap the More From tab and you can then tap the Subscribe button to subscribe to all movies from this source. View your subscriptions by tapping the Subscriptions button at the bottom of the YouTube screen.

Controlling video playback

The video playback controls in the YouTube app on your iPad sport all the familiar playback buttons you're used to, but just in case you haven't used a player in a few weeks, here's a quick rundown:

✔ The Play button is, logically enough, what you tap to get the video to play, as shown in Figure 3-11.

Play/Pause button   Playback progress bar

Figure 3-11: These playback tools look like those used in most video or music players.

✔ The Pause button is used (quite logically) to pause playback. (If the button is not visible, tap the screen in the black area on either side of the video once to display it.)

✔ The circular button on the Playback progress bar can be moved right or left to move forward or backward in the video.

 Was the video so good you have to watch it again? When the video is finished, you can replay it from the beginning by tapping the Play button once again.

Changing views

 You know that there are times when you just have to switch from a smaller view to a full screen view to watch a video. By default, you watch a YouTube video on your iPad in the smallest of three available views. To change to larger views, tap the Play button and then tap the Full Screen button. The video displays in a full screen version, as shown in Figure 3-12.

Figure 3-12: Full screen gets you the most screen real estate.

To go to an even larger view, tap the button in the top-right corner. The movie fills the screen, as in Figure 3-13.

To reduce the movie back to its smallest size, tap the button on the right side of the playback controls. Tap the button in the upper-right corner to return to the medium view.

You can use the double-tap method of enlarging the playback when in either of the two larger screen formats. Double-tapping the smaller of the two moves you to the largest full screen view. Double-tapping the largest full screen view zooms out farther. But be forewarned: depending on the quality of the video, the largest zoom factor could produce a rather grainy image.

Figure 3-13: A video shown in the full screen view.

Flagging content as inappropriate

If there's a chance your kids or younger sibling could get ahold of your iPad, you might appreciate the capability to flag inappropriate content on YouTube. First you have to set a restriction in your YouTube account using your computer, and then set a flag using the iPad YouTube app. A flag requires that a passcode be entered to access that content.

Here are the steps involved in flagging content on the iPad, after you've set a restriction using your computer:

1. **With a video open in the YouTube application, tap in the black area near the top of the screen to display tools, as shown in Figure 3-14.**

Display this toolbar

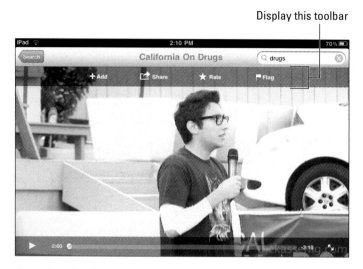

Figure 3-14: Displaying the toolbar in the YouTube app.

2. **Tap the Flag option.**

3. **Tap the Flag As Inappropriate button that appears (see Figure 3-15).**

Tap this option...

then tap this button

Figure 3-15: There's pretty much one choice here!

Rating videos

Part of the fun of YouTube is the fact that the masses can rate videos to express their opinions. This rating system also helps you find the best of the best videos, according to those who have recorded their opinion.

You can easily rate videos using the YouTube app on your iPad. Follow these steps to rate a video:

1. **Display a video you want to rate.**

2. **Tap the Rate button shown in Figure 3-16.**

Tap the Rate button...

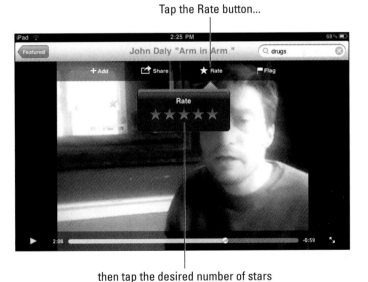

then tap the desired number of stars

Figure 3-16: A simple, but effective 5-star rating system.

3. **Tap the number of stars you want in the Rate field that appears (refer to Figure 3-16) to rate the video (if you're not sure, 1 is the lowest rating, 5 the highest).**

That's it! Your opinion has been noted and can help guide others to great content, or steer them away from the not so great.

Remember that you can view the highest rated videos on YouTube by tapping the Top Rated button at the bottom of the screen.

Sharing videos

Found a video you like? Just as you can use your computer to share YouTube videos you like, you can share links to videos with others from your iPad using e-mail. Here's how:

1. **Display a video you want to share.**

2. **Tap the Share button shown in Figure 3-17.**

Tap this button

Figure 3-17: Start sharing your favorite videos by e-mail.

3. **In the e-mail form shown in Figure 3-18, type a recipient in the To field and add to the message if you like.**

4. **Tap the Send button to send a link to the video.**

If you like a movie enough to share it, you might also be interested in sharing your opinions with the greater YouTube community using the Comments feature. With a video selection displayed, tap the Comments tab. Tap in the Add a Comment field, type your comment, and tap the Send button on your keyboard. Your comment is posted.

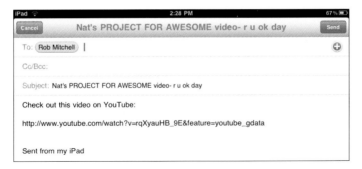

Figure 3-18: Fill out the simple e-mail form which has the subject already filled in for you.

Adding to video favorites

Have you discovered a video you want to play again and again? You can use the Favorites feature of the iPad YouTube app to save such videos to your Favorites folder for easy access.

Save a video to Favorites using these steps:

1. **Display a video you want to add to Favorites.**
2. **Tap the Add button shown in Figure 3-19.**
3. **In the menu shown (refer to Figure 3-19), tap Favorites.**
4. **To view your favorite movies, tap the Favorites button at the bottom of the YouTube screen.**

   Your favorite folder containing all your favorite videos is displayed (see Figure 3-20).

To delete a favorite while in the Favorites screen, tap the Edit button. Delete buttons appear on each movie. Tap the movie-specific Delete button to remove that movie. Tap the Done button to leave the editing mode.

Tap this button...

then tap Favorites

Figure 3-19: Fill up your Favorites folder.

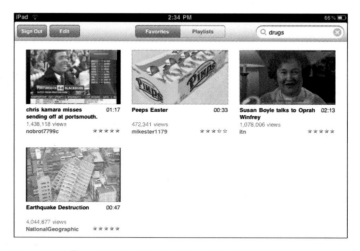

Figure 3-20: The eclectic collection in my Favorites folder.

Chapter 4: Playing with Photos

*W*ith its gorgeous screen, iPad is a natural for viewing photos. iPad supports most common photo formats, such as JPEG, TIFF, PNG, and GIF. You can get your photos from your computer, iPhone, or digital camera. You can also save images you find online to your iPad.

After you have photos to play with, the Photos app allows you to view them in albums, one-by-one, or in a slideshow. You can also e-mail a photo to a friend or use your expensive gadget as an electronic picture frame, all of which you read about in this chapter.

Getting Photos into iPad

Before you can play around with photos, you have to get them into iPad. There are a few different ways to accomplish this. You can buy an accessory to import them from your camera or iPhone, save a photo you find on the Web or receive as an e-mail attachment, or sync to your computer to download photos you've saved there. The whole syncing process is discussed in Book 1, Chapter 4. The two other methods are explained here.

Importing photos from a digital camera or iPhone

You can import photos from a digital camera and photos or videos from your iPhone if you buy the iPad Camera Connection Kit from Apple, which will set you back about $29.

The iPad Camera Connection Kit contains two adapters (see Figure 4-1): a USB Camera Connector you use to import photos from a digital camera or iPhone, and an SD Card Reader to import images from an SD card.

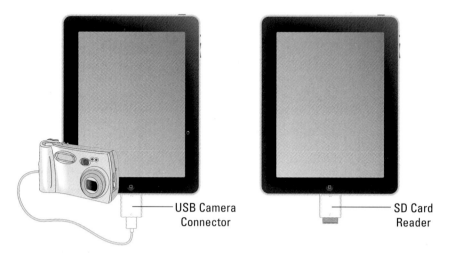

USB Camera Connector

SD Card Reader

Figure 4-1: These two adapters are included in the connector kit accessory.

If you've got an iPhone 3G or earlier model, sad to say, it isn't supported by the connector kit.

Follow these steps to import photos, after you have the connector kit in hand:

1. **Start the import process by locking your iPad's screen by using the screen locker on the top-right side of the iPad.**

2. **Insert the USB Camera Connector into the Dock connector slot of your iPad.**

3. **Connect the USB end of the cord that came with your digital camera or iPhone into the USB Camera Connector.**

4. **Connect the other end of the cord that came with your camera or iPhone into that device.**

5. **Unlock your iPad.**

   The Photos app opens and displays the photos on the digital camera or iPhone.

6. **Tap Import All on your iPad; if you only want to import selected photos, tap individual photos, and then tap Import. Finally, tap Import rather than Import All.**

   The photos are saved to the Last Import album.

7. **Disconnect the cord and the adapter and you're done!**

You can also import photos stored on an *SD* (secure digital) memory card often used by digital cameras as a storage medium. Simply lock the iPad, insert the SD Card Reader into the iPad, insert the SD card containing the photos, and then follow Steps 5–7 above.

Though not promoted as a feature by Apple, people have discovered that you can also use the USB connector in the connector kit to connect audio devices such as speakers or headphones, and to hook up some USB-connected keyboards that have lower power consumption.

Saving photos from the Web

The Web offers a wealth of images that you can download to your Photo Library on the iPad. The built-in Safari browser makes it simple to save any image you come across to your iPad. (Of course you should be careful not to violate copyrights when grabbing pictures online).

Several search engines have advanced search features that allow you to only search for non-licensed images, meaning, at least theoretically, you don't have to pay for the images. But it's always a good idea to get written permission to use an image, especially if you intend to use it to make money (as with a company brochure or online course).

Follow these steps to save images from the Web:

1. **Open Safari and navigate to the Web page containing the image you want.**

2. **Press and hold the image.**

   A menu appears, as shown in Figure 4-2.

3. **Tap Save Image.**

   The image is saved to your Saved Photos album in the Photos app, as shown in Figure 4-3.

For more about how to use Safari to navigate to or search for Web content, see Book I, Chapter 5.

Tap this option

Figure 4-2: Use this menu to save an image to your iPad.

The Saved Photos album

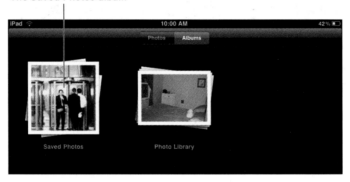

Figure 4-3: Photos you save from the Internet go into the Saved Photos album.

Looking at Photos

Pictures were made to be looked at, so knowing how to view the albums and individual photos you manage to get into your iPad is a way to tap into the key strength of the Photos app. In this section, you get some tips for taking your viewing experience to the max.

If you want to do more than look at photos, check out a few of these photo-editing apps that were designed to work with iPad: Photogene for iPad; Photoforge for iPad; and the free PhotoPad by Zagg. All three are available through the Apple App Store.

Viewing an album

The Photos app organizes your pictures into albums. The Saved Photos album contains images you have saved from the Web or received as Mail attachments. The Photo Library album stores images you import from your computer. There may also be albums for images you synced from devices such as your iPhone or digital camera.

To view albums, tap the Photos app icon in the Dock on the Home screen. If the Photos tab is selected when the Photos app opens, tap the Albums tab shown in Figure 4-4. Now you can tap an album and the photos in it are displayed, as shown in Figure 4-5.

Tap this tab to view albums

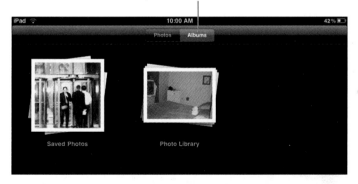

Figure 4-4: Switch between individual photos and albums using these buttons.

If you're a Mac user, try using iPhoto to create new albums before you sync to your iPad to create new albums for organizing your iPad content. If you're on a Windows machine, check out two products for managing and syncing photos to iPad: Lightroom from Adobe (www.adobe.com) or Adobe's Photoshop Elements.

Screenshots you take of your iPad screen are also saved to the Saved Pictures album. To take a screenshot, display what you want to shoot, press and hold the Home button, tap the Sleep/Wake button, and then release. You'll find your screenshot in the Photos app.

**Book II
Chapter 4**

Playing with Photos

Figure 4-5: My cottage, my cat, and some of my books (and if you look carefully, me).

Viewing individual photos

After you figure out what album your images are in, you have several fun ways to interact with individual photos. The iPad touchscreen is the key to this very tactile experience.

Tap the Photos app icon in the Dock on the Home screen and then tap the Photos tab (shown in Figure 4-6).

Now try out these techniques:

- To view a photo, pinch your fingers together, place them on the photo, and then spread your fingers apart. The picture expands, as shown in Figure 4-7.

- Flick your finger to the left or right to scroll through the individual photos in that album.

- To reduce the size of the individual photos and return to the multi-picture view, place two fingers on the photo and then pinch them together.

- Place two fingers on a photo and spin them to the left or right. This maneuver, known as grab and spin, twirls the photo on the screen (and it's lots of fun to do).

Tap this tab

Figure 4-6: Viewing individual photos.

Figure 4-7: An expanded photo.

Do you like to associate a face with a name? Doing so can help you keep your clients or other contacts straight. You can place a photo on a person's information page in the Contacts app on your iPad. For more about how to do this, see Book V, Chapter 4.

Sharing Photos

Part of the fun of taking photos is sharing those images with others. It's easy to share photos stored on your iPad by sending them as e-mail attachments. Follow these steps to do just that:

1. **Tap the Photos app icon in the Dock on the Home screen.**

2. **Tap the Photos tab and locate the photo you want to share.**

3. **Tap on the photo to select it and then tap the Sharing icon (it looks like a box with an arrow jumping out of it).**

   The menu shown in Figure 4-8 appears.

Tap the Sharing icon...

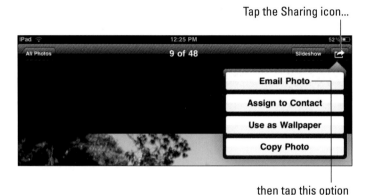

Figure 4-8: The Sharing menu offers different options.

4. **Tap the Email Photo option.**

5. **In the e-mail message form that appears (see Figure 4-9), make any modifications you want in the To, Cc/Bcc, or Subject fields. You can also tap within the body of the message and add more text.**

6. **Tap the Send button and the message and photo go on their way.**

You can also copy and paste a photo into documents, such as those created in the Pages word processor app that you can purchase for about $9.99. To do this, press and hold a photo in Photos until the Copy command appears. Tap Copy, and then in the destination app, press and hold the screen and tap Paste.

Figure 4-9: Your e-mailed photo will be labeled "Sent from my iPad."
How cool is that?

Running a Slideshow

You can run a slideshow of your images in Photos and even play music and
choose transition effects for the show. This is a great way to give a presentation to a client on your easy-to-carry iPad, or show your friends a slideshow
of your last adventure travel vacation.

To use the slideshow feature, follow these steps:

1. **Tap the Photos app icon to open the application.**

2. **Tap the Photos tab.**

3. **Tap the Slideshow button to see the Slideshow Options menu, shown in Figure 4-10.**

4. **If you want to play music along with the slideshow, tap the On/Off button in the Play Music field.**

Tap the Slideshow button

Figure 4-10: Use this menu to add transition effects and start the slideshow.

5. **To choose the music that will play along with the slideshow, tap the Music field and in the list that appears (see Figure 4-11), tap any selection from your iPod library.**

6. **Tap the transition effect you want to use for your slideshow (refer to Figure 4-10).**

7. **Tap the Start Slideshow button.**

The slideshow begins.

To run a slideshow that includes only the photos contained in a particular album, tap the Album tab, tap an album to open it, and then tap the Slideshow button to make settings and run a slideshow.

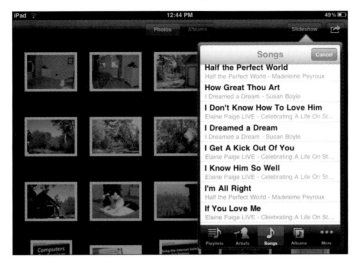

Figure 4-11: Pick a song that matches your slideshow's mood.

Displaying Picture Frame

You can use the slideshow settings you created in the previous section to run your slideshow while your iPad screen is locked so you can view a continuous display of your pictures. This feature can help you make good use of the time when your iPad is recharging or subliminally flash images of your products again and again at your client while you make your sales pitch.

Here's how to use the Picture Frame feature:

1. **Tap the Sleep/Wake button to lock iPad and then tap the Home button to go to the Lock screen; the bottom of this screen looks like Figure 4-12.**

The Picture Frame button

Figure 4-12: Picture Frame is a great feature for showing off your product line — or cool new car.

2. **Tap the Picture Frame button (refer to Figure 4-12). The slideshow begins (see Figure 4-13). To end the show, tap the Home button.**

If you don't like the effects used on the picture frame, go back to Photos and change the slideshow settings.

Figure 4-13: Use Picture Frame to show off several images at once.

In the category of questionable iPad accessories is The iPad Frame Dock. This item is a stand for your iPad that looks like a picture frame. You can even hang it and your iPad on a wall. That is, if you have nowhere else to place your several hundred dollar electronic device. Of course the dock does allow you to charge your iPad while it's hanging around (www.theipadframe.com).

Deleting Photos

You might find it's time to get rid of some of those old photos of the family reunion or the last project you worked on. If a photo wasn't transferred from your computer but instead was downloaded or captured as a screenshot on the iPad, you can delete it using this procedure:

1. **Tap the Photos app icon in the Dock on the Home screen.**
2. **Tap the Albums tab and then tap the Saved Photos album to open it.**
3. **Tap an individual photo to open it.**
4. **Tap the Trash Can button and then tap the Delete Photo button that appears, as shown in Figure 4-14.**

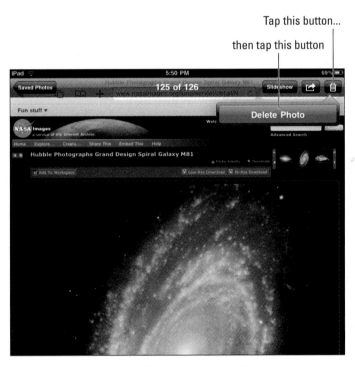

Figure 4-14: If you don't need it any more, delete it!

If you need to delete multiple photos, with the album open, just tap the Share button, select up to five images, tap Delete at the top left of the screen, and tap Delete Selected Photos. Repeat as desired!

Chapter 5: Using Your iPad as an eReader

Apple has touted iPad as a great eReader, so, though it isn't a traditional dedicated eReader device like Amazon's Kindle, you won't want to miss out on this very cool functionality.

Apple's free, downloadable application that turns your iPad into an eReader is called *iBooks*. iBooks enables you to buy and download books from Apple's iBookstore. You can use several other free eReader applications, such as Kindle, Stanza, and Barnes & Noble's Nook that you can use to download books to your iPad from a variety of online bookstores and read to your heart's content.

In this chapter, you discover the options available for reading material and how to buy books. You also find out about the iBooks app: how to navigate a book and adjust the brightness and type, as well as how to search books and organize your iBooks library.

Discovering How iPad Differs from Other eReaders

An *eReader* is any electronic device that enables you to download and read books, magazines, and newspapers. These devices are typically dedicated only to reading electronic content. They are very portable, and most use a technology called eInk to create a paper-like reading experience.

The iPad is a bit different: As you know, it isn't only used for reading books, and you have to download an application to enable it as an eReader (though every eReader app I've found is free). Also, it doesn't offer the paper-like reading experience — you read from a computer screen (though you can adjust the brightness of that screen).

When you buy a book or magazine online (or get one of many free publications), it downloads to your iPad in a few seconds using your Wi-Fi or 3G connection. After you've got your eReader app and some content, iPad offers several navigation tools to move around a book, all of which you explore in this chapter.

Finding and Buying eBooks

Before you can read books or other publications, you have to get your iPad's hands on them (so to speak). This involves downloading eReader software, and then using it to buy publications using the eReader. I'll start by introducing you to iBooks, a free eReader that you can download from iTunes.

Finding books at iBooks

In Book I, Chapter 4, I walk you through the process of downloading the apps, so you should go back and use those steps to download the iBooks app first, if you haven't already.

With iBooks downloaded, you can shop using iBooks by tapping on the iBooks application icon to open it. (Note that it is probably located on your second Home screen, so you may have to swipe your finger to the left on the Home screen to locate it.)

If you become addicted to iBooks, consider placing it on the iPad Dock for quick access from any Home screen. To do this, press and hold the app till all apps jiggle, then tap and drag the iBooks icon to the Dock. Tap the Home button and the jiggling stops.

The iBooks library opens (see Figure 5-1). At this point you see a bookshelf; yours probably has only one free book already downloaded to it. (If you don't see the bookshelf, tap the Library button to go there or, if no Library button is displayed on the screen, tap the Bookshelf button at the top-right corner of the screen — it sports four small squares.) For a cool effect, tap the Store button and the shelf pivots around 180 degrees to display the iBookstore.

Tap the Store button

Figure 5-1: Your virtual iBooks bookshelf.

**Book II
Chapter 5**

Using Your iPad
as an eReader

In the iBookstore shown in Figure 5-2, you can do any of the following to find a book:

- Tap the Search field and type a search word or phrase using the onscreen keyboard.
- Tap the right or left arrows located in the middle of the screen to scroll to more suggested titles.
- Tap the Categories button to see a list of types of books, as shown in Figure 5-3. Tap a category to view those selections.
- Tap See All to view more titles.
- Tap the appropriate button at the bottom of the screen to view Featured titles, the New York Times Bestseller List, books listed on Top Charts, or Purchases to review the titles you've already purchased.
- Tap a suggested selection or featured book ad to open more information about it.

TIP

To avoid buyer's remorse, you can download free samples before you buy. You get to read several pages of the book to see if it appeals to you, and it doesn't cost you a dime! Look for the Get Sample button when you view details about a book to get your free preview.

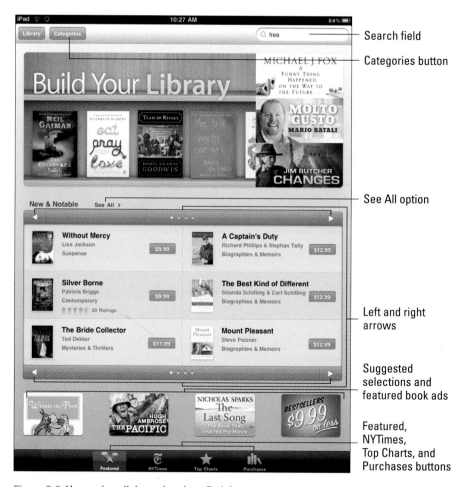

Figure 5-2: Use various links and tools to find the content you want.

Figure 5-3: Find your publication using the Categories feature.

Exploring other eBook sources

iPad is capable of reading book content from other bookstores, so you can get books from sources other than iBookstore. To do so, first download another eReader application such as Kindle from Amazon or the Barnes & Noble Nook from the iPad App Store (see Book I, Chapter 4, for how to download apps). Then use their features to search for, purchase, and download content.

The Kindle eReader application is shown in Figure 5-4. Any content you have already bought from Kindle is archived online and can be placed on your Kindle home page in iPad for you to read any time you like. Deleting an application from this reader works the same as for iBooks: Just swipe a title toward the right and the Delete button appears.

Figure 5-4: Kindle was one of the first to offer a free eReader for iPad.

Buying books

If you have set up an account with iTunes, you can buy books at the iBookstore easily (see Book I, Chapter 4 for more about setting up an account).

1. **When you find a book in the iBookstore that you'd like to buy, tap its Price button.**

   The button changes to a Buy Book button, as shown in Figure 5-5.

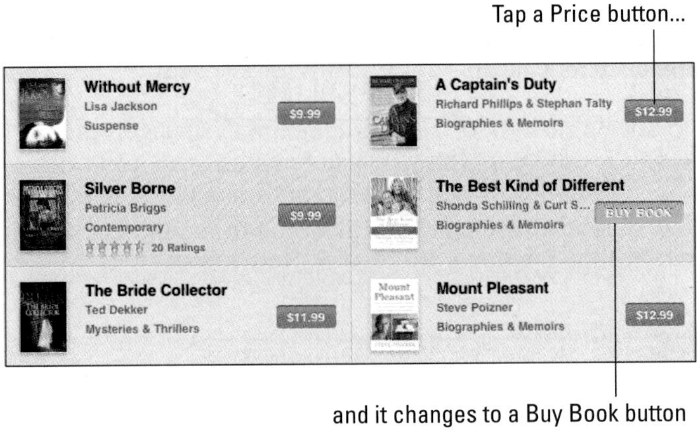

Tap a Price button...

Without Mercy Lisa Jackson Suspense $9.99	**A Captain's Duty** Richard Phillips & Stephan Talty Biographies & Memoirs $12.99
Silver Borne Patricia Briggs Contemporary ★★★★☆ 20 Ratings $9.99	**The Best Kind of Different** Shonda Schilling & Curt S... Biographies & Memoirs BUY BOOK
The Bride Collector Ted Dekker Mysteries & Thrillers $11.99	**Mount Pleasant** Steve Poizner Biographies & Memoirs $12.99

and it changes to a Buy Book button

Figure 5-5: Click the price to buy the book.

Book II
Chapter 5

Using Your iPad as an eReader

2. **Tap the Buy Book button.**

   The iTunes Password dialog shown in Figure 5-6 appears.

iTunes Password

ipadsenior@gmail.com

Password

Cancel   OK

Figure 5-6: Enter your iTunes password to buy anything.

3. **Enter your password and tap OK.**

   The book appears on your bookshelf, and the cost has been charged to whatever credit card you provided when you opened your iTunes account.

You can also sync books you've downloaded to your computer to your iPad using the data connection cord and your iTunes account. Using this method, you can find lots of free books from various sources online as long as they are in the ePub or PDF format, and drag them into your iTunes Books library;

Adjusting brightness

iPad doesn't offer a simulated page surface as some dedicated eReaders such as Kindle do, so it's important that you make the reading experience as comfortable on your eyes as possible by adjusting the brightness.

iBooks offers an adjustable brightness setting that you can use to make your book pages comfortable for you to read. Follow these steps to make an adjustment:

1. **With a book open, tap the Brightness button shown in Figure 5-9.**

   The Brightness dialog appears.

Tap the Brightness button...

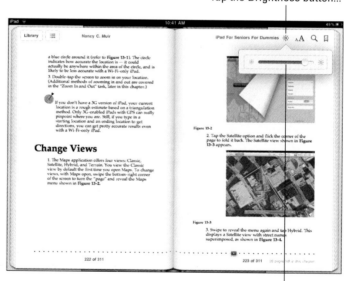

and adjust the screen brightness

Figure 5-9: Adjusting brightness can ease eye strain.

2. **Tap and drag the slider to the right to make the screen brighter, or to the left to dim the screen.**

3. **Tap anywhere in the book to close the Brightness dialog.**

You have to experiment with the brightness that works for you. It's commonly thought that bright white computer screens are hard on the eyes, so going with the halfway default setting or below is probably a good idea.

Changing the font size and type

If the type on your screen is a bit small for your taste, you can change to a larger font size, or choose a different font for readability.

1. **With a book open, tap the Font button (it sports a small and a large capital A, as shown in Figure 5-10).**

Tap the Font button to change font size and type

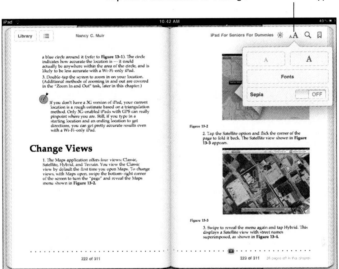

Figure 5-10: Need larger type? Set that up here.

2. **In the Font dialog that appears (refer to Figure 5-10), tap the A button on the left to use smaller text, or the A button on the right to use larger text.**

3. **Tap the Fonts button.**

   The list of fonts shown in Figure 5-11 appears.

4. **Tap a font name to select it.**

   The font changes on the book page.

5. **Tap outside the Fonts dialog to return to your book.**

Some fonts appear a bit larger on your screen than others because of their design. If you want the largest fonts, use Cochin or Verdana.

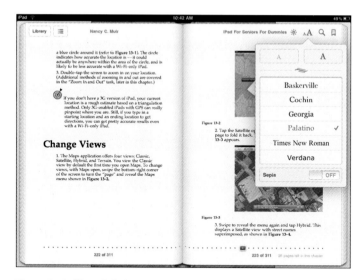

Figure 5-11: Though limited, there is a selection of fonts available in iBooks.

Searching in your book

You may want to find a certain sentence or reference in your book. To search for a word or phrase, follow these steps:

1. **With the book displayed, tap the Search button shown in Figure 5-12.**

   The onscreen keyboard displays.

2. **Enter a search term and then tap the Search key on the keyboard.**

   iBooks searches for any matching entries.

3. **Use your finger to scroll down the entries (see Figure 5-13).**

4. **If you want, you can use the Search Google or Search Wikipedia buttons at the bottom of the Search dialog to search for information about the search term online.**

You can also search for other instances of a particular word while in the book pages by pressing your finger on the word and tapping Search in the toolbar that appears.

The Search button

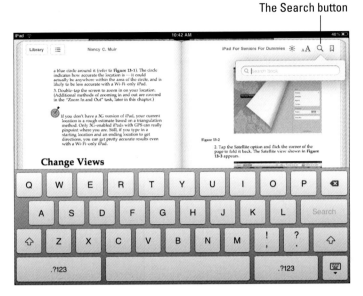

Figure 5-12: Find the content you need using the iBooks search feature.

Scroll through the entries

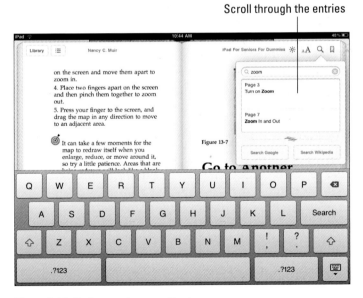

Figure 5-13: Find a spot in your eBook.

Using bookmarks

Bookmarks in your eBooks are like favorites you save in your Web browser: They enable you to revisit a favorite page or refresh your memory about a character or plot point. Note that iBooks can retain these bookmarks across iDevices such as iPad and iPhone.

1. **With a book open to a page you want to bookmark, tap the Bookmark button in the upper-left corner as shown in Figure 5-14.**

   A colored bookmark is placed on the page as shown in Figure 5-15.

The Bookmark button

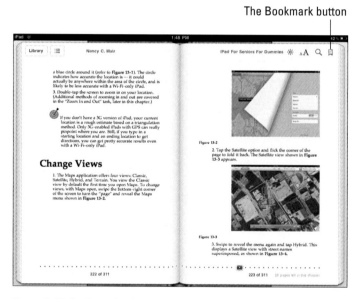

Figure 5-14: Assign a bookmark to a page.

2. **To remove a bookmark, tap it.**

3. **To go to bookmarks, tap the Table of Contents button on a book page.**

4. **In the Table of Contents, tap the Bookmarks tab.**

   As shown in Figure 5-16, all bookmarks are displayed.

5. **Tap a bookmark in this list to go there.**

iPad automatically bookmarks the page where you left off reading in a book so you don't have to do that manually.

The bookmark

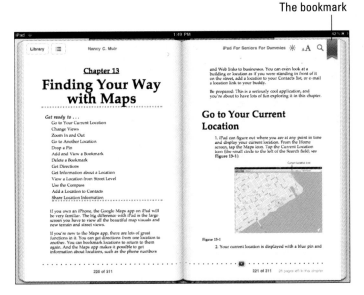

Figure 5-15: A bookmarked page.

Bookmarks are displayed here

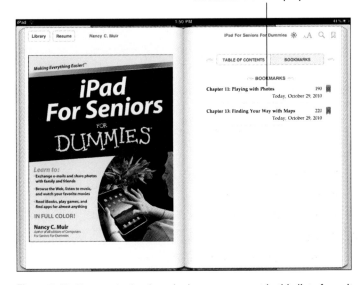

Figure 5-16: Choose the bookmarked page you want in this list of results.

TIP

Although you can't bookmark illustrations in a bookyou can add notes to them. To do so, hold your finger on an illustration or word until it is selected. On the toolbar that appears tap Note, and then type your note in the sticky pad that appears. A small sticky note appears in the margin of the page with the date it was created showing, to help you find all your notes at a later time.

Checking Words in the Dictionary

I know some people just skip over words they don't understand when reading, but being a writer I like to know what every word means. If you do, too, you'll appreciate the iPad's built-in dictionary. As you read a book, if you come across unfamiliar words, don't skip over them — take the opportunity to learn a word!

1. **With a book open, press your finger on a word and hold it until the toolbar shown in Figure 5-17 appears.**

Tap this button

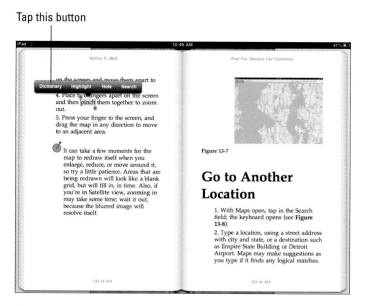

Figure 5-17: Check a selected word in the built-in dictionary.

2. **Tap the Dictionary button.**

   A definition dialog appears, as shown in Figure 5-18.

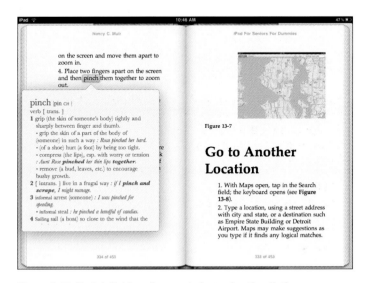

Figure 5-18: Find definitions for words fast using the dictionary.

3. **Tap the definition and scroll down to view more.**

4. **When you finish reviewing the definition, tap anywhere on the page, and the definition disappears.**

Organizing Your Library

Your library looks like a bookshelf with books stored on it, with the most recently downloaded title in the top-left corner. However, if you prefer, you can view your library in a few other ways.

1. **With the bookshelf version of the library displayed, tap the List button shown in Figure 5-19.**

   Your books appear in a list, as shown in Figure 5-20.

List button

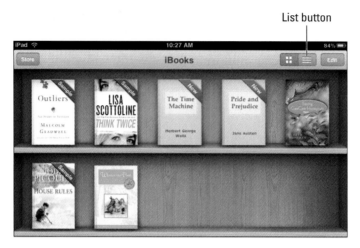

Figure 5-19: Switch back and forth between a bookshelf and list view using these buttons.

Figure 5-20: Organize your titles in various ways.

2. **To organize the list alphabetically by Titles, Categories such as Series, or Authors, tap the appropriate button on the bottom of the screen.**

3. **To organize by categories, tap the Categories button.**

   Your titles are divided by category titles such as Fiction, Mysteries & Thrillers, or Literary, as shown in Figure 5-21.

4. **To return to the bookshelf view at any time, tap the Bookshelf view button.**

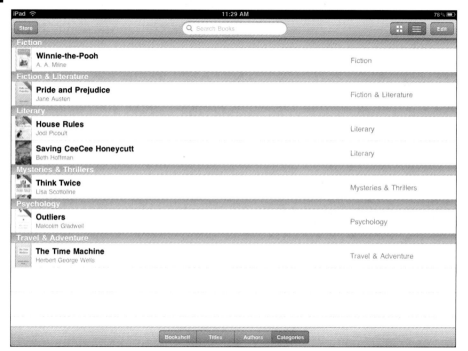

Figure 5-21: Titles neatly divided by topic.

The Bookshelf button in the list view displays the bookshelf order, which lists the most recently downloaded book first.

Use the Edit button in the list view to display Delete buttons for all books in the list. Tap the book-specific Delete buttons (which look like minus signs) to delete books, and then tap the Donc button to exit the Edit function.

Chapter 6: Playing Games

In This Chapter

✓ **Appreciating iPad's gaming strengths**

✓ **Finding games of all kinds**

✓ **Exploring iTunes Game Center**

*i*Pad is, after all, a close relative of the iPhone and no matter who tells you that they use their iPhone to get work done, they're probably spending most of their time gaming. iPad outstrips iPhone as the ultimate portable gaming machine because of its beautiful screen and unique features.

In this chapter you discover why iPad is such a great mobile gaming device, what kinds of games are out there, and what cool accessories you must get to be a completely awesome iPad gamer.

Let the games begin!

Appreciating iPad's Gaming Strengths

The iPhone is a fun gaming device, but the screen is too small. Your computer is a good gaming device, but it lacks some of the tactile input of a touchscreen. iPad may be just right as the ultimate gaming device (once enough iPad-specific games surface) for many reasons, including:

✓ iPad's fantastic screen. You've got a few things going for you here. First, the high resolution, 9.7-inch screen has a backlit LED display. As Apple describes it, it's "remarkably crisp and vivid." They're not lying. The in plane switching or IPS technology means you can hold it at almost any angle (it has a 178-degree viewing angle) and still get good color and contrast.

✓ Faster processor. The Λ1 chip in your iPad is a super-fast processor that can run rings around your iPhone, making it ideal for gaming.

✔ Playing games in full screen. Rather than playing on a small iPhone screen, you can play most games designed for the iPad in full-screen mode on your iPad. Having a full screen brings the gaming experience to you in an even more engaging way than a small screen ever could.

✔ Dragging elements around the screen. The Multi-Touch screen in iPad may be based on the same technology as the iPhone, but it's been redone from the ground up for iPad. It's responsive, and if you're about to be zapped by aliens in a fight to the death computer game, that responsiveness counts.

✔ The ten-hour battery life of an iPad. This long battery life means you can suck energy out of it playing games into the wee hours of the night.

✔ Specialized game playing features. Some games are coming out with features that take advantage of iPad's capabilities. For example, Gameloft came out with a version of its Nova game that includes a feature called Multiple Target Acquisition, which lets you target multiple bad guys in a single move to blow them out of the water with one shot. The Need for Speed racing game allows you to look in your rear mirror to see what's coming up behind you, a feature made possible by iPad's larger screen.

✔ Great sound. The built-in speaker is a powerful little thing, but if you want things even more up-close and personal, you can plug in a headphone or microphone using the built-in jack.

Understanding the Accelerometer

iPad has a built-in motion sensor called a 3-axis accelerometer. This device allows those developing apps for iPad to have lots of fun as they use the automatically rotating screen to become part of the gaming experience. For example, they can build in a compass device that reorients itself automatically if you switch your iPad from landscape to portrait mode. Some racing games allow you to grab the iPad as if it were a steering wheel and rotate the device to simulate the driving experience.

Check out Firemint's Real Racing HD app ($9.99) to try out the cool motion sensor feature.

As you can see in Figure 6-1 and 6-2, this is a very fun gaming environment.

Figure 6-1: Move the iPad around to steer left or right.

Figure 6-2: Size up your competitors in this cool racing game that takes advantage of iPad's accelerometer.

Finding Some Very Cool Games

Now it's time to tell you about some of my favorite iPad games (the part of the book where you wonder why I get paid for what I do, 'cause reviewing games is so fun).

Check out some cool downloadable games at sites such as ipadgamestore. org and tcgeeks.com for free iPad games.

Looking at what's out there

First, take a look at the gaming landscape. Several types of games are available (some ported over from iPhone and some customized for iPad), for example:

- Arcade games include apps such as Arcade Bowling Lite, Arcade Spinball Lite, Foosball HD, and The Simpsons Arcade.

- Kids' games are sometimes educational, but almost always entertaining. These include Ace Kids Math Games, Addition UnderSea Adventure, and Word Monkey.

- Card and board games, such as 12 Solitaire Card Games from Astraware Scrabble (see Figure 6-3), Mahjong Epic HD, and Payday Roulette.

- Adventure games like Plants vs. Zombies (see Figure 6-4), Everest Hidden Expedition, AirAttack, Amazon: Hidden Expedition, and Carnivore Dinosaur Hunter.

- Sports games, such as Snocross, Stick Golf, and Pool Bar.

Exploring a half dozen games

Narrowing down choices to just a few must-have games is hard because we all like different kinds of fun. To add to the choices, there are both iPhone and iPad engineered games you can use on your iPad, and more coming out all the time.

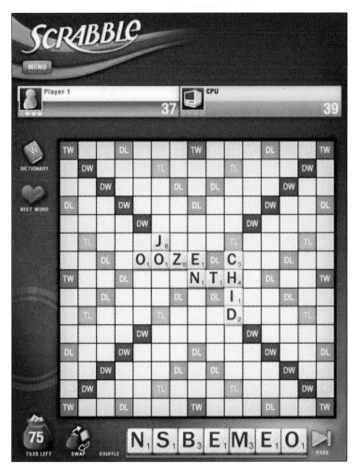

Figure 6-3: Scrabble is awesome on iPad.

Figure 6-4: Plants vs. Zombies: May the best man (thing?) win!

Still, the following list is a sampling of six recommended games for you to try that won't break the bank:

✐ **Scrabble for iPad ($9.99).** You remember Scrabble, that favorite old board game that can let you shine or put you to shame for your spelling and vocabulary skills? Scrabble is now available on iPad and it's hot. Shake your iPad to shuffle tiles. Use the drag-and-drop motion to play your letters. Want to share the fun? Reach out to your Facebook friends to take the game to the multiplayer level.

✐ **Broken Sword HD ($7.99).** This classic adventure game lets you virtually become the main character to experience all the game has to offer. Great art and animation distinguish this game, and the iPad version (see Figure 6-5) has a handy hint system you'll appreciate.

✐ **Civilization Revolution for iPad ($12.99).** If you like a world-building type of game, you'll find Civilization Revolution right up your alley. It's been fine-tuned for iPad to be even better than the iPhone version. The game also offers a feature called Scenario Creator. Scenario Creator lets you create your own unique challenges, essentially allowing for unlimited variety in the game.

✐ **Flight Control HD ($4.99).** Ever wanted to be an airline pilot? This game gives you a taste of the experience. Create flight paths that ensure your plane lands safely. A favorite with iPhone gamers, this one translates well to iPad. This game has lots of multiplayer options including the option of using a split screen to keep both players in the action.

Figure 6-5: Broken Sword is a classic game updated from its iPhone version for iPad.

✏ **Monkey Island 2 ($9.99).** A point and click adventure game classic on iPhone, in its iPad incarnation Monkey Island (see Figure 6-6) has great graphics and sound, and an engaging story at its heart. If you like adventure games, don't miss this one.

Figure 6-6: Monkey Island is a very fun adventure game.

✔ **T-Chess Pro ($7.99).** This game is another app designed for iPhone that works just great on iPad (see Figure 6-7). You can play against the computer or another player. You can modify the appearance of the chess pieces. It even sports features that help chess beginners learn the game painlessly, but more advanced players will enjoy it as well.

As well as costing money, games take up a lot of memory, so choose the games you buy wisely. If you no longer want to play a game, delete it from your iPad to save space, keeping a backup on your Mac or PC in case you change your mind at a later date.

Figure 6-7: If you love chess, this is one of the better apps for your iPad.

Special mention: Marvel Comics isn't a game, but it's a blast of an app that most gamers can appreciate. The iPad screen is perfect for those bright, crisp graphics, and iPad's navigation tools let you swipe your way through the panes in several interesting ways.

Getting Gaming Accessories

Some interesting accessories are coming out in the wake of iPad. No doubt more will appear over time, and Apple itself may add features in a next edition device. For example, a new iPad might sport control buttons so you don't have to cover up your onscreen game to use onscreen control mechanisms, and they might add rumble to simulate gaming sounds.

For now, here are a few iPad gaming accessories in the works that caught my attention:

✔ iCade is a pretty pricey ($150) accessory for die-hard arcade game enthusiasts who happen to own an iPad (see Figure 6-8). However, if you miss the old days of arcade gaming (before you played everything on your mobile phone screen) it might just be worth it. The only catch? It's a phantom product from ThinkGeek that hasn't yet seen the light of day, though I think it would be very cool if it did. (It probably never will appear— ThinkGeek regularly promotes nonexistent products. Gotcha!).

Figure 6-8: iCade makes an arcade of your iPad.

✒ Griffin Party Dock was announced in August, 2010 (no price yet available as of this writing). Dock your iPad here (see Figure 6-9) and you've got a mighty cool gaming peripheral with some basic but useful controls. You can also hook the device up to your television and enable multiple player action.

Figure 6-9: Dock your iPad here for lots of gaming fun.

✒ If you have kids, check out CinemaSeat from Griffin ($39.99). Use it to strap your iPad onto the back of your car seat so your kids can use it as an entertainment center to watch videos or play games as you travel. The ultimate "Are we there yet" squelcher.

iTunes Games Center

The Game Center is an app that comes pre-installed with iPad (iOS 4.2 and later). If you're into gaming you'll enjoy the features it offers that allow you to invite friends to play games, buy games, and keep track of your games, friends, and achievements.

Think of the Game Center as a kind of social networking site for gamers, where you can compare your scores and find players to go a few rounds with. The app can automatically match you with other players who have a similar ability. Say you need three other people to play a certain game, Game Center can find them for you. And the Achievements listing shows you your score history for all the games you play. Finally, Leaderboards allow you to compare your performance with your gaming friends.

Figure 6-10 shows you the Game Center interface with the following four choices along the bottom:

✔ Me contains your profile and summary of number of friends, games, and achievements.

✔ Friends is what you tap to invite friends to play.

✔ Games takes you to iTunes to shop for games.

✔ Requests shows you any requests from your friends for a game.

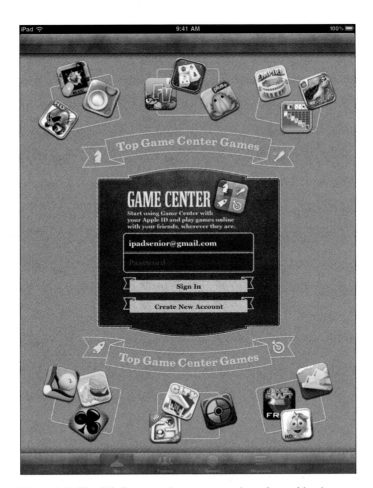

Figure 6-10: The "Me" screen shows an overview of your friends, games, and achievements.

Book III
iPad on the Go

The 5th Wave   By Rich Tennant

iPad

"In fact it does come with a compass."

1 f you like to hit the road — whether on a vacation or business trip — one of the great attractions of iPad is its portability and long battery life. The chapters in this minibook get you on the road with your iPad. Using Wi-Fi or 3G connections, you can stay in touch with others and with your home office.

In this minibook I also help you discover some awesome uses of iPad that make travelling more convenient, from using the Maps app for directions to making travel arrangements or finding that great hotel, restaurant, or the nearest ATM.

Chapter 1: Configuring iPad to Connect Everywhere

In This Chapter

✔ **Making Wi-Fi settings**

✔ **Making 3G settings**

✔ **Tethering your iPad to your smartphone**

✔ **Setting up a Microsoft Exchange account**

This chapter is all about connecting, whether you're connecting to the Internet via Wi-Fi or 3G, or connecting to your company network. Apple has made an effort over the years with iPhone to support enterprises, meaning that you can use the phone to connect with your company network and vital work data. The iPad continues that tradition with support for Microsoft Exchange Server, virtual private networks, and LDAP accounts.

Your best ally in setting up the more technical of these is your network administrator. In this chapter, I give you an overview of the capabilities of iPad to connect and some guidance in making the settings you need to make.

Making Wi-Fi and 3G Settings

The way people with iPads can connect to the Internet, the grandmother of all networks, is via its Wi-Fi or 3G capabilities (assuming they have a 3G model). In this section, I go into the settings you can make to manage your Wi-Fi or 3G connection.

Making Wi-Fi settings

Book I, Chapter 4 gives you the information you need to connect to a Wi-Fi network, a matter of simply signing into the network with a password if necessary. Now it's time to go over some of the finer points of your Wi-Fi connection.

A basic Wi-Fi setting is the one that tells iPad to automatically search for and join networks that are in range. If several networks are in range, using this setting, iPad will join the one that it used most recently.

After iPad has joined a network, a little Wi-Fi icon appears in the Status bar. The number of bars indicates the strength of the signal, just as you're used to on your cellphone.

To get to Wi-Fi settings, tap Settings on your Home screen and then tap Wi-Fi (see Figure 1-1). Here's a rundown of the items you can work with in Settings for your Wi-Fi configuration:

- **Wi-Fi On/Off:** Simply tap and slide this to On to turn Wi-Fi on. If you want it off, perhaps because you're on an airplane and the pilot tells you to, set this to Off. (Note that 3G models have an Airplane Mode setting, which I discuss in the next section.)

- **Ask to Join Networks:** iPad automatically connects to the previously joined network, but does not go looking for other networks unless this setting is on. Tap and slide this to the On position, and iPad will display all possible network connections in this dialog. If a network requires a password, it will spot a little padlock symbol. To forget a network so iPad doesn't join it automatically, tap the arrow on the right of the network name and then tap Forget this Network.

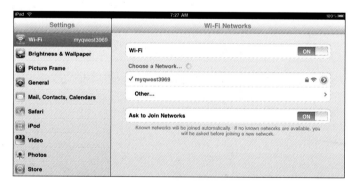

Figure 1-1: Wi-Fi settings.

- **Other:** If you want to join a network that doesn't show up on the list, tap Other under the Choose A Network section of these settings. In the dialog that appears, enter the network name and choose a type of security, such as WEP or WPA. When you choose a form of security and return to the dialog shown in Figure 1-2, a Password field appears. Some networks might need other information, such as a username or static IP address to complete this dialog. Check with your administrator for any information you can't provide.

To adjust settings for individual Wi-Fi networks, tap the arrow icon at the right of a listed network.

Figure 1-2: Accessing a closed network.

Making 3G Settings

When you own a Wi-Fi/3G model of iPad, in addition to modifying Wi-Fi settings as covered in the previous section, you can make changes to your cellular data in Settings. Cellular data settings enable you to manage data roaming and your account information (see Figure 1-3).

You can find the following items under the Cellular Data category in Settings:

 - **Cellular Data Network** On or Off: Turn 3G on or off here.

 - **Data Roaming** On or Off: Data Roaming is a feature of cellular networks that takes advantage of other carriers' networks if you're out of range of your primary carrier's network. Using data roaming can result in additional charges, so you may want to turn it off here at times.

 - **View Account**: Tap this setting to view account information.

 - **Add a SIM PIN**: If you want to protect the data on your SIM card from prying eyes, you can assign it a PIN number here. Don't forget your PIN, though, or you won't be able to unlock your SIM card.

Though you're pretty much stuck with AT&T at the moment, that could change. If you change your cellular data carrier, you might need to remove the SIM card and replace it with another. To do this you need to use a SIM eject tool to press and open the SIM tray located on the left side of 3G-enabled iPads. (Don't have a SIM eject tool? Don't worry: Apple recommends using a very high tech paperclip). Replace the SIM card and push the tray back in. That's it!

**Book III
Chapter 1**

Configuring
iPad to Connect
Everywhere

Figure 1-3: Cellular Data account dialog.

With a Wi-Fi and 3G model iPad, you also have access to the Airplane Mode setting. This setting allows you to disable wireless features of your device as required by airline regulations when you're flying. With Airplane Mode turned on in Settings, you won't be able to browse, e-mail, sync, buy stuff online, or stream videos. Also, the GPS locator of Maps won't work, but you can play content you've downloaded, play games, and create documents in apps like Pages and Numbers. Just don't forget to turn the Airplane Mode setting off when you land!

To Tether or Not to Tether, That Is the Question

If you want to avoid those 3G data charges, you have to tether your iPad to your smartphone. That way, you can use your phone's data connection to go online and not pay for two data plans. You can also get a connection anywhere your phone gets a connection — even if you have a Wi-Fi-only iPad model.

To tether involves a few challenges. First, you should probably have an unlimited data plan for your smartphone or you'll quickly exceed any limits. You won't go online instantly, because you have to complete a few steps to do so, and the connection speed might be a tad slow. Finally— and this is a big one — you may have to jailbreak your iPad, invalidating your warranty, to tether.

To get going, you need a tethering app, which will vary depending on your carrier. For example, if you're with AT&T, MyWi should work for you. Verizon customers should check into WiFiTether or pdanet. Download the app, and tethering then typically involves selecting your phone from the connections list.

Connecting to an Enterprise Remotely

When previewed in early 2010, iPad had no support for Microsoft Exchange. Between that time and its release in April 2010, somebody got smart and added Exchange support. That opened up possibilities for connecting with an enterprise network and its data remotely. If you work and use an iPad, this is very good news.

Thanks to these enterprise features, here are some of the things you can do to connect to your organization's network and data.

Setting up a Microsoft Exchange account

Microsoft Exchange is a messaging standard that allows exchange of information between networks. Many companies use Microsoft Exchange and a feature called ActiveSync to exchange their e-mail, contacts, and calendar information with devices. iPhone has supported Microsoft Exchange for a while now, and iPad carries on the tradition. You can use Microsoft Exchange to wirelessly sync that information to your iPad from your corporate network.

One benefit of a connection with Microsoft Exchange is that you can wipe the data and settings off a device remotely by using a command in Exchange if it's lost or stolen, keeping those company confidential contacts private.

With a configuration profile in place, you can set up a Microsoft Exchange account on your iPad. To set up an Exchange account on your iPad, follow these steps:

1. **Tap Settings.**

2. **Tap Mail, Contacts, Calendars.**

3. **Tap Add Account.**

4. **Tap Microsoft Exchange.**

5. **Enter your account information in the dialog shown in Figure 1-4 (e-mail address, domain such as IT or Marketing, username, password, and a description) and then tap Next.**

Figure 1-4: The Exchange dialog box.

iPad then uses Microsoft's Autodiscovery feature to verify your Exchange server. If it can verify your information, tap Save and you're all set. If it can't, you may have to enter additional information yourself. Check with your network administrator to get what you need.

When you're setting up a Microsoft Exchange account, you can choose which items you want to sync with, e-mail, contacts, or calendar. You get choices for how existing data on your iPad will be handled (merged, kept in a separate account, or overwritten).

Setting up a configuration profile

A configuration profile is a way for the network administrator at your enterprise to set up your iPad to use the systems in your company, which might include Microsoft Exchange, a VPN, or control access to corporate e-mail or contacts.

Your administrator should check out the Enterprise Deployment Guide and iPad Configuration Utility from Apple to get a configuration profile set up. After a configuration profile is in place, it can be e-mailed to you or placed on a secure Web page. Also, your company's network administrator can install a configuration profile on your iPad.

If you receive a configuration profile, you can install it yourself by opening the message and tapping the file. Tap Install and enter any information that's requested, such as your password.

You can't change the settings in a configuration profile. To set up a different configuration profile, first remove the existing configuration profile, have the new profile sent to you, and then install it. To remove a profile, in Settings, choose General, then Profile, and then select the configuration profile you want to get rid of and tap Remove.

LDAP accounts

If you are set up to access an Exchange server, you can also set up an LDAP (Lightweight Directory Access Protocol) account. LDAP accounts allow you to search for contacts on an LDAP server, which many companies use to store data, and access them through iPad Contacts.

Here's how to set up an LDAP account on your iPad:

1. **In Settings, tap Mail, Contacts, Calendars.**

2. **Tap Add Account.**

3. **Tap Other.**

4. **Tap Add LDAP Account.**

5. **Enter your LDAP account information (see Figure 1-5), and then tap Next to verify the account.**

6. **Tap Save.**

Figure 1-5: The LDAP dialog.

When you have set up such an account, it will appear as a group in the iPad Contacts app. To see these contacts, you have to be connected to the Internet, since they aren't stored locally on your iPad. If necessary, check with your company's network administrator for information about your network and LDAP requirements.

Virtual private networks

If you want to be able to connect to your organization's network, you can use a virtual private network or VPN. VPN works over both Wi-Fi and 3G cellular data connections. A VPN allows you to access data securely, even if you're on a public Wi-Fi connection. After a VPN is set up at your company, you can then use Network Settings on your iPad to modify your VPN settings and connect to your network.

You might need to ask your network administrator for information on making settings for accessing a VPN. If you've set up VPN on your computer, you should be able to use the same VPN settings on your iPad. You might want to let your admin know that iPad can connect to VPNs that use the L2TP, PPTP, or Cisco IPSec protocols.

To add a new VPN configuration, go to iPad Settings. Tap General, Network, VPN and if necessary tap and slide to turn on VPN. Then tap Add VPN Configuration to access the dialog shown in Figure 1-6. Fill in the information requested and tap Save.

To delete a VPN configuration, tap the blue arrow to the right of the configuration name in the Network settings and then tap Delete VPN.

Figure 1-6: Add Configuration dialog.

Some third-party tools are available that your administrator might want to check out to enable use of the corporate network by remote iPad users. Good for Enterprise helps them manage and update smartphone-like standards if their company has no single standard. Array Networks Desktop Direct is an iPad app that, along with Citrix Receiver software, helps users access their Desktop from afar.

For the latest iPad updates, be sure to check out my Web site at www. iPadMadeClear.com.

Status icons

In case you're wondering what all the icons in the Status bar on the top of the iPad screen mean relative to your connections, here's a rundown.

Icon	Meaning
✈	Airplane Mode is on and your Wi-Fi and 3G connection capabilities are turned off.
3G	3G network is available.
E	A carrier's EDGE network is available.
O	A GPRS network is available.
📶	Your iPad has a Wi-Fi Internet connection. The more bars that are showing, the stronger your connection.
✳	Network or other activity involving some third-party apps.
VPN	You are connected to a network.

Chapter 2: Finding Your Way with Maps

In This Chapter

↙ **Going to your current location**

↙ **Changing views**

↙ **Zoom in and out**

↙ **Going to another location**

*1*f you own an iPhone, the Google Maps app on iPad will be very familiar. The big difference with iPad is the large screen on which you can view all the beautiful map visuals and new terrain and street views.

You can find lots of great functions in the Maps app, including getting directions from one location to another by foot, car, or public transportation. You can bookmark locations to return to them again. And the Maps app makes it possible to get information about locations, such as the phone numbers and Web links to businesses. You can even look at a building or location as if you were standing in front of it on the street, add a location to your Contacts list, or e-mail a location link to your buddy.

Be prepared: This app is seriously cool, and you're about to have lots of fun exploring it in this chapter.

Getting Where You're Going

The first duty of a map is to get you where you want to go. The Maps app can go right to wherever you are or any other location you wish to visit. You can also use tools that help you find different views of locales, by displaying streets, terrain, or aerial views, or zooming in and out for various levels of detail. In this section, you find out how to use Maps to get around.

Going to your current location

iPad is pretty smart: it can figure out where you are at any point in time and display your current location using GPS technology (or a triangulation method if you have a wi-fi model). You must have an Internet connection; your location can be pinpointed more exactly if you have a 3G iPad, but even Wi-Fi models do a pretty good job.

To display your current location in Maps, follow these steps:

1. **From the Home screen, tap the Maps icon. Tap the Current Location icon (the small circle to the left of the Search field; see Figure 2-1).**

   Your current location is displayed with a blue pin and a blue circle around it (see Figure 2-1). The circle indicates how accurate the location is — it could actually be anywhere within the area of the circle.

Current Location icon

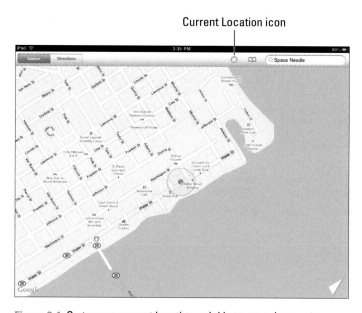

Figure 2-1: Go to your current location quickly to see where you are.

2. **Double-tap the screen to zoom in on your location.**

   (Additional methods of zooming in and out are covered in the "Zoom In and Out" section, later in this chapter.)

 If you don't have a 3G version of iPad, your current location is a rough estimate based on a triangulation method. Only 3G-enabled iPads with GPS can really pinpoint your location. Still, if you type in a starting location and an ending location to get directions, you can get pretty accurate results even with a Wi-Fi–only iPad.

Changing views

The Maps app offers four views: Classic, Satellite, Hybrid, and Terrain. You view the Classic view by default the first time you open Maps. Here's what these views offer:

- ✔ Classic is your basic street map you might find in any road atlas.
- ✔ Satellite is an aerial view.
- ✔ Hybrid offers a satellite view with street names included.
- ✔ Terrain is a topographical map showing mountains and other variations in the landscape.

Another cool app for those who like their maps of the topographical variety is Top Maps for iPad from Phil Endecott ($7.99). This app taps into the USGS and Canadian topographical maps and is great for planning that next trek into the wilderness.

Follow these steps to switch among the views in Maps:

1. **To change views, with Maps open, swipe the bottom-right corner of the screen to turn the "page" and reveal the Maps menu shown in Figure 2-2.**

Book III Chapter 2

Finding Your Way with Maps

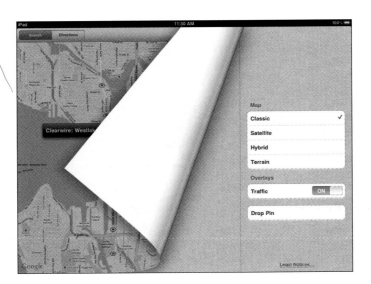

Figure 2-2: The controls for Maps are tucked away underneath the map display page.

2. Tap the Satellite option and flick the corner of the page to fold it back.

The Satellite view shown in Figure 2-3 appears.

Figure 2-3: Satellite is like looking at a location from the sky.

3. Swipe to reveal the menu again and tap Hybrid.

Doing this displays a Satellite view with street names superimposed, as shown in Figure 2-4.

4. Swipe to reveal the menu one more time and tap Terrain.

A topographical version of the map is displayed (see Figure 2-5), show-ing hills, mountains, and valleys. (Seeing this is very helpful if you want to walk around San Francisco and avoid those steep streets!)

Having trouble getting Maps to work? Note that if you turn Location Services off in iPad Settings, Maps can't find you. Go to Settings and under General settings, make sure Location Services is set to On.

You can drop a pin to mark a location on a map that you can return to. See the "Dropping a pin," section later in this chapter, for more about this feature.

You can also turn on a feature that displays an overlay on the Classic map to show current traffic conditions. (The setting for this feature is shown in Figure 2-2.) This feature shows roads in red, yellow, or green to indicate any obstructions (red for serious, yellow for caution) or roads on which cars are moving right along (green).

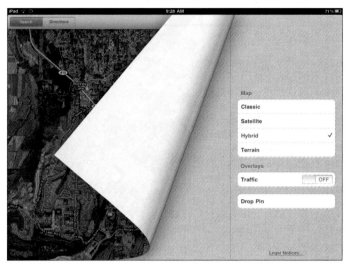

Figure 2-4: Street names or highway numbers appear in Hybrid view.

Figure 2-5: Terrain is a great view for hikers — if you get reception out in the woods!

Zooming in and out

If you've used an online mapping program, you know that you frequently have to move to more or less detailed views of the map to find what you're looking for: the street detail doesn't show the nearest highway, and the region level doesn't let you see that all important next turn. You'll appreciate the feature in the Maps app that allows you to zoom in and out to see more or less detailed maps and to move around a displayed map.

Here are the methods you can use to zoom in and out and move around a map:

✔ With a map displayed, you can double-tap with a single finger to zoom in (see Figure 2-6).

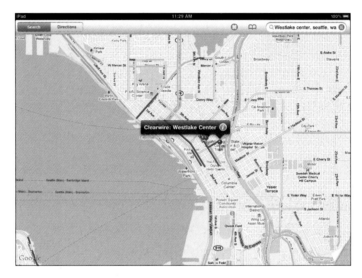

Figure 2-6: Zoom in to get more details.

✔ Double-tap with two fingers to zoom out, revealing less detail (see Figure 2-7).

✔ Place two fingers positioned together on the screen and move them apart to zoom in.

✔ Place two fingers apart on the screen and then pinch them together to zoom out.

✔ Press your finger to the screen, and drag the map in any direction to move to an adjacent area.

It can take a few moments for the map to redraw itself when you enlarge, reduce, or move around it, so have a little patience. Areas that are being redrawn will look like a blank grid, but will fill in, in time. Also, if you're in Satellite view, zooming in may take some time; wait it out, because the blurred image will resolve itself.

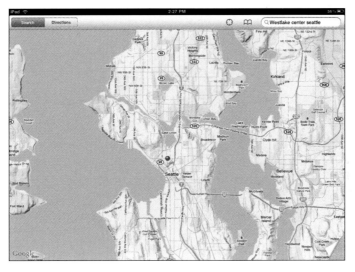

Figure 2-7: Get a good view of the region — but less detail — by zooming out.

Going to another location

If you're at Point A and want to get to Point B, Calcutta, DesMoines, or wherever, you need to know how to find any location other than your current location using Maps. Doing this involves using a Search feature in which you enter as much information as you have about the location's address.

Try going to another location using these steps:

1. **With Maps open, tap in the Search field.**

   The keyboard opens (see Figure 2-8).

2. **Type a location, using a street address with city and state, or a destination, such as Empire State Building or Detroit Airport.**

   Maps may make suggestions as you type if it finds any logical matches. Tap the Search button, and the location appears with a red pin inserted in it and a label with the location, an Information icon, and in some cases, a Street view icon (see Figure 2-9). Note that if several locations match your search term, you may see several pins on the map.

Tap in the Search field...

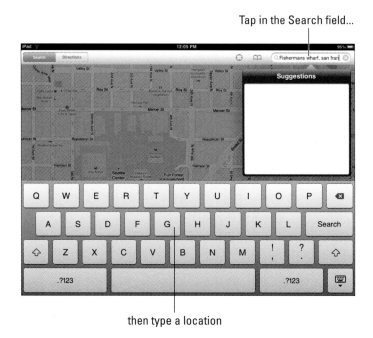

then type a location

Figure 2-8: You can use the onscreen keyboard to enter location information.

3. You can also tap the screen and drag in any direction to move to a nearby location.

4. Tap the Bookmark icon (the little book symbol to the left of the Search field; refer to Figure 2-9), and then tap the Recent tab to reveal recently visited sites.

5. Tap on a bookmark to go there.

As you discover later in this chapter in the "Adding a bookmark" section, you can also quickly go to any location you've previously visited and saved using the Bookmarks feature.

If you enter a destination, such as Bronx Zoo, you might want to also enter the city and state. Bronx Zoo landed me in the Woodland Park Zoo in Tacoma because the search uses the individual words and the closest "Zoo" match to find results!

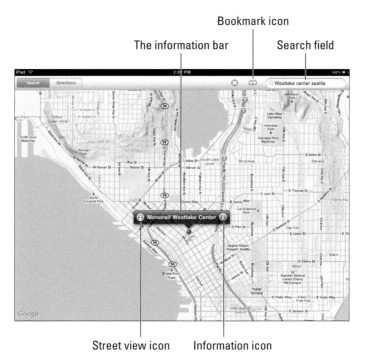

Figure 2-9: The more specific the address information you enter, the more likely you are to find just the right location.

Remembering Where You've Been

Why reinvent the (mapping) wheel? One of the great capabilities of a mapping program is the ability to store locations you like to go to for future reference. In Maps you can do this in a few different ways. You can drop a pin on a map, which marks a beginning point for getting directions from one site to another. Or, you can place a bookmark for a site you want to revisit often.

Dropping a pin

With iPad, pins act like the pins you might place on a paper map to note routes or favorite locations. With iPad, pins are also markers; a green pin marks a start location, red pins mark search results, while a blue pin (referred to as the blue marker) marks your iPad's current location.

Use these steps to try out the pin feature of iPad:

1. **Display a map that contains a spot where you'd like to drop a pin to help you get directions to or from that site.**

   If you need to, you can zoom in to a more detailed map to get a better view of the location you'd like to pin using the techniques I cover in the earlier Zoom In and Out section.

2. **Press and hold your finger on the screen at the location where you want to place the pin.**

   The pin appears, together with an information bar (see Figure 2-10).

The information bar

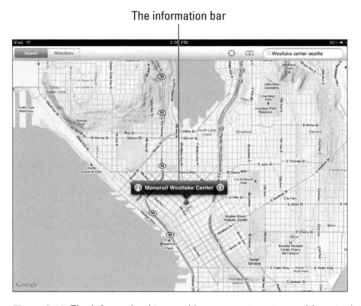

Figure 2-10: The Information bar provides access to yet more Maps tools.

3. **Tap the Information icon (refer to Figure 2-10) on the information bar to display details about the pin location (see Figure 2-11).**

To delete a pin you've dropped, tap the pin to display the information bar, and then tap the Information icon. In the information dialog that opens, tap Remove Pin. This only works with pinned sites that aren't bookmarked.

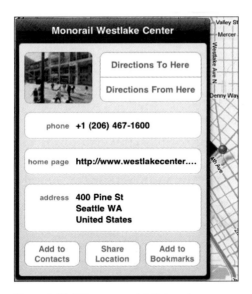

Figure 2-11: This very useful dialog gives you information and lets you share what you know.

Adding and Viewing a Bookmark

Bookmarks are a tried and true way to save a destination so that you can display a map or directions to that spot quickly. You've probably used a bookmark feature in a Web browser that works similarly. With Maps, you can save bookmarks and access those locations from a drop down list.

Here's how to add a bookmark in Maps:

1. **Place a pin on a location, as described in the preceding section.**
2. **Tap the Information icon to display the information dialog.**
3. **Tap the Add to Bookmarks button (see Figure 2-12).**

   The Add Bookmark dialog and the keyboard appear (see Figure 2-13). If you like, you can modify the name of the bookmark.
4. **Tap Save.**

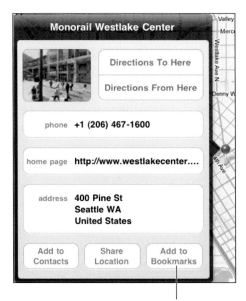

Tap the Add to Bookmarks button

Figure 2-12: Grab a destination you like and add it to Bookmarks

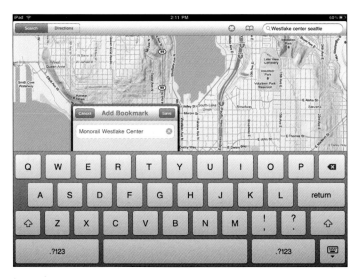

Figure 2-13: Name your bookmark

5. **To view your bookmarks, tap the Bookmarks icon (it looks like a little open book; refer to Figure 2-9) at the top of the Maps screen.**

Be sure the Bookmarks tab is selected; a list of bookmarks is displayed, as shown in Figure 2-14.

Figure 2-14: The list of saved bookmarks

6. **Tap on a bookmark to go to the location.**

You can also view recently viewed locations even if you haven't bookmarked them. Tap the Bookmark icon, and then, on the bottom of the Bookmarks dialog that appears, tap Recent. Locations you've visited recently are listed there. Tap on one to return to it.

Deleting a bookmark

There comes a time when a place you wanted to go gets crossed off your list. At that point you might want to delete a bookmark, which you can easily do by following these steps:

The line indicating your route

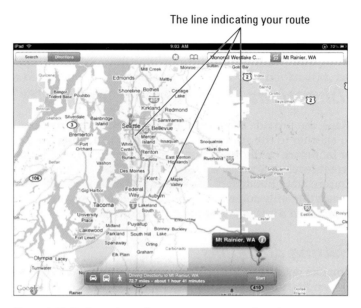

Figure 2-16: Go from pin to pin on your map to get directions

Current Location field   Destination field

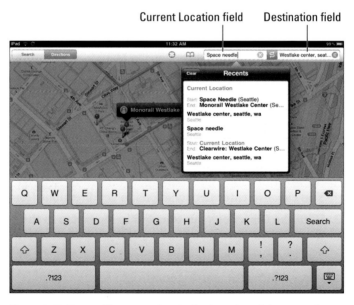

Figure 2-17: Enter addresses using the keyboard or pick a recently visited location from this list.

5. **Tap in the Destination field, enter a destination location, and then press the Search button on the keyboard.**

   The route between the two locations is displayed.

6. **You can also tap the Information icon on the information bar that appears above any selected pin and use the Directions To Here or Directions From Here button to generate directions (see Figure 2-18).**

Tap either of these buttons
to generate directions

Figure 2-18: Use these buttons to go to or from
someplace

Book III
Chapter 2

Finding Your Way
with Maps

7. **With a route displayed, a blue bar appears along the bottom of the Maps screen with information about the distance and time it takes to travel between the two locations.**

   Here's what you can do with this informational display:

   • Tap the car, bus, or pedestrian logo to get driving, public transportation, or walking directions (see Figure 2-19).

   • Tap Start to change the tools offered: The icon on the left showing several lines of text as if in a small document takes you to step-by-step directions (see Figure 2-20). The arrow keys take you through the directions one step at a time.

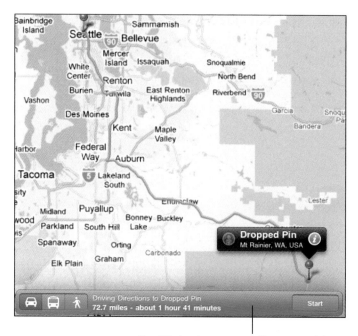

Use this bar to get travel distance and time

Figure 2-19: Find out how long a trip you're in for

In the directions view of Maps, notice the button with a zig-zag line between the Current Location and Destination fields (refer to Figure 3-17). After you generate directions from one location to another, tap this button to generate reverse directions. Believe me, they aren't always the same — especially when one-way streets are involved!

Getting information about a location

You've displayed the Information dialog for locations to add a bookmark or get directions in previous sections of this chapter. It's time to focus on the other useful information displayed there. Using the Information button for any location you can get the street address, phone number, and even Web site URL for some businesses or landmarks.

To get to the Information dialog go to a location and tap the pin. In the information bar that appears above the pinned location, tap the Information icon (see Figure 2-21).

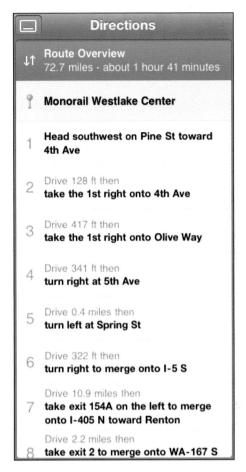

Book III
Chapter 2

Finding Your Way
with Maps

Figure 2-20: Get a blow by blow description of your route

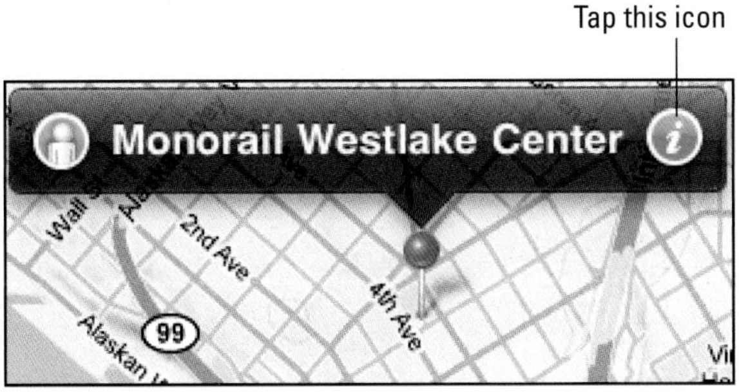

Tap this icon

Figure 2-21: Display the Information dialog.

At this point in the information dialog (see Figure 2-22), you can tap the Web address listed in the Home Page field to be taken to the location's Web page, if it has one associated with it.

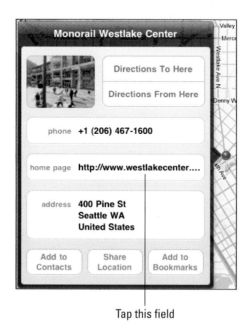

Tap this field

Figure 2-22: Going to a business's website with a tap.

You can also press and hold the Phone or Address fields and use the Copy button to copy the phone number, for example, so you can place it in a Notes document for future reference. When you've got all the information you need, tap anywhere outside of the information dialog to close it.

Rather than copy and paste information, you can easily save all the information about a location in your Contacts address book. See the "Adding a location to contacts" section, later in this chapter, to find out how that's done.

Viewing a location from street level

Street level view is seriously cool. You can not only get a picture of what the location looks like from the street, you can pan all around it to look up at tall skyscrapers, around to get a feel for the neighborhood, or down to see the actual street. You can only view certain locations from street level (see Figure 2-23), so you'll have to explore to try this out.

Street view is available for this location

Figure 2-23: The red icon with a little person in it indicates that street level view is available

If you want to give it a try, follow these steps and use the Monorail Westlake Center in Seattle (which is shown in these figures) to explore one location at street level:

1. **In the Search tab of Maps, tap the Search field and enter a location, such as your favorite local shopping mall.**

   (Enter Monorail Westlake Center if you have trouble finding a location that offers a street level view, indicated by a little red icon on the information bar for the location.)

2. **When the location appears, tap the Street view icon on its information bar.**

   The Street view appears.

3. **When you're in Street view (see Figure 2-24), you can tap and drag the screen to look around you in all directions.**

4. **Tap the small circular map in the bottom-right corner (refer to Figure 2-24) to return to the standard map view.**

You can also drag the screen down to get a better look at tall skyscrapers or up to view the street and manhole covers. The small circular map in the bottom-right corner highlights what you're looking at in the specific moment. In addition, street names are displayed down the center of streets.

Using the Compass

Sometimes it helps you to find your way if you know the direction that you're headed in. The Compass feature of Maps displays a small compass on screen that helps you figure out if you're going north, south, east, or west or any combination such as Southeast.

Book III
Chapter 2

Finding Your Way
with Maps

Tap here to return to the standard map view

Figure 2-24: The Monorail station in downtown Seattle

Note that the Compass feature only works from your current location, so start by tapping the Current Location icon at the top of the Maps screen (refer to Figure 2-1).Tap the icon again to turn the Compass on. A small compass appears in the top-right corner of the screen (see Figure 2-25).

Now move your iPad around in different directions and note that the compass symbol moves as well, indicating which direction you're facing. To turn the Compass off, tap the Current Location icon one more time.

You may get a message that there's interference and the Compass needs resetting. You can deal with this by moving away from any electronic equipment that might be causing interference, and moving the iPad around in what Apple describes as a figure 8 motion.

The Compass

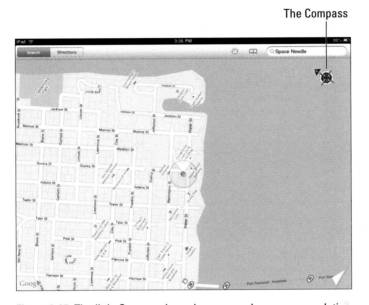

Figure 2-25: The little Compass icon shows you where you are relative to the rest of the world

Location Services has to be turned on in iPad Settings for the Compass feature to be available.

Sending Location Info beyond Maps

When you find a location you want to come back to or tell others about, you can use features of Maps that help you out. You can save a location to the Contacts app, which also saves the address, phone number, and Web site URL, if any. You can also share a link to locations with friends via e-mail. They can then access the location information by using Google Maps.

Adding a location to contacts

The beauty of this feature is that not only can you store valuable information such as phone numbers and street addresses in Contacts quickly and easily, but you can also use stored contacts to quickly find locations in Maps.

Here's how this works:

1. **Tap on a pin to display the information bar.**
2. **Tap on the Information icon.**
3. **In the information dialog that appears (see Figure 2-26), tap Add to Contacts.**

   A dialog appears.

Tap this button

Figure 2-26: Use handy buttons in the Information dialog to add a location to Contacts

4. **In the following dialog, tap Create New Contact.**

   The New Contact dialog appears (see Figure 2-27). Whatever information was available about the location has been entered.

5. **Enter any additional information, you need such as name, phone, or e-mail.**

6. **Tap Done.**

   The information is stored in your Contacts address book.

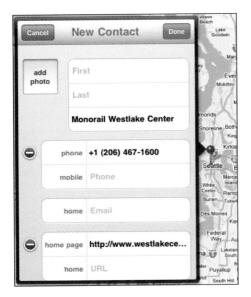

Figure 2-27: Any available information can be stored to Contacts

After you store information in Contacts, you can also share it with friends from there by tapping the Share button in the address record. See Book V, Chapter 4 for more about using Contacts.

Sharing location information

Have you found a fantastic restaurant or movie theater you absolutely have to share with a friend? From within Maps, you can use a simple procedure to e-mail a link to your friend. When your friend, who is connected to the Internet, taps on the link, it opens the map to the location in Google Maps (a free service).

Take these steps to share a location:

1. **Tap on a pin to display the information bar.**

2. **Tap on the Information icon.**

3. **In the information dialog that appears, tap Share Location.**

4. **In the e-mail form that appears (see Figure 2-28), use the onscreen keyboard to enter a recipient's e-mail address, any Cc/Bcc addresses, and add or change the subject or message as you like.**

5. Tap Send.

A link to the location information in Google Maps is sent to your designated recipient(s).

Use this feature to share your current location so a friend or emergency service can find you. However, beware of sharing your current information with strangers!

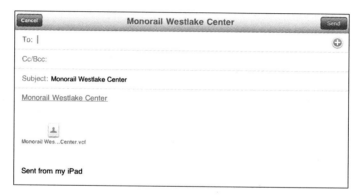

Figure 2-28: Your basic e-mail form, ready for you to fill pertinent information.

Chapter 3: Apps for Road Warriors

In This Chapter

✔ **Arranging travel**

✔ **Finding the best hotels**

✔ **Locating restaurants**

*i*Pad is practically perfect for people who have to travel a lot for business or who choose to travel for pleasure. It's lightweight, slender, and stays powered up for about 10 hours at a time. Depending on the model, you can connect around the world using 3G or Wi-Fi (or both) to stay in touch or browse the Internet for whatever you need. You have an onscreen keyboard so you don't have to tote around a keyboard. Robust business apps such as iWork let you get work done as you travel. You may never drag a laptop on a trip again!

That's why in this chapter the focus is on how people on the road can use iPad. I start out by pointing out the built-in apps that work for travellers, and then provide some general advice and specific app suggestions for making travel arrangements, finding great hotels and restaurants, getting maps and travel guides, and keeping track of what you spend as you travel.

Starting with What You Have

Before I get into the marvelous world of apps for travellers, you should consider the tools that come with the iPad out of the box. You could find your way around the world quite nicely with these little gems, including:

✔ **Maps:** This app allows to you locate worldwide locations and get detailed street maps, view buildings from street level, show directions from one point to another, and bookmark favorite locations. You can navigate as you drive, take public transportation, or walk around by using an onscreen compass (see Figure 3-1), and share location information with others by e-mail. (See Book III, Chapter 2, for details about how to use Maps.)

11:39 AM

Destinations

...re Street, V8V 3E7 Victoria (British Columbia) Show map

| Overview | Photos | How to Book |

Elegantly blending historic charm with state-of-the-art including a full-service spa and gourmet dining options and breakfast-style hotel is in the heart of Victoria, on major attractions.

Abigail's Hotel is situated only a short stroll from down Victoria's scenic Inner Harbor. The Royal BC Museum, Gardens and numerous shops and restaurants are all r
Guests can also enjoy top-rated golf courses and exciting whale watching tours.

Originally built in 1930, Abigail's combines charming antiques, including claw-foo modern amenities such as wireless internet and flat-screen TVs. Uniquely decora accommodations are also furnished with soft goose-down duvets and Italian mar bathrooms.

Guests staying at Abigail's can enjoy a delicious free daily breakfast as well as f appetizers. The hotel also features a Library Lounge, providing games, books, m cocktail.
Rooms: 23

vailability

• from **Tue 17 Aug 2010** to **Wed 18 Aug 2010** (Change date
...n rooms available for the dates of your sta

The Compass

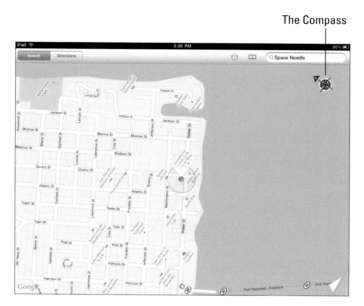

Figure 3-1: If your rental car doesn't have a navigation feature, use iPad instead!

✔ **Contacts:** If you're going on the road to visit clients or friends, if you have their address information in Contacts you can click on the address and be taken to it instantly in the Maps app. Keep phone numbers handy to get in touch when you hit town, and even use the contact notes field to keep track of your business activities with that person or company. Remember that you can add fields to business contact records including job title, department, and birthday using editing tools in Contacts. (See Book V, Chapter 4 for more about Contacts features).

✔ **Safari browser:** Don't forget that, if you have an Internet connection, you can use the Safari browser to get online and tap into all the travel-related information and sites on the Web. Use sites such as Expedia.com shown in Figure 3-2 or Kayak.com to book travel, check flight information at airline Web sites, go to sites such as Mapquest to get directions and maps, and so on. (For more about using Safari, go to Book I, Chapter 5).

✔ **Mail:** This built-in e-mail client lets you keep in touch through any accounts you set up in iPad as long as you have an Internet connection. Find out more about setting up e-mail accounts in Book I, Chapter 6.

✔ **Notes:** Although there isn't a travel expense tracker in iPad, you can always use Notes to keep a record of what you spend or any other information about your trip you need to recall after you get home. You can even e-mail a note to yourself or your accountant so it's on your office computer when you get back.

Figure 3-2: Expedia offers travel booking services for flights, hotel, car rental, and more.

TIP

Travel can get tedious with long waits in line or terminals. Don't forget that you have a built-in music player in iPod and a built-in video player in the Videos app to keep you entertained.

Making Travel Arrangements

Now I can move on to apps that don't reside on your iPad when you buy it. This chapter features just a few of the available apps — more are covered in Book VI, Chapter 2. Some are actually iPhone apps that work on iPad, and some were built specifically for iPad.

Start at the beginning when you are planning your trip. You need to book flights or other modes of travel and check to see that your flight is on time. You may need a rental car when you arrive and perhaps maps of public transit to help you plan your route. All these are covered in this section.

Getting there by air

This list is a mixed bag of travel booking tools and apps that help you check on your seat assignment or flight status. Try these:

- **Travelocity:** This nicely designed app shown in Figure 3-3 lets you book travel online, save itineraries, and get flight information. My favorite feature is the ability to explore destinations by great deals, upcoming events, or available travel guides. You can even check out hotels and sort the results by distance, price, or rating.

- **Airline Seat Guide:** You know how you always get on the plane thinking your seat will be fine just to find out you're three blocks from the restroom or can't see the in-flight movie on those older aircraft with no

If you're a frequent flier, check out the Air Mileage Calculator app. For $1.89, you can get the mileage for travel between airports worldwide with up to three legs for each trip. You can also have the app calculate bonuses based on your frequent flier status and the class of travel.

If packing is a challenge for you and you don't have a valet to help you out, try PackingPro. Keep track of lists of what you need by trip, including your passport, clothing, and vital accessories such as an umbrella for that trip to Seattle. It costs you $2.99, but if you're organizationally challenged, it might save your neck as you prepare for trips.

Renting a car

If you want to deal with your car rentals from your iPad, you'll be glad to hear that there are apps that help you do just that. Consider sites such as these that help you find the right rental deal:

✔ Priceline Hotel & Car Negotiator (see Figure 3-6) helps you find the best deal on airport car rentals. If you're in a rush, you can book up to 30 minutes before you need your car using this app. And Priceline lets you bid on the best price to save you the most money on your rental car.

Figure 3-6: Priceline helps you get the best deal on your rental car.

✔ Car Rentals lets you search among 15,000 national and international car rental options. You can sort your options by their distance from you, and book the car of your choice from major car rental companies.

You can also get individual apps for your favorite car rental companies, such as Avis Reservation App or Hertz Car Rental.

Road Trip Lite is a free utility that helps you track your mileage and fuel economy, which may help you estimate your costs if your rental car doesn't include unlimited miles. It sports a nice visual graph of fuel economy, and if you use your own car on the road, the feature that lets you track mileage and fuel cost by trip could be a neat way to sum up your travel expenses every month.

Finding your way around town

Before you set off on your trip to cities such as New York, San Francisco, or Chicago, you might want to download one of these apps to get local transit system maps, schedules, and more.

Transit Maps comes with one transit map, but enables you to download transit maps as graphics files from the Internet using its own browser feature.

iTransit Buddy is a series of $0.99 apps for various metro areas designed for iPhone but usable on iPad. If you want lots of transit maps, you can subscribe to iTransitBuddy and get access to all their map apps. This app has a helpful feature for looking up free transfers and schedule updates. Maps are downloaded to your device so you don't have to have an Internet connection to use the map. This one is handy for commuters as well as those who travel to metro areas on business or pleasure.

There's a Google Transit app that is available for mobile phones, though I couldn't find information on support for iPads yet — though I'd bet it's coming. Meanwhile, visit m.google.com/maps from your cellphone to download this handy app for transit travellers.

As you're exploring a new town make sure you're dressed right for the weather. SBSH Pocket Weather 2.3.0 Mobile lets you get weather reports on the go.

Finding Just the Right Hotels

Though airlines are jumping on the iPad app bandwagon, individual hotel chains don't seem to have gotten the app memo. Therefore, you may not find a Holiday Inn app or a Marriott app (though I did find an Annapolis,

**Book III
Chapter 3**

**Apps for Road
Warriors**

If you're concerned about your waistline, here are a few more helpful food-oriented apps:

- Crazymenu.com allows you to view restaurant menus and get and give recommendations to Facebook friends.

- Fast Food Calories Hunter can help you control how many calories you ingest along with your fast food meal.

- Restaurant Nutrition shows you carbohydrates, calories, and fat for more than 80 chain restaurants, such as TGI Fridays and The Cheesecake Factory. (Well, forget what I said about watching your waist!)

Using Maps and Travel Guides

One important part of the road warrior experience is finding your way around and connecting with the local culture. For that you can explore some mapping apps and travel guides. These will get you started:

- **World Atlas w/Factbook & Travel for iPad:** For only $0.99, you get high-definition country maps you can browse using your finger and touchscreen. There's also a link to the CIA's World Fact book for different countries and a cool graphical compass that gives a direction in both analog and digital form.

- **Cityscouter.com guides:** These handy little guides run about $3.99 per city and can be used offline. That's useful if you're on a plane, wandering around a foreign city nowhere near a Hotspot, or out of range of your 3G provider's services. Find out about top attractions, take advantage of a currency converter, find a Wiki article, photos, or maps (see Figure 3-9). Many include up-to-date information about local public transportation, as well.

- **WorldTravel Guide Deluxe:** This guide is free and gives you lots of information on about 23,000 destinations. Again, after you download it, you don't need an Internet connection to read all about your travel locations. Suggested itineraries and even a phrasebook to help you with the local lingo are included. This app supports full-screen iPad display, unlike some iPhone clone apps.

- **World Customs and Cultures:** Do you know whether it's appropriate to tip in Turkey? Or whether you should bring a gift to a host of a dinner in Japan? It's important to understand local customs to shine at international business interactions or just appear polite. This app covers more than 165 countries, giving you tips on common greetings, eye contact, acceptable (and unacceptable) gestures and local laws, among other things.

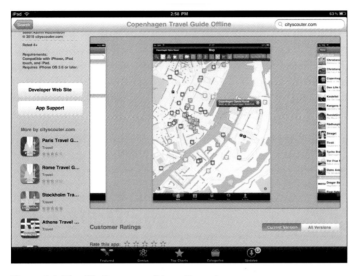

Figure 3-9: The CityScouter guide to Copenhagen.

In addition to the above, check out popular travel guides and tools with an iPad presence, including:

- Lonely Planet Travel Guides
- Frommer's Travel Tools
- Footprint Travel Guide

Tracking Your Expenses

My favorite part of any business trip is when I get that expense reimbursement check. Of course, to get that check I go through my receipt collection trying to figure out what I spent where and itemize it for my client.

To make your iPad travel experience easier, try out these great apps that help you keep all your trip expenses in order:

- **JetSet Expenses and JetSet Expenses Lite:** These are identical, except that the Lite version is free and supported by advertising. They allow you to track expenses in 15 expense categories and more than 100 sub-categories. Use either app to track mileage, calculate business expense percentages, and generate a daily summary of expenses.

- **myExpenses:** Again with a regular and lite version, this app designed for the iPhone is easy to use for tracking expenses and has some very nice

Among the day-one iPad apps available at the launch where Numbers, Keynote, and Pages: the three components of Apple's iWork office suite. (They're sold as independent apps on iPad; you buy them as a single boxed set for Mac OS X.) They shot to the list of top ten paid iPad apps, and they've remained there pretty consistently ever since. These apps let you create and edit word processing documents, spreadsheets, and presentation on your iPad. In addition, they let you share those documents with friends via e-mail, on your MobileMe iDisk or a WebDAV server, and with Apple's own iwork.com site. In all cases you can save and share your iWork documents using standard formats:

- Word processing documents can be saved as native .pages files or as PDF files or .doc files.

- Spreadsheets can be saved as native .numbers files or as PDF files or as .xls files.

- Presentations can be saved as native .key files or as PDF files or as .ppt files.

A large part of the power and popularity of the three iWork apps is that they all use a common interface which you find out about in Chapter 1. Then, you move on to each of the apps to see how to create and edit your own documents — often starting from the powerful and sophisticated templates provided within the app. Finally, you see how to use the power of the iWork apps to work with inserted graphics, movies, text, and other objects.

So get to work . . . and play!

Chapter 1: Introducing the iWork for iPad Apps

In This Chapter

✔ **Getting familiar with the iWork for iPad apps**

✔ **Discovering the basics of the iWork apps**

✔ **Utilizing photos and images**

✔ **Managing your iWork documents**

*W*ord processing and spreadsheet applications are among the most widely used software products on personal computers; presentation software is a close runner-up. Having started from scratch on the hardware side and then the operating system side, people at Apple started dreaming about what they could do if they were to start from scratch to write modern versions of word processing, spreadsheet, and presentation programs. They knew they'd have to follow one of their advertising campaign themes: *Think Different.*

The result was the iWork suite of applications (a collection of applications that can work together) for the Mac — Pages, Numbers, and Keynote — that were developed one by one over a period of several years.

Then Apple thought different again. They questioned everything and came up with iPad — a new type of device that dispenses with things that once seemed so miraculous, like the mouse, menus, and scroll-bars. Today, iWork is a terrific suite of programs for Mac OS X as well as a trio of dynamite apps for iPad.

In this chapter, you'll find an introduction to the three iWork for iPad apps including how to get them and how to use the common interface elements. You'll also find a summary of differences between iWork for iPad and iWork for Mac in those cases where it matters.

Presenting the iWork for iPad Apps

iWork is an *office suite,* like Microsoft Office. Office suites provide applications that are, well, office-oriented. The iWork office suite includes three applications that are similar to Microsoft Office applications (but way cooler, I think):

- **Pages:** A word processing application (similar to Microsoft Word)
- **Numbers:** A spreadsheet application (similar to Microsoft Excel)
- **Keynote:** A presentation application (similar to Microsoft PowerPoint)

On Mac OS X, all three programs are sold together in iWork. On iPad, each of the programs is sold on its own. The same day that iPad was launched on its blockbuster career, Apple announced three iWork apps for $10 each. You can purchase the iWork for iPad apps from the App Store (see Book I, Chapter 4, for more information). Their features and integration are almost the same on both platforms.

The following sections take a quick look at the three iWork for iPad apps.

Pages

For many people, word processing is the core of an office suite. In fact, many people don't get beyond it. A key feature of a word processing document is that the text flows from one page to the next as needed. (For example, adding a paragraph on page three causes the text at the bottom of page three to flow onto the top of page four automatically.) In general, the automatic flowing of word processed documents is used for documents that will be read in the way in which letters and memos are read.

Pages for the Mac adds a big desktop publishing plus in that it also allows you to create page layout documents. They have the type of structure you see in newspapers and magazines — articles don't just flow one after the other. Instead, an article on page one may be continued on page four, while another article on the first page may be continued on page eight. Also, objects such as photos are often placed in a specific position on a page, and they don't move as text is added or deleted.

iWork provides you with a variety of sophisticated tools to create your Pages documents. These include advanced font handling, color, tables, and charts, as well as the ability to place QuickTime movies and hypertext links in your Pages documents. iWork applications also provide a variety of template options for your documents. Figure 1-1 shows some of the templates available with Pages for iPad.

Figure 1-1: Choose a Pages template as a starting point.

For more on the Pages app, see Book IV, Chapter 2.

Numbers

Spreadsheet programs let you enter data in rows and columns. One of their main features is that they can perform calculations by means of formulas. For example, if you have a column listing your grocery expenditures for a week, the addition of another grocery bill will cause the program to recalculate the column's total. Spreadsheets are about data (usually numbers) and fast calculation updates, but they can also help you organize data such as address lists and even generate charts to show data trends.

Playing the name game

The word *documents* is a generic word for the data that an application program stores. As you see in the iWork apps, while you can use the term "document" to refer to an iWork file there are more specific terms that are used for each of the iWork file types:

✔ **Documents** are created and read by Pages. They can be page layout or word processing documents, as you'll see later in Book IV, Chapter 2.

✔ **Spreadsheets** are documents created by and used by Numbers; they can be imported from and exported to Excel. I give you more details on Numbers in Book IV, Chapter 3.

✔ **Presentations** are documents used by Keynote. I tell you more about Keynote in Book IV, Chapter 4.

You probably think you know what a spreadsheet looks like, but take a look at the Numbers document in Figure 1-2. This is a Numbers document based on the Travel Planner template. A single document can have a number of *sheets* (like sheets in a Microsoft Excel workbook). On iPad, sheets appear as tabs, as shown in the figure.

Sheets in a Numbers document

Figure 1-2: A typical Numbers document.

But the similarity to Microsoft Excel soon ends. A Numbers sheet can contain a variety of objects such as tables and charts, but it can also contain other iWork objects, such as graphics, text boxes, movies, and audio. In Figure 1-2, the sheet is shown with a table and five pictures above it.

For more on the Numbers app, see Book IV, Chapter 3.

Keynote

It's only been a few thousand years since people starting giving presentations. Call them lectures, classes, sermons, or sales pitches, they're all pretty much the same: Someone stands in front of a large or small group of people and explains, teaches, or informs them. Today, the presentation often has multimedia elements: slides in an architecture class, music in a history lecture about a composer, and movies in a talk about Uncle Charlie's summer vacation.

Keynote was the original iWork application. Built by Apple engineers for MacWorld and Worldwide Developers Conference keynote speeches delivered by Steve Jobs, Keynote has been refined over the years to become the powerful tool it is today. (See Figure 1-3.)

For more on the Keynote app, see Book IV, Chapter 4.

Figure 1-3: A Keynote document being edited.

Getting Familiar with the iWork Interface

Throughout this chapter, you've seen some images of iWork in action. Before continuing, take a minute to consider what you've been seeing. You'll find that each of the iWork apps has a very similar look and feel. One of the coolest advantages of iWork is that major features — not just small operations such as changing a font or selecting a color — are available in the same way in all its applications. You really have only one program to understand when you're using iWork.

The iWork apps are updated periodically. In these cases, you'll see the App Store on your iPad Home screen with a number indicating downloads are available. If your iWork screens do not match the images in this book, check the App Store to see if you have downloads waiting (see Book I, Chapter 4).

Creating a new document

You create a new document in the same way for each of the iWork apps. To create a new iWork document, follow these steps:

1. **Tap any of the iWork app icons to launch the application.**

   The documents screen appears. This screen is titled My Documents in the Pages app (see Figure 1-4), My Spreadsheets in Numbers, and My Presentations in Keynote.

   Note that when you first open one of the iWork apps, you should see a single document that contains basic information and instructions for that app.

   If you see My Documents on the button in the top-left corner, you're not on the documents screen. You're on the screen for working with an individual document, and tapping My Documents (or My Spreadsheets or My Presentations) will bring you to the documents screen.

2. **Depending on the application you're working in, tap the New Document (Pages), New Spreadsheet (Numbers), or New Presentation (Keynote) button in the top-left corner of the My Documents screen.**

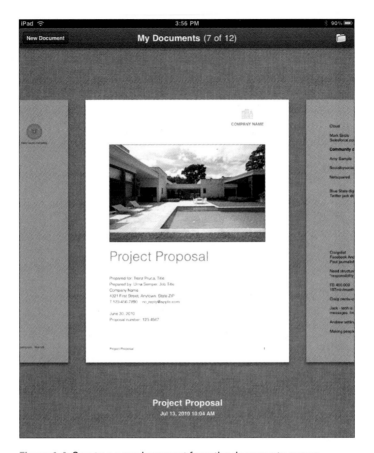

Figure 1-4: Create a new document from the documents screen.

The Choose a Template screen appears. (Figure 1-5 shows the Pages templates.)

3. **Tap the template you want to use as a starting point, or tap Blank to start working with a completely clean document.**

If you change your mind, you can click the Cancel button (which replaces the New button) and you'll be returned to the documents screen.

Figure 1-5: Select a template.

The templates are different for each of the iWork apps, so they are discussed in the appropriate chapters in this minibook.

4. **Your new document opens on the screen.**

Locating a document

Before long, you'll have created several documents, and chances are you're going to want to go back and work on some of them. As with creating new documents, locating a document is done the same way in each of the iWork apps.

To locate a document to work on, follow these steps:

1. **Tap any of the iWork app icons to launch the application.**

The documents screen appears. (Refer to Figure 1-4.)

2. **View the documents and find the one you want to work with.**

   You'll see your current documents in the center of the screen. Browse through the documents by flicking to the right or left as you do to turn pages. Below the document, you see its title and the date it was last worked on.

3. **Tap the document you want to work with.**

   The document opens, and you can begin working in it.

In addition to using the document screen to locate a document, you can use the four buttons at the bottom of the screen to take other actions. The two on the left let you share documents and use documents that others have shared: you'll find out more about this later in this chapter in the "Managing Your iWork Documents" section. You should recognize the two buttons at the right from other software you have used:

✐ **New Document (+):** Click this to create a new document from a template or duplicate the current document, as shown in Figure 1-6.

✐ **Trash:** This button lets you move the current document to the trash. Don't worry. You're asked to confirm it.

Identifying other common iWork features

As I mentioned earlier, one of the coolest advantages of iWork is that major features are available in the same way in all its applications. For example, there's an important interface element in action in the Pages document shown in Figure 1-7 called a *popover*. It's like a dialog on Mac OS X and other operating systems, but it's redesigned for iPad. Here are three aspects to note about popovers:

✐ **Knowing what the popover is for:** Each popover includes an arrow that points to the button that opened it.

✐ **Dismissing the popover:** If you want to dismiss the popover (the equivalent of a Close or Cancel button on your Mac), tap anywhere outside the popover.

✐ **Making a selection on the popover:** When you tap a choice in a popover, it is carried out and the popover closes automatically.

Also visible in Figure 1-7 is the toolbar, which runs along the top of the screen. On the far-left side of the toolbar, the My Documents button lets you see all of your Pages documents. Next to My Documents is the Undo button. (It is the same as the Edit⇨Undo command you have on Mac OS X for iWork and most other apps.) In the center of the window is the document's name — this too is the same for all iWork apps.

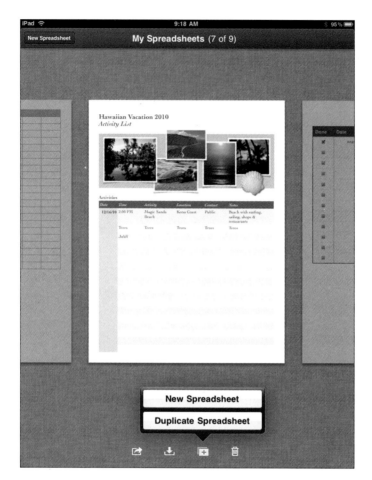

Figure 1-6: Create a new or duplicate document.

At the right of the iWork toolbar are four or five buttons.

- ✔ **Info:** This provides info and choices about the current selection in the document. For example, it lets you choose a style, a list format, or a layout (alignment, columns, and line spacing) for a selected paragraph. If nothing is selected, this button is dimmed.

- ✔ **Insert:** This button lets you insert images from your photo albums on iPad. If you want to insert a photo into your iWork document, add it to your album by synchronizing it in iTunes. (There's more on this later in this chapter in "Working with Photos and Images" section.)

- ✔ **Animation:** The double-diamond button shown in Figure 1-8 appears only in Keynote. It's used to add an animation to slide transitions.

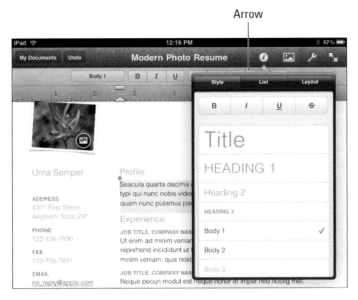

Figure 1-7: The iWork popover.

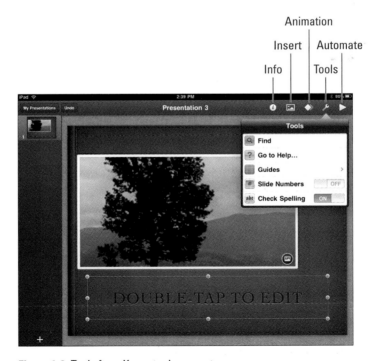

Figure 1-8: Tools for a Keynote document.

✓ **Tools:** The wrench opens a popover containing tools that are based on the document as a whole rather than the current selection within the document. Figure 1-9 shows the tools for a Pages document.

✓ **Full-screen:** The double arrows expand the document to fill your iPad screen, hiding the toolbar and other features. Tap in the full-screen document to return to the editable view with the toolbar.

Keynote also has an Automate button to the right of the Tools button (refer to Figure 1-8). Tapping the Automate button begins playing your presentation.

The ruler that you have seen in Pages is used by its word processing features. Similar tools at the top of the screen are used in Numbers and Keynote depending on what you're trying to do. I discuss them in the relevant chapters in this minibook.

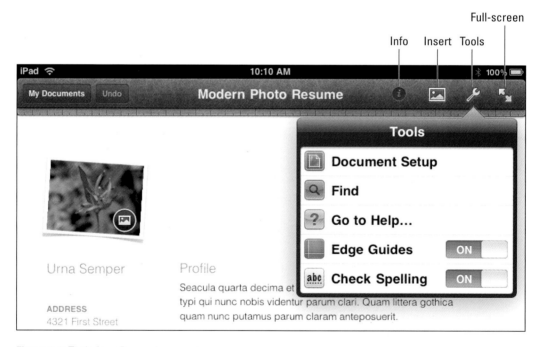

Figure 1-9: Tools for a Pages document.

Another interface element that you'll encounter from time to time is known as a *modal view*. Think of this as a dialog that appears on top of the screen (sometimes covering all of it) with the background appearing to be slightly dimmed. Often, a button in the upper-right corner (usually with a blue background) lets you accept the information in the view. Sometimes a modal view presents you with a choice — there will be buttons in both the upper-right and upper-left corners. In these instances, tap the button of the action you want to take.

Working with Photos and Images

One important feature that distinguishes Apple software from many other products is how easily you can use graphics and video in the documents you create. It's probably not surprising for you to see Pages templates with photo placeholders in them, and it certainly makes sense that Keynote templates often include photos. In today's world, you expect images in word processing documents and presentations. But spreadsheets? Take a look at the Numbers templates to see how the people at Apple are suggesting you rethink your understanding of spreadsheets.

In short, photos, images, and video can be added — easily and productively — to any iWork for iPad document. There are two ways to do this:

- Use the Insert button at the right of the toolbar.
- Use a template that includes a placeholder image.

Because using a template with a placeholder image requires one more step than the Insert button, that's the technique described here.

1. **Create a document based on a template that includes a placeholder image.**

   Some templates have several placeholder images on various pages, slides, or spreadsheets. Figure 1-10 shows the Photo Portfolio template in Keynote.

   Notice in the lower-right corner of the image that there's a button that matches the Insert button at the right of the toolbar at the top of the Keynote window. This indicates that the image is a placeholder.

2. **Tap the placeholder button to open a list of your photo albums as shown in Figure 1-11.**

   You can browse photos you have saved on your iPad as well as albums you have created in iPhoto and synchronized to your iPad. Select the image you want to use instead of the placeholder.

Figure 1-10: Create a document with placeholder images.

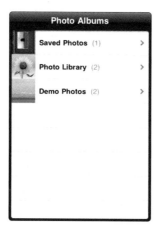

Figure 1-11: Choose a photo.

3. **Double-tap the image to show the masking control (see Figure 1-12).**

4. **Adjust the slider to change the image mask.**

   The slider adjusts the size of the image. It starts being the same size as the frame, but if you move it all the way to the right as you see in Figure 1-13, the image is shown dimly filling the entire screen. You can drag the image around so that the part you want is inside the frame.

You can also use the eight handles on the frame to change its size and shape. This is a hands-on way to handle tasks such as cropping images. Rest assured that the image itself is unchanged by these steps: you are only changing the image's appearance within the document.

Figure 1-12: Double-tap to mask the image.

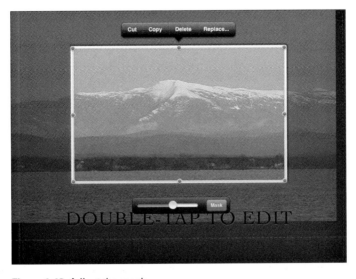

Figure 1-13: Adjust the mask.

Managing Your iWork Documents

The data for your iWork documents is stored in files on your iPad, possibly on your Mac or PC, and also sometimes on shared WebDAV servers, your MobileMe iDisk, and, as you will see, on iWork.com if you choose.

You can store iWork files on a PC, but iWork only runs on iPad and Mac OS X. As you'll see you can easily convert your iWork files to the comparable Microsoft Office file types so that you can work on them on a PC in that format.

One of the features that makes iWork for iPad so successful is that the iWork team has made it so easy for you to move documents around and work on them in whatever environment you want. That can be a mobile hand-held device such as your iPad or a server that's somewhere far away (quick, do you know where your iDisk is actually located?).

What matters is that you can get to your documents, read and write them, and share them with people. It's also critical that you can get to documents that other people want to share with you without either one of you having to jump through hoops.

Deep down inside the iPad operating system (iOS), there are files and folders, but most of the time you manipulate them indirectly through apps. When it comes to apps, the files and folders are in a special area reserved just for that app. Some apps such as the iWork apps can read files from servers such as iDisk and WebDAV; if you select one of those files as you'll see later in this section, it will be copied into the appropriate place on your iPad for you to work on it.

The storage areas for files on your iPad are kept separate for each app. iPad further keeps the storage areas separate by identifying them internally by a specific app's installation. If you install Pages and then remove it from your iPad, your Pages documents will disappear along with the Pages app. If you reinstall Pages . . . you reinstall Pages — the documents that you used to have for the copy of Pages that you removed are still removed. Before uninstalling any app from your iPad, make certain that you have backed up any files you have created. For many apps, the procedure is exactly the same as it is for iWork's apps.

Copying a file into an iWork for iPad app

If you have a file on your Mac or on a server (an iDisk or WebDAV server) you can copy it into an iWork app to work on it there. Of course, the document needs to be saved as a compatible file type. That means:

✔ **Numbers:** .numbers, .xls, .xlsx

✔ **Keynote:** .key, .ppt, .pptx

✔ **Pages:** .pages, .doc, .docx

These are the primary document types. You can import other files such as JPEG image files by adding them to your iPhoto library, music files in iTunes, and so forth.

1. **From your documents page (My Documents, My Spreadsheets, or My Presentations), tap the Copy From button (see Figure 1-14).**

Figure 1-14: Begin to copy a file into iWork for iPad.

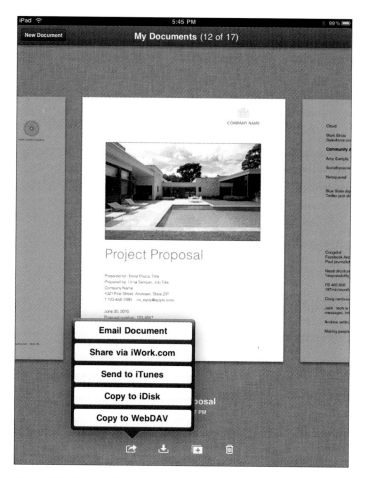

Figure 1-19: Export a file.

2. **In all cases of exporting, you will be asked to choose the export format.**

   In the case of an iDisk or WebDAV server you may be prompted to log in as you saw in the previous steps. Figure 1-20 shows the export formats for Pages documents.

3. **Your document is on its way.**

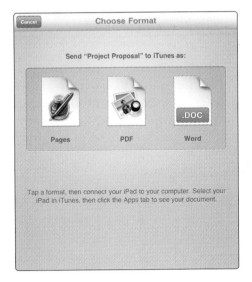

Figure 1-20: Choose a format.

Moving files with iTunes

Unlike moving documents to and from iDisk and WebDAV servers, the moving of documents between iTunes on your PC or Mac and your iPad requires a direct connection, not a wireless connection, so make certain you have your cable handy.

Moving files to your computer from your iPad

Each iWork app has its own storage area for your files. You move files from your iPad to your computer using iTunes and these steps:

1. **Connect your iPad to the computer where you want to movethe files.**

   Yes, your computer can be a Mac or a PC. It must have iTunes installed. If iTunes isn't installed, see Book I, Chapter 4, and then come back here.

2. **When iTunes launches, find your iPad in the left pane of the window under Devices (see Figure 1-21) and select it by clicking once.**

   If you look carefully, you'll notice the menus such as File, Edit, and View at the top of the window in Figure 1-21. This is iTunes running on Windows and connecting to an iPad to be able to transfer iWork files back and forth.

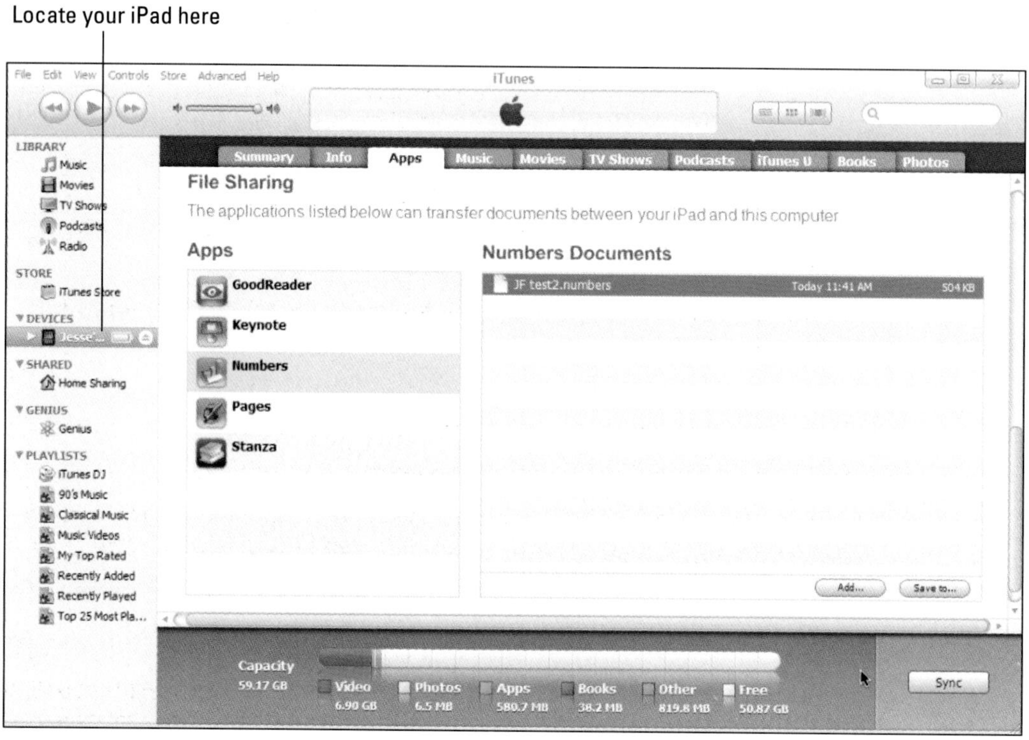

Locate your iPad here

Figure 1-21: Connecting your iPad to iTunes on your Mac or PC.

3. **Select the Apps tab from the group of tabs running across the top of the window.**

4. **Scroll down to the bottom of the window and select the iWork app you're interested in.**

   The documents on your iPad for that app are shown.

5. **Select the document you want and click Save To.**

6. **Choose the folder and the name you want to use for the saved file.**

   The file is moved to your computer.

Moving files to your iPad from your computer

This process for moving files from your computer to your iPad is very similar to the process in the previous section. To copy files from your computer to your iPad follow these steps:

1. **Connect your iPad to the computer from which the files are to be moved.**

   Yes, it can be a Mac or a PC. It must have iTunes installed. If iTunes isn't installed, see Book I, Chapter 4, and then come back here.

2. **Find your iPad in the left pane of the window under Devices (refer to Figure 1-21) and select it by clicking once.**

3. **Select the Apps tab from the group of tabs running across the top of the window.**

4. **Scroll down to the bottom of the window and select the iWork app you're interested in.**

   The documents on your iPad for that app are shown.

5. **Click Add in the lower-right portion of the window.**

6. **When prompted, select the file on your computer's disk.**

   When you select it, it is moved to the list of files in iTunes and usually moves immediately to your iPad. If it doesn't move immediately, click Sync.

iWork.com: Playing well together

iWork.com lets you work together with other people and let devices such as iPads, Macs, and iWork.com work together. Want to work with two colleagues on a presentation? No problem: Start by uploading your Keynote document to iWork.com on the Internet. Then a friend can download it and make changes in the document as a Microsoft PowerPoint document. Back it goes to iWork.com, and someone else can download it in yet another format. This is an example of a process called *cloud computing*. When working in the cloud people can work together on their own terms. They don't have to get together and decide which presentation (or spreadsheet or word processing) application they'll all use.

Now, with the advent of iPad, iWork.com is ready to play a new role. Exactly the same process that lets you share a document with a friend who will edit it on another computer also lets you share a document with yourself on another computer so that you can create it on your Mac, edit it on a PC, and then continue the edit on an iPad. One of the benefits of cloud computing is that it doesn't matter what computer and what software each person is using. As long as you use the standard file formats, iWork.com works equally well for iPad, PCs, and Macs.

You can post an iWork document to your iWork.com area, where it is visible to you and the people you invite to view it. Those people can then add notes and comments to the documents on the Web.

You can share your iWork documents with people using other cloud services such as Live.com or Google.

You can download documents from iWork.com in a variety of formats. This makes two types of actions possible:

- **Comments and notes on iWork documents:** You can add comments to specific parts of iWork documents (a section of text, for example); you can also add notes to the document as a whole (rather than to a specific part of it). As a result, a number of people can work together on a document.

- **Multiple revisions to iWork documents:** You can download the documents to your own computer in a variety of formats. Many of these formats include the comments that you and others have added. Once you've downloaded a document, it can be modified and you can add more comments describing the modifications.

All of this is made possible by the iWork.com site; the actual sharing of documents is handled by your Web browser and by your iWork software. Here's the division of labor:

- **Uploading to iWork.com:** This is done from your iWork software: the Share menu on Mac OS X and from your documents screen as shown previously in Figure 1-19.

- **Downloading from iWork.com:** You do this by connecting to iWork.com with your browser and logging in with your iWork ID and password. This works with a browser that can run on Mac OS X, your iPad, your iPhone, and Windows (among other operating systems). If you can run a browser, and if your device and its operating system support downloading through browsers, you can receive a shared file. You can find a list of supported browsers at www.apple.com/iwork/iwork-dot-com/.

  Once you have downloaded an iWork file, you can get to work. Even if iWork doesn't run on your computer, you may have another application that does run and can read the standard formats (including the Microsoft Office formats). That means you can edit downloaded iWork documents using Microsoft Office on Windows or Mac OS X, or by using Google Docs on any platform it runs on.

iWork.com is designed to be the bridge across various platforms and formats so that you can share your iWork documents. You may want to share your documents with yourself as you switch from your iPad to your Mac or to Windows. For that reason, the following sections show how to log on to iWork.com from iWork on Mac OS X as well as iPad.

Sharing a document on iWork.com

You need an Apple ID to log on to iWork.com. If you have a MobileMe sub-scription account with an e-mail address, your Apple ID is your e-mail address (for example, `jfeiler@me.com`). And if you've activated an iPhone or iPad, you also have an Apple ID. You log in to iWork.com to upload (share) documents and to retrieve documents. Here, I tell you about sharing documents. In the next section, I tell you how to log in to retrieve documents.

1. **Open the document you want to share in the appropriate iWork for iPad app.**

2. **On your documents screen, share it via iWork.com as shown previously in Figure 1-19.**

3. **If asked, log in as shown in Figure 1-22.**

Figure 1-22: Log in to iWork.com

4. **Address the e-mail to the person (or several people) you want to be notified of the file.**

   You can type in a message if you want (see Figure 1-23).

5. **If you want, tap Sharing Options at the right to change default sharing settings as you see in Figure 1-24.**

6. **You're done.**

   The file will be uploaded and your e-mail will be sent.

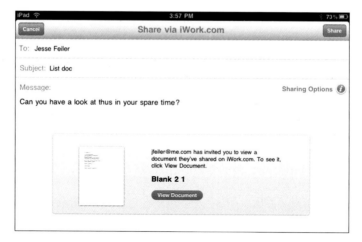

Figure 1-23: Let people know the document is ready to be shared.

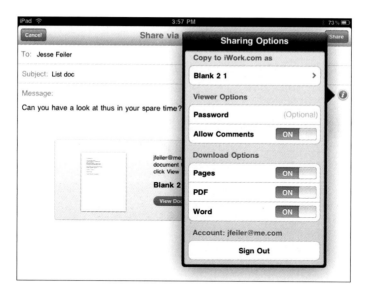

Figure 1-24: If you want, change Sharing Options.

Accessing shared documents on iWork.com

Your message, together with a download link, will be delivered to all of the addressees you have listed. All people have to do is click the link in the e-mail. If a recipient has an iWork.com account, there are more options.

If you have an iWork.com account, you can access shared documents by following these steps:

1. **You are notified of the newly shared file; you also have an option to view your shared files as shown in Figure 1-25.**

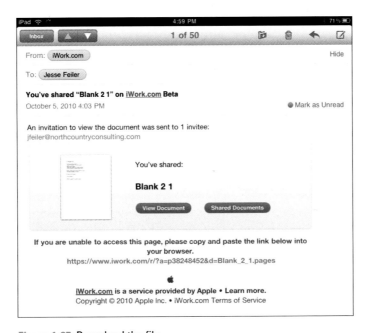

Figure 1-25: Download the file.

2. **If the Sharing Options permit, the blue arrow lets people download the file in various formats (see Figure 1-26).**

   Tapping anywhere in the box will download the native iWork version of the document.

   To find out more about iWork.com (such as how to download and modify iWork.com documents), check out *iWork '09 For Dummies* by Jesse Feiler (Wiley Publishing).

Figure 1-26: Download the file.

Knowing the Differences: iWork on the iPad Versus on a Mac

You can work happily and productively with just your iWork for iPad apps, but you may want to use your Mac for some additional work that iWork for Mac supports. They key to this is the ability to share documents between your Mac (or even your PC) and your iPad as described earlier in the "Managing Your iWork Documents" section.

On iPad, you have a subset of the templates available on Mac OS X. For example, the project proposal template on Mac OS X has half a dozen sample pages (budget, schedule, executive summary, and so forth); on iPad, there are only a couple. You can certainly add more if you want. Also, some of the large document features (track changes and automatic table of contents creation) are available only on Mac OS X.

You may find that for much if not all of your work, you can happily do it on your iPad. Other people may find that they need some of the large document features of Mac OS X. Most people probably use both.

The range of document features available on iPad is amazing: spell-checking, fonts and styles, the ability to add and manipulate images, charts and tables (not just in Numbers!), columns and pagination, and much, much, more. It's just some of the features that tend to be used by large and complex documents that are not supported.

Don't make the mistake of thinking that iWork documents on iPad are small documents. Because of the way in which the iPad apps are designed, there are essentially no practical limits to document size. There's no reason to think that you can't write your 1,000 page novel on the Pages iPad app (but you'd better get busy).

In fact, even for the features such as tables of contents that you only get in the Mac OS X version, you may find that it's easy for you (and others) to work on iPad and Mac OS X as you're developing the document. Then all you have to do is put it together on Mac OS X to generate the table of contents.

Chapter 2: Pages Has a Way with Words

This chapter addresses the Pages app. Pages is the primary word processing tool in the iWork suite of apps. Pages gives you powerful tools for creating documents that may be complex or lengthy. Pages also gives you some tools that can come in very handy for specific tasks that apply to even short and simple documents.

In this chapter you find out how to work with text and text boxes, how to format your document, and how to use the simplified Pages for iPad interface. Whether you are creating documents from scratch using Pages for iPad or editing existing documents created elsewhere with Pages for Mac, Pages for iPad, or even existing documents in the .doc format from Microsoft Office and Google Docs, you'll be able to get right to work by using the advice in this chapter.

For the basics of managing documents, sharing them with MobileMe, WebDAV, or iWork.com, via e-mail, or through iTunes, see Book IV, Chapter 1.

Editing a Pages Document

After you open a Pages document, you edit it in the document editing view shown in Figure 2-1.

To find out how to create a new Pages document, see Book IV, Chapter 1.

Figure 2-1: The document editing view.

When you are editing a document, this view remains open until you move to another document, return to the My Documents view, or leave Pages. Remember that when you leave an iWork for iPad app and then come back to it, you usually come back to exactly where you were when you left; if you were in the middle of editing something, it will be right there when you return.

Note that when you're in the editing view, a My Documents button is visible in the upper-left corner of the screen. The label of this button switches between My Documents and New Document, depending on the view you're currently in: When you're in My Documents, the button is labeled New Document; when you're in a document, the button reads My Documents.

When working on a multipage document in the document editing view, you can quickly move through the document by swiping or flicking up or down.

In Pages, you can touch and hold your finger anywhere at the right side of a page to bring up the *navigator* (see Figure 2-2). The navigator shows a thumbnail of a page, and you can move the navigator very quickly through the document by dragging up or down on the screen. When you're on the page you want, just lift your finger off the screen. If you don't want to leave the page you started from, swipe to the right from the navigator and it will disappear.

Figure 2-2: Using the navigator.

You don't have to select the paragraph with a triple-tap for this to work. If you have selected a word or an insertion point, the paragraph containing either item is the selected paragraph.

✓ **Tabs and Breaks:** This button brings up a popover where you can choose to insert a tab, line break, column break, or page break.

Feel free to experiment with the formatting within your Pages documents, and remember that the Undo button in the upper-left corner is there to help you out. When you tap Undo, you're given the option to undo or redo the last steps. (Undo or Redo may be grayed out and unavailable if there is no step to undo or redo, as shown in Figure 2-5.)

Figure 2-5: Use Undo and Redo.

Most of the buttons in the ruler just require you to tap them, but some (for example, the Styles and Tab buttons) open their own popovers for further selections; Figure 2-6 shows the Styles popover.

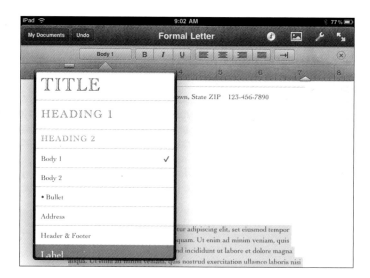

Figure 2-6: Set styles from the ruler.

You can also use the ruler to set the margins for paragraphs. Just slide the indicators along the ruler, as shown in Figure 2-7. Note that the top indicator for the left margin reflects the margin for the first line of a paragraph; the lower indicator is the left margin for all other lines in the paragraph. You can indent the first line of a paragraph, but you can also outdent it (or provide a hanging first line); this works very well in lists.

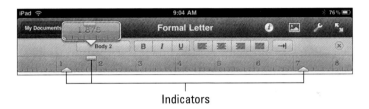

Indicators

Figure 2-7: Set margins from the ruler.

Getting and Setting Info about the Selection

The Info button at the right of the ruler opens a popover that provides additional settings beyond those shown in the ruler. When you select text and tap the Info button, you see a popover with three buttons along the top: Style, List, and Layout. You click one of those buttons to access various formatting options that I describe in the sections that follow.

Setting character style: font, size, and colors

One of the settings you can adjust using the Info button is character style. Tap the Info button, and the popover shown in Figure 2-8 opens. (The Style button in the top-left corner of the popover is selected by default.)

Compare the list of styles to those shown previously in Figure 2-6. They're the same styles, but look at the top of this popover: You have buttons to let you set the bold, italic, and underlined styles. However, as is often the case with the Info popover, you've got more choices. In this case, you have a strike-through style at the right in addition to the other character styles.

Scroll down to the bottom of the list of styles, and you'll see Text Options, as shown in Figure 2-9.

Figure 2-12: Handle indents and lists.

The advantage of using a list style is that, if you add or delete an element to or from the list, Pages automatically handles the renumbering for you.

Establishing alignment, columns, and line spacing

The Layout button in the top-right corner of the Info popover lets you set layout options, as shown in Figure 2-13. These include the alignment options available from the ruler as well as creating columns and adjusting line spacing.

Figure 2-13: Adjust layout settings.

Formatting the Document

You can format the text in your document, but there's one other bit of formatting you should attend to: the formatting of the document itself. This includes page headers and footers, page numbers, and backgrounds that appear on all of the pages. Here's how to proceed:

1. **With a Pages document open, tap Tools.**

   The Tools popover appears (see Figure 2-14).

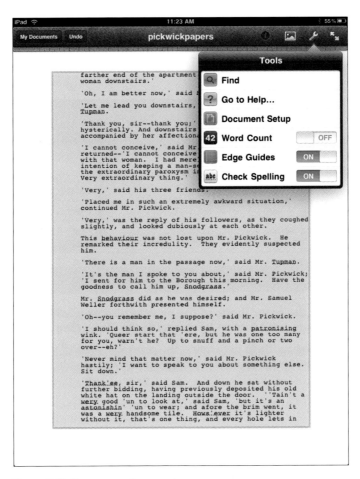

Figure 2-14: Set up your document.

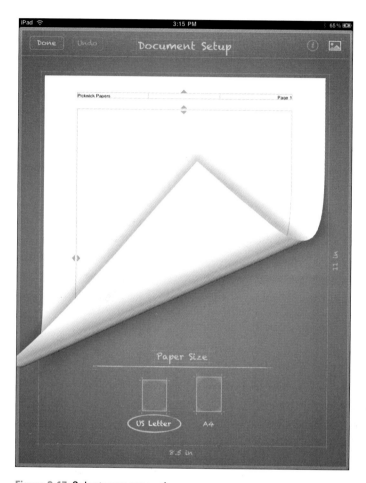

Figure 2-17: Select your paper size.

Now that your page is set up, you're ready to finish entering text in your document and print it when it's done.

Chapter 3: Counting on Numbers

*N*umbers is a different approach to the concept of spreadsheets. Not only does it bring structure to spreadsheets, but it also brings data formats you may not have seen before. In addition to numbers and text in your spreadsheets, you can use on/off checkboxes and star ratings as part of your data. Think of an inventory spreadsheet with checkboxes for in-stock items and star ratings based on reviews or user feedback. Before long, what you may have thought of as just a bunch of numbers can really provide meaning and context to users.

First launched as part of iWork '08, Numbers now joins the other iWork apps on iPad. Tables and charts are built into Keynote and Pages, but Numbers is the main number crunching tool on iPad.

In this chapter, you discover how Numbers helps you organize your data into manageable units. Once you can manage your data, you can display it in charts and graphs. (In order to help yourself and others make sense of the data, you find out how to add graphics, text, and charts to your documents in Book IV, Chapter 5.)

Introducing Numbers

Because Numbers is so much more advanced than many spreadsheet programs you may know, it's worth taking a moment to look at Numbers for Mac and its concepts and comparing them to Numbers for iPad. The concepts are alive and well on Numbers for iPad, and you'll be able to move your Numbers documents back and forth between your iPad and Mac. (See Book IV, Chapter 1, for document management information.)

When you create a Numbers document, you work with three things:

- ✔ **A Numbers document:** This is the container for everything, including worksheets (sheets) and their data. It's similar to a Microsoft Excel workbook.

- ✔ **One or more sheets:** There are one or more spreadsheets (called *sheets* in the Numbers world of simplicity).

- ✔ **Zero or more tables:** The subspreadsheets or tables that people have been creating in other spreadsheet programs exist in Numbers as formal, structured tables rather than a range of cells within a spreadsheet. Numbers gives them a specific name — *tables.* (And yes, you can have a Numbers document with no tables, but you have to have at least one sheet.)

The simple idea of making tables into an actual part of the Numbers application rather than letting people create them any which way leads to a major change in the way you can use Numbers when compared to other spreadsheet programs. Because a table is an entity of its own and not a range of cells, you don't break the tables you've organized in a spreadsheet when you reformat some other part of the spreadsheet. You can work within any of the tables, and you can reorganize them within a sheet, but you can't break them by simply adding a row or column to your spreadsheet.

Figure 3-1 shows you one of the Numbers for Mac templates (Team Organization). It's a single document with six sheets visible at the left in the *Sheets pane:*

- ✔ **Roster**
- ✔ **Stats**
- ✔ **Schedule**
- ✔ **Field and Positions**
- ✔ **Playoff Bracket**
- ✔ **Budget**

Some of the sheets have tables or charts within them, and you see them listed in the Sheets pane under their corresponding documents. For example, the Roster sheet has the Team Roster and Admin. Info tables within it. Down at the bottom, the Budget sheet contains two tables (Cost Breakdown and Cost per Player) as well as a chart (Team Costs). The idea that a single sheet can have defined charts and tables within it that do not depend on ranges of cells is the biggest difference between Numbers and other spreadsheet programs.

Figure 3-1: The Team Organization template in Numbers for Mac.

As you can see in Figure 3-1, sheets can also contain images and other graphics; they are not part of the structure of charts and tables. You simply insert them as you insert any other objects in iWork documents.

In this figure, the Team Roster table on the Roster sheet is selected. You can select it with a mouse click in the Sheets pane at the left or by clicking in the table itself. Notice in Figure 3-1 that a selected table has a frame with its column and row titles as well as some other controls. It's also important to note that each table within a sheet has its own row and column numbers (you can also name them, if you want) and that each table you deal with starts with cell A1. (The first row is 1, and the first column is A.)

Apple's iWork team moved the Numbers concepts elegantly to iPad. Figure 3-2 shows the comparable template on iPad. Each sheet is a tab. When you tap a table on iPad, you get a frame that lets you manipulate the table just as on Numbers for Mac. (See the section "Using Tables" later in this chapter for more information.)

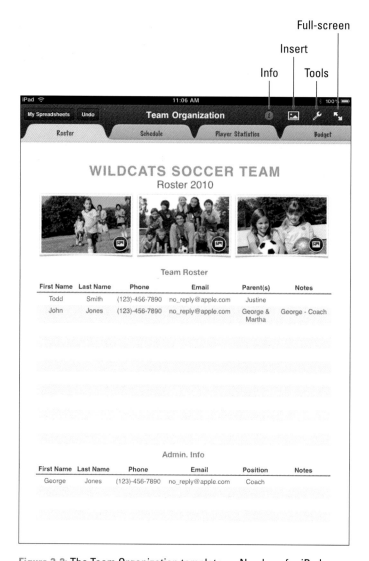

Figure 3-2: The Team Organization template on Numbers for iPad.

Numbers for Mac lets you insert charts along with tables on your sheets, as you see in Figure 3-3. (Remember that you can also insert graphics and other objects on your sheet.) The same functionality is available on Numbers for iPad, as you see in Figure 3-4.

Numbers for iPad also includes the ability to create *forms,* which simplify data entry. When you create a form, you select a table and you're taken to a tab that displays each column heading with a text entry box next to it. This allows you to focus on entering data for one row at a time and eliminates the possibility of accidentally tapping and entering data in the wrong row. You can find more about forms in the "Utilizing Forms" section later in this chapter.

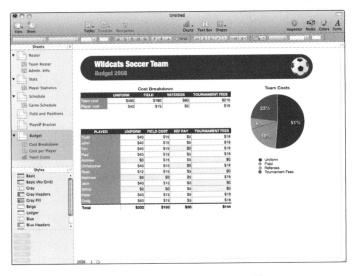

Figure 3-3: You can add charts to your sheets on a Mac.

Tap the + tab and Numbers asks if you want to add a new sheet or a form. (See Figure 3-6.) Tap New Sheet, and Numbers creates a new tab for that sheet that contains one table. The sheet is labeled Sheet N where N is the next number in the internal list of sheets you have created. See "Changing a tab's name" later in this section if you want to rename the tab. (If you're interested in forms, I tell you about that later in this chapter in the "Utilizing Forms" section.)

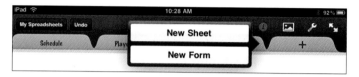

Figure 3-6: Add a new sheet or form.

Deleting or duplicating a tab

If you add a tab by mistake, Numbers allows you to remove it. Also, if you have a tab that you'd like to reuse for a new tab, Numbers allows you to duplicate it. To do either of these actions, tap the tab you want to delete or duplicate, and selection buttons appear above it. (See Figure 3-7.) All you have to do now is tap the option (Duplicate or Delete) for the action you want to take.

Figure 3-7: Duplicate or delete a tab.

Remember that a double-tap starts editing. A single tap brings up your selection buttons, if they are available for the object you've tapped.

Rearranging tabs

Don't like the order of your tabs? Tap and hold a tab to rearrange the tab order. You simply drag the tab to the right or left in the row of tabs, and then remove your finger when the tab is in the position you want it. (See Figure 3-8.)

Figure 3-8: Rearrange tabs.

Navigating through tabs

If you have more tabs than can be shown on the screen, just flick right or left to slide along the tabs. Remember to flick in the row of tabs. Flicking on the body of the sheet scrolls over to the right or left of the content on that sheet.

If you're holding your iPad in portrait orientation, turn it to landscape to allow more tabs to display on the screen.

Changing a tab's name

Double-tapping text anywhere on your iPad allows you to edit it. That goes for tabs, too. Double-tap the name of a tab to begin editing it; you'll also see standard editing commands, such as Select, Select All, and Paste in the selection buttons just above the tab. (See Figure 3-9.)

Figure 3-9: Edit a tab's name.

Using Tables

Tables are at the heart of Numbers — they're where your data is entered. This section shows you how to work with a table as a whole; the following section, "Working with Cells," shows you how to work with individual cells within the table.

Selecting a table

In order to work on a table, you need to select it. To select a table in Numbers, tap it. If it's not visible in the current tab, just tap the tab it's in.

If you need to find an entry within a table, it's easy to do. Tap the wrench in the top right to open the Tools popover. Tap Find to search your entire Numbers document for a word or phrase that may be in the table you're looking for.

As is the case with Numbers for Mac, when a table is selected its appearance changes. (See Figure 3-10.) A selected table is framed with gray bars above (the column frame) and to its left (the row frame). To the left of the column frame, a button with concentric circles lets you move the table. To the right of the column frame as well as beneath the row frame are two other buttons, each with four small squares (looking a bit like table cells) These are the

Cutting and pasting a table

You can select a table and then drag it around on a sheet by using the round button to the left of the column frame; you can resize it as described in the "Resizing a table" section later in this chapter. But what if you want to place the table on a different sheet? To copy and paste a table onto a different sheet follow these steps:

1. **Select the table by tapping inside the table bounds but outside the cells.**

   You see the Cut, Copy, and Delete buttons shown earlier in Figure 3-10.

2. **Tap Cut from the selection buttons that appear above the table.**

3. **Tap the tab of the sheet you want to add the table to.**

4. **Tap in the sheet (but not in an existing table).**

   This brings up new selection buttons.

5. **Tap Paste.**

   Then move and resize the table as you want.

Adjusting columns or rows

If you've ever used a spreadsheet program, you know that columns and rows don't always fit the data within them. In Numbers, you can select the columns or rows that you want to work on and then rearrange or resize them.

Selecting a row or column

Tap in the row frame to select the corresponding row, as shown in Figure 3-12.

Tap in the column frame to select the corresponding column.

Once you've selected a row or column, you can adjust the selection by dragging the handles (the round buttons) at the top and bottom (or left and right for columns), as shown in Figure 3-13.

Tap in this bar to select a row

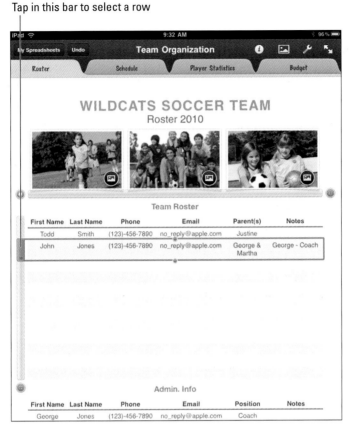

Figure 3-12: Select a row.

The selection buttons (Cut, Copy, Paste, Delete, Insert, and Sort) appear above a selected column or row. Make certain that you have the right object selected. In Figure 3-14, the image on the left shows an entire column selected; note that the selection border extends into the column or row frame and the section within the column or row frame is broader than the other three borders. The image on the right shows several cells within a column selected. When cells within a row or column are selected, all four borders of the selection are the same width.

Use the handles to adjust the selection

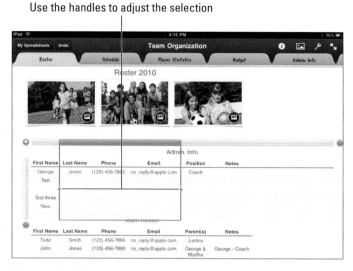

Figure 3-13: Adjust a selection.

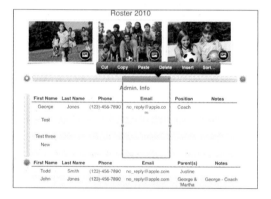

Figure 3-14: Select a column (left) or a single cell in a column (right).

The selection button you tap will affect the column or the single cell you have selected.

You can also use the selection button to sort a column (or row). Tap Sort in the selection button and then choose ascending or descending sort order.

Resizing a row or column

The two vertical lines (known as the Cells button) in the upper-right corner of the column frame (refer to the left image in Figure 3-14) and the bottom-left corner of the row frame (refer to Figure 3-12) let you resize the selected columns or rows. You always resize a column to its right and a row to its bottom whether you are making it larger or smaller. The contents are automatically adjusted, and the adjoining rows or columns are moved aside.

Resizing rows or columns is a good task to try. There's nothing like seeing how Numbers automatically just does the right thing.

Moving a row or column

Sometimes you will want to rearrange the rows or columns in a sheet. With one or more rows or columns selected, drag it (or them) to the new position. All the selected rows or columns move as a unit and the other rows or columns move aside as necessary.

Resizing a table

There are two ways to resize a table. You can add or remove rows or columns to or from the table, but you can also leave the number of rows and columns the same and change the overall size of the table. You often want to do both.

Adding or removing rows and columns at the right or bottom

Tap the Cells button in the upper-right corner of the column frame to add a new column at the right of the table. To add a new row at the bottom, tap the Cells button in the lower-left corner of the row frame, and a new row is added to the bottom of the table.

To remove a blank column or row at the right side or bottom of a table, drag the appropriate Cells button to the left or to the top of the frame — the extra rows or columns disappear.

Adding or removing rows and columns inside the table

Select the row or column that you want to be below or to the right of the new row or column. From the selection buttons, tap Insert. This adds a new row above the selected row or a new column to the left of the selected column.

Changing a table's size

Select the table so that the handles (small blue dots) are visible at the right side and bottom. These handles work like any other resizing handles in Numbers — just drag them horizontally or vertically to change the table's size. The content of the table automatically resizes to fit the new table size. The numbers of rows and columns remain unchanged, but their sizes may be adjusted.

You can select the table by tapping anywhere outside of a cell (such as near the title). If you have already selected a cell, row, or column, tap the round button to the left of the column frame to show the handles. (You can see them in Figure 3-10.)

There's more information on formatting tables in the "Working with New Tables" section, later in this chapter.

Working with Cells

You tap or double-tap a cell to work with it. If you want to add or edit data, double-tap the cell. A blue outline appears around the cell, and the keyboard appears so that you can begin entering data. Single tap if you want to select a cell. The cell is outlined, and the table-selection elements (the column and row frames, the Cells button, the round button to the left of the column frame, and the button to the right of the column frame as well as beneath the row frame) are shown.

A double-tap always makes the cell available for editing. Figure 3-15 shows that after a double-tap in a cell, the keyboard appears.

Once you have set up your spreadsheet, most of your work consists of entering and editing data of all types. That's what you'll find out about in this section.

Entering and editing data

The keyboard for entering data into a Numbers cell is a powerful and flexible tool — it's actually four keyboards in one. Above the keyboard is a formula bar that lets you quickly and easily enter formulas. (Refer to Figure 3-15.) At the left of the formula bar are four buttons that let you switch from one keyboard to another. Starting from the left, you can choose the following keyboards:

- **42:** The first button, labeled 42, lets you use the numeric keyboard.
- **Clock:** The second button, with the image of a clock, lets you enter dates and times.

✓ **Text:** The letter T displays a standard text keyboard.

✓ **Formulas:** The = sign brings up the formula editing keyboard.

Whichever keyboard you're using, you see what you're typing in the formula bar above the keyboard. To the right of the oblong area is a button labeled Done (or OK, depending on which keyboard you're using) that moves your typing into the selected cell and then hides the keyboard.

You can bring up a keyboard only when you double-tap a cell or other text field (such as a tab name). That means it's selected, and it also means that the keyboard always knows where the data should go when you tap OK or Done.

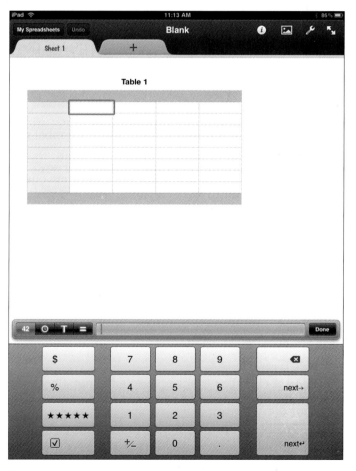

Figure 3-15: Start to edit a cell's data.

With a cell selected and the Checkbox formatting button selected, you'll see the true/false value above the keyboard and the checkbox itself in the table cell. Tap the checkbox in the table cell: The true/false value is reversed, as is the checkbox itself.

Likewise, if you tap the word true or false in the display above the keyboard, the checkbox will flip its value, and true/false will reverse.

When you tap one of the formatting buttons, it turns blue and formats the number in the selected cell (or cells). You can tap another formatting button to switch to another format (from stars to a percentage, for example). Tapping a highlighted formatting button turns it off without selecting another: Your numbers are displayed the way you type them in.

Entering date/time data

Tap the clock to enter date/time or duration data, as shown in Figure 3-19. The Date & Time button lets you specify a specific moment, and the Duration button lets you specify (or calculate) a length of time.

Figure 3-19: Enter date or duration data.

In the display above the keyboard, the units of a date or duration are displayed. To enter or edit a date and/or time, tap Month in the formula bar and use the keypad to select the month (the keys have both the month name abbreviations and the month numbers on them). Similarly, tap any of the other components and enter a value. As you do so, the display changes to show the value. (Tapping AM or PM just toggles that value — you don't type anything.)

If you select a cell containing Date & Time or Duration data, you can use the Info button to choose the formatting to use. There's a particularly interesting user interface for the duration formatting shown in Figure 3-20. The possible components of duration are shown at the top of the view (week, day, hour, minute, second, and millisecond). Above them, a display lets you know which ones you currently have selected. Drag the left or right border to display the units you want displayed. They will always be in sequence, so you can display hours, minutes, and seconds, but not hours and seconds.

Play around with the various formats, and you'll discover something else that's very useful: What you display is not what's stored. The duration value that is entered (or calculated) is unchanged as you change the formatting. If you change hours and minutes to minutes only, you can change it back to hours and minutes, and the value is kept intact.

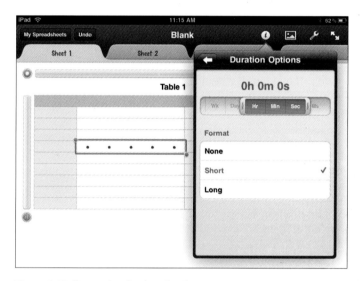

Figure 3-20: Customize the duration format.

Entering text data

When you tap T to enter text data, the QWERTY keyboard appears, as shown in Figure 3-21.

As with most onscreen keyboards, you can switch among letters, numbers, and special characters. (If you need a refresher on how to do that, see Book I, Chapter 2.) Unlike the other specialized Numbers keyboards, you don't have the Next (adjacent and next line) buttons to the right of the keyboard. The reason is that everything you type goes into the selected cell until you tap the Done button to the right of the display above the keyboard. If you enter a Return character, that's part of the text in the cell. The cell automatically grows vertically to accommodate the text you type, and you can resize the column so that the cell is the appropriate size.

Figure 3-21: Enter text.

Entering formulas

Tapping the = button lets you enter a formula, which automatically computes values based on the data you type in. The result of the formula can be displayed in a cell in any of the usual formats, and, as is the case with any cell, that value can be used in a chart.

When you are entering a formula, the four buttons controlling the date/time, text, and numeric keyboards disappear. In their place, a button with three dots appears. Tapping it returns you to the display that includes the other three keyboards. It's just a matter of Numbers saving space.

There's good news and bad news when it comes to formulas. The good news is that you don't have to type in many common formulas: Almost all spreadsheets have the same built-in list of formulas. The bad news is that it's a very long list of formulas.

Formulas can consist of numbers, text, dates, durations, and true/false values. They can also include the results of formulas and the values of individual cells.

Here are the basics of creating a very simple formula in Numbers. The example in this section is about as simple as you can get. It takes the value of an existing cell, adds a number to it, and then displays it as a result in the cell that contains the formula. In this example, I'm using the Team Organization template that you see in the figures throughout this chapter. I've added a new table to the Game Schedule sheet to use as an experiment. (You'll see more about adding tables in the "Creating a new table" section later in this chapter. The cell that contains the formula can be in the same table or another one. It's easier to use a separate table here so that you can see the formula in action.)

The formula takes the starting time of a game from the existing table, adds two and a half hours to it, and displays the estimated completion time in a cell in the new table. This is what you do to get there:

1. **Select the cell into which you want to put the formula by double-tapping it.**

   I selected B2 in Table 1.

2. **Tap the = button at the top-left side of the keyboard.**

   The keyboard changes to the formula keyboard shown in Figure 3-22. (Note that Figure 3-22 shows the keyboard as it will appear after Step 4.)

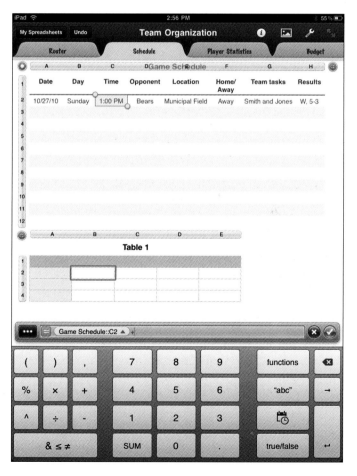

Figure 3-22: Begin to create a formula.

Note that the tables' column and row frames now contain row and column identifiers. The columns are labeled A, B, C, and so forth; the rows are labeled 1, 2, 3, and so forth. Every cell can be identified by its coordinates (such as A1 for the top-left cell). Each table on the sheet also contains a title — in this case, the table on the top is called Game Schedule. That identifies the table, which is important when you create a formula that references a table other than the one that the formula is contained in.

Also note that, at the right of the keyboard, you have a different set of buttons than in the text, date, and number keyboards. To the immediate right of the keypad, you'll find four buttons which do the following:

- *Functions:* Brings up a list of functions, as you'll see in Step 3.

- *abc:* Displays the text keyboard. You can type in text, tap Done, and the text is added to the formula you are constructing. You will be returned to the formula keyboard.

- *Date/Time:* This button (the one with the calendar and clock on it) takes you to the date keyboard. The date or duration that you enter uses the same interface you saw in Figure 3-19. When you tap Done, the date or duration is added to the formula, and you are returned to the formula keyboard.

- *True/False:* Utilizes the same interface as checkboxes; the result is added to the formula you are constructing, and you are returned to the formula keyboard.

3. **Add the game starting time to the formula.**

   Just tap the cell containing the game start time. The formula reflects the name of the table and the cell referenced. In this case, that reference is

   ```
   Game Schedule::C2
   ```

   That means column C, row 2 in the Game Schedule table. You don't have to type a thing — just tap, and the correct cell is referenced.

   You now need the formula to add two and a half hours to the starting time.

4. **Tap + from the operators on the left side of the keyboard.**

   The formula bar now looks like the one in Figure 3-22.)

5. **Tap the Date/Time button to the right of the keyboard and then tap the Duration button at the left.**

6. **On the formula bar, tap Hours and enter 2.**

7. **Tap Minutes and enter** 30.

Figure 3-23 shows what the screen should look like now.

Figure 3-23: Enter the formula.

8. **Tap Done.**

This means you're done with entering the duration. You return to the formula keyboard.

9. **Finish the formula by tapping the button with a check mark on it.**

Figure 3-24 shows the formula as it is now. Note that instead of a Done button, as you have with the other keyboards, you have a button with a check mark and a button with an X at the right. The X cancels the formula, and the check mark completes it. If you want to modify the formula with the keys (including Delete) on the keyboard, feel free.

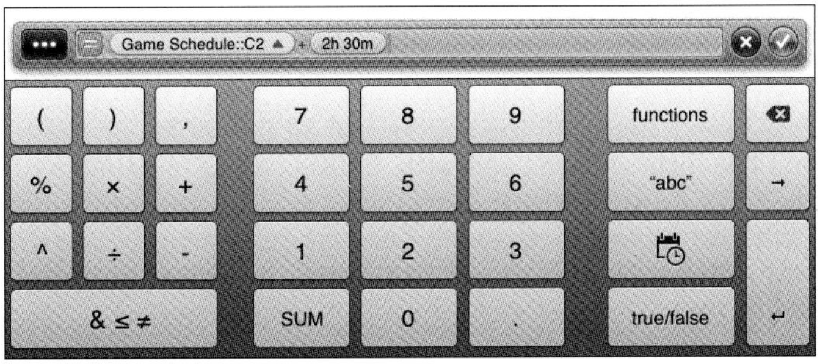

Figure 3-24: Tap the check mark to accept the formula.

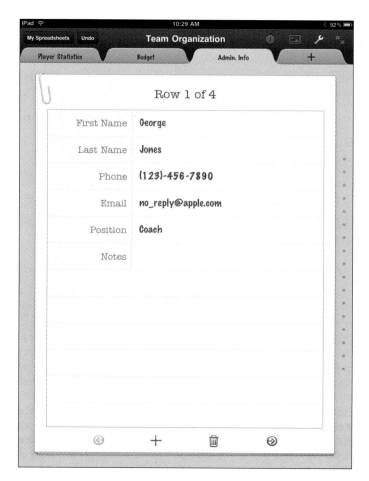

Figure 3-26: Use a form to browse, enter, and delete data.

Working with New Tables

Tables contain the data for your spreadsheets and charts, so it may be a bit surprising to have gotten nearly to the end of the chapter without creating a single table. The reason is the same reason that so much of Numbers for iPad is simple: You've got a lot of templates to work with. You don't have to start from the beginning; instead, you can start from pretty far along in the development process.

Tables can be relatively small and focused. You can use formulas to link them together, and that's a much better strategy than putting every single piece of data into an enormous spreadsheet.

Tables are not just repositories of data; they also drive charts. When you are organizing data in a table, you may want to think about how you want to transform it to create the kind of charts you want. (For more on charts, see Book IV, Chapter 5.)

As you're planning the structure of your tables and sheets, pay attention to the moments when you realize you have to add more data to a table. Ask yourself if you really need more data in that table or if you need a table that can be linked to the first table with a calculation.

Tables often have a *header row* above the data rows; the header row usually contains titles but may also contain calculations such as sums or averages. Numbers tables can have several header rows. There's also a column to the left of the table that has the same functionality — it's called a *header column*. Some people are confused because they think that a header is at the top, but in this usage, it's at whichever side is appropriate.

Creating a new table

Here are the basic steps to create a new table:

1. **Go to the sheet you want the table on.**

   This can be an existing sheet from a template or a new sheet you create just for the table. Remember that tables can be cut and pasted, so you have a second (and third, and fourth . . .) chance to determine the sheet for your table.

2. **Tap the Insert button (the one with the mountain view) on the right side of the toolbar at the top of the window.**

   The Insert popover will open.

3. **Select Tables from the top row of the popover.**

4. **Swipe from one page to another to find the table layout you like.**

   While you can change anything in the table layout, it's a good idea to start with something close to what you want.

   There are six pages of templates — each of the six pages has the same layouts but with different color schemes. From the upper left, as shown in Figure 3-27, they are

Book IV
Chapter 3

Counting on Numbers

- *Header row and a header column at the left:* This is one of the most common table layouts.

- *Header row at the top:* This works well for a list such as students in a class.

- *No header row or header column:* This is a blank spreadsheet. Before choosing it, reconsider. Headers and titles for the tables make your spreadsheet more useable. You can add (or delete) them later and change them, but take a few moments to identify the table along with its rows and columns as soon as you create it.

- *Header and footer rows and a label column:* This works well for titles at the top and left and sums or other calculations at the bottom.

- *Checkboxes in the left column:* This makes a great list of things to do.

5. **Tap the table layout you like and it will be placed on the sheet you have open.**

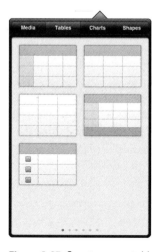

Figure 3-27: Create a new table.

Formatting a table's look

Whether you have just created a new table or created a table long ago, you might want to change its appearance. Here's how:

1. **Select the table you want to format (to select the table, tap inside the table bounds but outside the cells) and tap the Info button in the toolbar.**

   The Info popover opens. (See Figure 3-28.) You can change the basic color scheme and layout by tapping the design you want to use.

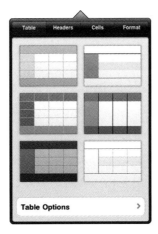

Figure 3-28: Use Info to reformat a table.

2. **Tap Table Options to fine-tune the table. (See Figure 3-29.)**

   Every table has a name (it starts as Table N with the next sequence number for all your tables). The Table Option simply controls whether the title is shown. It's a good idea to change the name to something meaningful. Likewise, each table has a certain size. The Table Border option determines whether a thin line is applied as the table's border or not. Alternating Rows is an option in which every other row is shaded with a contrasting color.

   For large tables, alternating the shading of the rows can make it easier for users to follow the data.

Figure 3-29: Set table options.

3. **Tap Grid Options to show or hide the cell dividers.**

   Many people think that showing the lines in the main table and hiding them in the headers looks best. Experiment. As you tap Yes or No, the display changes so you can see the effect.

4. **Tap Text Size and Table Font to format the text in the table.**

5. **Tap Headers to modify headers for rows and columns.**

   You can set the number of header rows or columns (you either have zero or one footer row). These are created using the existing color scheme. To change the scheme, tap Table in the popover and choose a new one.

   Freezing rows and columns keeps the header rows and columns on each page. As you scroll through data, the data itself moves, but the headers never scroll out of sight. This is often the best option unless the table's content is self-explanatory.

6. **When you are finished, tap anywhere outside the popover to close it.**

Chapter 4: Presenting Keynote

In This Chapter

📑 **Things to consider before you create your presentation**

📑 **Working with Keynote**

📑 **Animating your presentation with transitions and builds**

📑 **Preparing to present**

📑 **Playing your presentation**

Keynote was the first component of iWork. It was originally written for Steve Jobs to use when he gave presentations at conferences and trade shows, including Apple's Worldwide Developers Conference and the Macworld conferences. After these "trials by fire," Keynote and Pages became the first two components of iWork.

Presentation software is a different type of product. It's really not paper-based like word processing or page layout software, and it's not designed for the kind of interactivity provided by a spreadsheet. A presentation definitely requires content presented by a speaker (whether in person or in absentia) and audience.

Keynote for Mac is a reinvention of presentation software Apple style. Now, with the Keynote for iPad app, there are new possibilities. Small group or one-on-one presentations using iPad are made possible in a new way because you can easily present short but impressive presentations just about anywhere. In addition, you can connect the iPad Dock Connector to a VGA adapter and present to larger groups from your smaller machine.

In this chapter, you find out how to prepare and give a presentation with Keynote. As is the case with all the iWork for iPad apps, you can start your Keynote presentation by creating a blank slide or by choosing from a variety of Keynote's templates. Between adding any text that you need onto the slides and using animated transitions, you'll soon have a sophisticated and useful presentation.

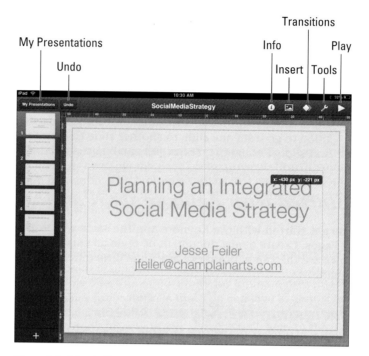

Figure 4-1: A basic Keynote screen.

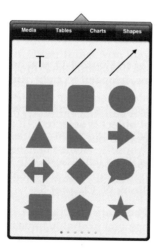

Figure 4-2: Insert objects into your slides.

✔ **Tools:** Tapping the Tools button gives you the popover shown in Figure 4-3. You can select Find to search the Keynote document, Go to Help for assistance with using the application, or Guides that can appear as you move an object toward the center of the slide or of other objects, at the edges of the slide, or at 10% increments horizontally and vertically along the slide. There's one new tool here just for Keynote. You can turn automatic slide numbering on and off. Just as with pages of a Pages document, it's best to let the app handle the numbering so that the slide (or page) numbers are correct even if you move things around, delete slides, or add slides. And notice one last thing in the Tools popover: Check Spelling, which you use to find and correct spelling mistakes.

Figure 4-3: Use the Keynote tools.

✔ **Play:** This starts the presentation playing; if you have a VGA adapter, the slides appear on the external display while the iPad screen shows the controls.

One difference between Keynote and the other iWork apps is that it always appears in landscape (horizontal) orientation; as you rotate the iPad, the image does not rotate. This is because the slides are all designed to be shown horizontally. It's not really a Keynote limitation but rather a nod to the realities of projectors and displays.

On the left side of the screen are thumbnail views of the slides in your presentation. (This is the *navigator.*) To go to any slide in your presentation, just tap the thumbnail.

Creating your first Keynote slide and adding text

The templates in all of the iWork apps provide you with great starting points. When it comes to Keynote, you're almost certain to find pre-built slides you can use so it's just a matter of organizing your own data.

1. To begin a new presentation, tap Keynote on the Home screen.

2. On the New Presentations screen (it should appear when you first open Keynote; if not, tap the My Presentations button in the top-left corner) tap the + button and then tap New Presentation.

3. In the Choose a Theme screen, tap on a theme for your presentation (note that the themes determine the background color and font that will be used). The presentation appears with one slide in it.

4. Double-tap a text placeholder on the slide to edit it; the text placeholder opens for editing and the onscreen keyboard appears.

5. Enter any text you'd like and then tap the slide itself to close the keyboard when you're done.

Formatting text

With Keynote — perhaps more than with the other iWork apps — it's more fill-in-the-blanks than fuss around with formatting. You can get right to work. The font is determined by the theme you choose, but you can modify its size and add effects such as bold and italic. Here's how:

- Double-tap text to select it.

- Tap the Info button and choose a text style option (Title or Subtitle, for example) and tap any of the formatting choices (Bold, Italic, Underline, or Strikethrough) to apply them to the selected text.

- Tap on the slide again to hide the Info options.

You want your presentation text to be perfect, so take advantage of the Check Spelling feature. Tap the Tools button to turn on Check Spelling. Select text and then choose More. In the next bar of commands that appears, tap Replace and Keynote suggests alternate spellings.

Adding a new slide

To add a new slide, tap the + button in the lower-left corner (see Figure 4-4) and choose the style of slide from the gallery that appears. Want to add a bulleted list? Just choose a slide style with a bulleted list already on it.

You can choose the layout for the slide you're adding from the thumbnails shown in the popover. As Figure 4-5 demonstrates, the layouts for new slides vary from template to template.

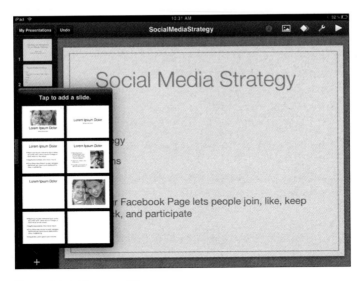

Figure 4-4: Add a new slide.

Figure 4-5: Slides vary by template.

Adding media

Themes provide some slides with image placeholders in them. When you insert a slide, choose a layout with an image placeholder. To change a placeholder image simply double-tap it. A dialog opens showing media sources, such as your Photo Albums. Locate an item and tap to insert it.

If you want to add an image outside of a placeholder, make sure no placeholder is selected, and then tap the Insert button. Tap any of the four tabs: Media, Tables, Charts, or Shapes. Choose the item you want to insert and it appears on your slide.

You can now move the object around with your finger. You select an object on a slide with a single tap (the same as in Numbers and Pages). You can drag the object around; Keynote provides the coordinates for precise positioning, and also provides you with guidelines as you align the object with the center of the screen or the edge of other objects. To resize an object, drag on a corner handle till it's the size you want and then let it go.

See Book IV, Chapter 5, for more on adding text boxes, media, tables, charts, and shapes to your iWork documents.

Managing slides

Tap a slide in the navigator to select it. Then tap the slide again to bring up the selection buttons shown in Figure 4-6. You can now take your desired action; for example, tap Delete, and the slide is gone. (Remember, if it's a mistake, just tap Undo at the top left of the screen.)

Figure 4-6: Delete a slide.

You can also use the selection buttons to cut, copy, and paste slides. After you have cut or copied a slide (tap it and tap Cut or Copy), tap the slide after which you want it to appear, and then tap Paste. (You always paste the contents of the clipboard after the slide you select.)

There's a new option in the selection buttons: Skip. This collapses the selected slide in the navigator into a thin line. When you play the presentation, the slide is skipped over. The thin line in the navigator is big enough for you to tap it to bring up its selection buttons: It will now have a Don't Skip button which lets you bring it back to full size and include it in the presentation as it plays.

Remember to select the slide from the navigator. If you tap the slide itself, the selection buttons act on the selected object within the slide.

Using Transitions and Builds

You can enliven your presentation and make it a better communication tool by using Keynote animations. These let you animate the transition from one slide to another; you can also use animations to *build* a slide. Building refers to the process of animating the appearance of each bullet or other object within a single slide. The process of creating transitions and builds is much the same, and I cover them in this section.

A little animation is a good thing. Feel free to try out all the options but then decide which one — or maybe two — you want for your presentation. Too many animations are distracting and become the focus of your presentation rather than the content you are presenting.

Working with transitions

Use the Transitions button (refer to Figure 4-1) at the right of the toolbar at the top of the Keynote screen to begin setting a transition. When you tap it, you'll be in the transition editor. Notice the Done button in the top-right corner of the screen — until you tap the Done button, you're working on a transition.

Transitions can work on slides as a whole or they can work on parts of slides; when they work on parts of slides, they are often called *builds*. Note that a transition consists of two parts:

- **Effect:** This is the visual effect that is displayed.
- **Options:** Options include the direction in which the animation moves as well as whether it starts in response to a tap or after a previous transition is finished. Options also include the duration of the transition.

Also note that while a transition may appear to happen between two slides it actually happens when you tap a slide to go to the next one. The transition is attached to the from, or first, slide in the sequence of two adjacent slides.

Here's how to build a transition:

1. Tap the Transitions button to enter the transition editor.

The screen will look similar to Figure 4-7.

Figure 4-7: Begin building a transition.

2. In the navigator on the left side of the screen, tap the slide for which you want to build a transition.

The list of transition effects appears in a popover, as shown in Figure 4-8. There are a number of transition effects available. Swipe up and down to see them all. (The list of transitions is controlled by the Effects button at the bottom-left corner of the popover.)

Figure 4-8: Choose an effect.

3. When you find a transition effect that interests you, tap the name to select it and see a preview.

4. **You can tap the triangle in the top-right corner of the popover to repeat the preview.**

   Once you apply a transition effect to a slide, it appears whenever you select that slide in the navigator, as shown in Figure 4-9.

Figure 4-9: The effect is shown on the slide in the navigator.

5. **Tap the Options button in the bottom-right corner of the popover (refer to Figure 4-8) to set the effect options.**

   Use the big circle in the middle of the popover to select the direction the animation moves, as you see in Figure 4-10.

Figure 4-10: Select the direction option.

6. **Swipe down on the popover to see the remaining options shown in Figure 4-11.**

   You can set the duration and when the effect starts.

Figure 4-11: Set the duration and start.

7. Continue to change the effects and options until you're satisfied.

You'll probably want to try out the combinations with the triangle in the upper right of the popover several times.

Working with builds

Builds are much like transitions except that they work within a single slide and control how elements such as bullets display. Here's how to set a build:

1. Tap the Transitions button.

Until you tap the Done button, you'll be creating a transition. Because builds are done within a slide, you'll work on the slide itself (not the navigator).

2. In the display portion of the screen, tap the object you want to build, as shown in Figure 4-12.

Each object can have two sets of builds: effects to build it *into the slide* (when the slide is shown) and effects to build it *out* of the slide (when the slide is closed).

3. Tap the appropriate button for the type of build you want to apply — either a build in or a build out.

4. Select the build effect you want to use, as shown in Figure 4-13.

Just as with slide-to-slide transitions, as soon as you select an effect, it is previewed for you. You can repeat the preview with the triangle in the upper right.

Figure 4-12: Set builds for an object.

Figure 4-13: Select the build effect.

5. **As soon as you select a build effect, you can set options, as shown in Figure 4-14.**

   Note that a number in a yellow circle is created on the object you are applying the build to; you can tap it later to go back and change the effect or options.

6. **Tap the Delivery button on the bottom of the popover to select whether the build happens all at one time or with the addition of each component, as shown in Figure 4-15.**

Figure 4-14: Choose an option.

Depending on what the selected object is, this can build each item in a bulleted list separately or each wedge in a pie chart in sequence. (Delivery options may not be available if they do not apply.)

Figure 4-15: Set the delivery options.

Managing multiple builds on a single slide

As you create builds, each one is numbered. The numbers appear in small yellow circles as soon as you have chosen an effect.

You can manage the sequence of these builds. To do so, follow these steps:

1. **Select the appropriate slide and tap the Transitions button.**

   You'll see the yellow circles around the numbers of the builds on that slide.

2. **Tap any build to edit it using the techniques you used to create the build. (See the previous section.)**

   The yellow circle for a build is shown in Figure 4-16. You can see that there are two transitions for the selected object. In this case, transition 1 is the build in, and transition 2 is the build out. (That happens to be the order they were created in: They don't have to be in that order.) Thus, you can separately tap either transition number to changes its settings or even delete it if you've gone transition-crazy.

Figure 4-16: Edit an existing build.

3. **To reorder the builds, tap the Order button in the bottom-right corner of the popover.**

   Using the horizontal bars at the right of each build (see Figure 4-17), drag them to the order you want them to be executed. The numbers automatically change. Keynote picks up identifying text, such as the title, so that you can keep them straight.

4. **When you are finished, tap Options again to review the reordered builds.**

   You can use the arrow in the top-right corner of the popover to test the builds. When you're satisfied, click Done.

Book IV
Chapter 4

Presenting Keynote

Figure 4-17: Set the build order.

Preparing to Present

You have dotted every i and crossed every t in your presentation, added all the great ideas you've got, tweaked the animations and are happy with what you've got. Now, you need to prepare for a great presentation.

Using a projector

The Apple iPad Dock Connector to VGA Adapter ($29 from the Apple Store at the time of this writing) is a cable that connects your iPad to any VGA device such as a projector. With it, you can use Keynote to give your presentation.

When you connect a projector (or any other display) to your iPad with the iPad Dock Connector to VGA Adapter, the Keynote app can sense that it has a second display. It uses that display when you start a slide show in the Keynote app (see the "Playing a Presentation" section later in this chapter). While it's sending the presentation to the external display, it lets you control it from your iPad. Figure 4-18 shows what you see on the iPad as it plays a presentation on an external display.

The slides are displayed on the external display, but on your iPad you can control the presentation. On the left side of the screen is a navigator show-ing thumbnail images of your slides. This is really important for giving a smooth presentation. Being able to see the next slide helps you make an ele-gant transition to it without shuffling papers and distracting your audience and yourself. You can tap the arrows in the center of the iPad screen to go forward and back from one slide to another.

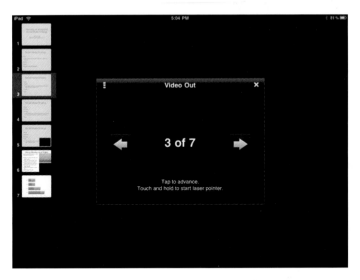

Figure 4-18: Control a presentation on an external display.

Keeping track of time

When you're giving a presentation, you should always keep track of time so that you cover everything and don't exhaust your audience's patience. There's one method you should not use to keep track of time: Don't look at your watch. Half of your audience will reflexively look at their own watches, and a significant number of them are likely to decide that it's time to leave.

At the top of your iPad screen, the time is displayed. When you're giving a presentation (particularly to a large group) that display may be a bit too small to read easily. Even if you can read it easily, look around the room to find a clock you can look at. It's a great idea to look up at a clock (ideally at the back of the audience). It helps you keep track of time and it also avoids you looking down and away from the audience all the time.

If you're speaking in a room that's not familiar to you, try to take a minute or two to "case the joint" before you speak and even before the audience arrives. Look for the clock — there usually is one in an auditorium or meeting room — and make certain you know where the doors are (so that when they open or close they don't distract you). Try to arrange your iPad and its connections in advance. Remember that if you're using a projector, there will be a short cable from your iPad to the projector unless the projector is mounted on the ceiling, in which case the cable will go from your iPad to a connector that may be in the wall. Look to see the location of the cables, and if any of them run over the floor, make certain they are taped down. If that's not an option, just put a chair over the cable. It will remind you that you shouldn't walk in that area.

Using nanopresentations

iPad is a game-changer in many ways. Its size (and therefore its portability) and its remarkably clear screen are just two of the features that open great new opportunities. Keynote for iPad can help you take advantage of a new opportunity — *nanopresentations* (presentations to a small group of people).

Whether you're used to presentations as a presenter or an audience member, you'll probably be pleasantly surprised at how well presentations to small groups can work. Perhaps the most interesting difference is the very simplest one: The speaker can sit down and join the audience around a table or in a circle or just in a group of chairs. Right away, this breaks the speaker/audience or teacher/student paradigm of so many presentations, and it can be a breath of fresh air. It certainly does seem to make discussions and audience questions more lively.

For presentations to large (or even medium-size) groups, your iPad and a projector work very well. But for a smaller group, a projector is often a bit of overkill (and you often hear the groans when it's brought out). You can use your iPad for a presentation to a few people seated around a table or — to be more iPad-like — seated or standing anywhere they want. This really isn't something that most people have thought about very much because the mechanics of a presentation have been bulky; you wouldn't normally think of offering short presentations of a few minutes to informal groups who may not even be seated for a formal presentation.

But think about the possibilities. If you're selling something that's not easy to carry around, a photo album on your iPad is a great way to show prospective customers what you're talking about. But a Keynote presentation — even just a handful of slides — can be much more effective and impressive than a photo album.

Are you canvassing door-to-door for a politician or a cause? Again, a Keynote presentation of perhaps half a dozen slides can present the issue with pictures, text, and diagrams. You can fill in the gaps and answer questions, but it's certainly more effective than knocking on a door and asking if you can come in and set up a computer and a projector.

One of the great advantages of nanopresentations is that the points raised previously about keeping your audience's attention and being careful about a room that's too dark can be ignored. There's not enough time for people to doze off or be distracted.

Here are a few final presentation pointers:

- ✔ **Avoid the dark:** If you are using a projector, use the least amount of room-darkening you can for your presentation. Make certain you can see your audience.

- ✔ **Use Q&A sections:** Use frequent short Q&A sections in your presentations to involve your audience as much as possible.

- ✔ **Use a roadmap:** Let people know where they're going in your presentation and where they are at any moment. When you're reading a book, the heft of the unread pages gives you an idea of how far you've come. With a presentation, one slide after another can come out of the dark without any clue as to how each fits into the presentation.

- ✔ **Time and rehearse your presentation:** Fortunately, Keynote has excellent presentation tools so you can make your presentation as efficient as possible. Depending on your topic, your experience with presentations, and who you are, you may find it more important to work on timing or to rehearse your presentation. Some presenters need no more than a few minutes' rehearsal, but many others need hours to come up with a 15-minute presentation.

Playing Your Presentation

After all of this, there's little to do when you want to play your presentation. Tap the Play button at the right side of the toolbar to begin playing. The transitions and builds happen automatically.

Tap to advance to the next slide. If you're using an external monitor and a VGA adapter, tap the Next and Previous buttons. (Refer to Figure 4-18.)

If your presentation contains hyperlinks, just tap them to open them in Safari on iPad. (Keynote automatically detects hyperlinks by the presence of an Internet schema such as `http://`.)

The Keynote app has a built-in laser pointer, so to speak. Just tap and hold the iPad screen, and a red pointer appears on the display. (If you're using an external display or projector, it appears on that display as well.) You can then emphasize parts of the slide to the audience.

Book IV
Chapter 4

Presenting Keynote

One of the advantages of this is that you can continue to face your audience while pointing out details on the slides. The alternative is to walk over to the slide, turn your back on the audience, and point. Not a really good idea. (They tend to sneak out the moment you turn your back.)

Chapter 5: Working with Text Boxes, Media, Tables, Charts, and Shapes

In This Chapter

↗ **Adding photos and video to your documents**

↗ **Inserting charts and tables in your documents**

↗ **Embedding shapes and text in your documents**

*E*ach of the three iWork apps has its own specialty: text for Pages, spreadsheets for Numbers, and presentations for Keynote. All three apps share a basic interface and common functionality features. One of the common features is the ability to add media (in the form of photos and video), tables, charts, and shapes (including shapes with text) to any document.

The fact that these are common features that are available in all the iWork programs means that you only have to learn how to use them once. In addition, the basic principles of media, tables, charts, and shapes (including shapes with text) to your iWork documents are the same. This means that, although photos and charts have different settings that you can control, you move them around your iWork documents in exactly the same way.

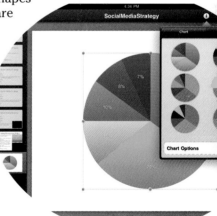

This chapter shows you how to use each of the items that you can add to your iWork documents. It also shows you how to position them and resize them as necessary.

We talk about *embedding* or *inserting objects* into iWork documents. That's the way programmers talk about it, and in this case, techno-speak is a bit easier than plain English.

Getting Started with Embedded Objects

The process of embedding objects into your documents is basically the same whether you are adding them to Pages, Numbers, or Keynote. There are a few differences that you should know about:

- ✓ **Tables in Numbers have more functionality than they do in Pages and Keynote.** For example, formulas and calculations are only available in Numbers.

- ✓ **Charts in Keynote and Pages are associated with a table that you edit by double-tapping a chart.** When you double-tap the chart, it flips over to show the table. In Numbers, you can associate a chart with any table in your spreadsheet.

- ✓ **In Pages, the entire document consists of flowing text.** When you embed an object, you can place it in a specific spot on a specific page, or you can place it at a specific spot in the text. When you place it in the text, it flows with that text and moves from page to page as you add or delete text.

Bear these few differences in mind as you explore the world of embedded objects.

Don't look for differences where they do not occur. The figures in this chapter show you how to embed objects in various types of iWork for iPad documents. Unless otherwise noted, the fact that the process is shown in the context of a Numbers, Pages, or Keynote document is irrelevant.

Begin by tapping the Insert button (the button that looks like a landscape) on the right side of the toolbar in any of the iWork apps. (See Figure 5-1.)

When you insert an object into a document, it is selected by default. It has handles that let you resize it; you can move it by dragging it from the middle (or, in fact, from any area of the object except a handle). Most objects have eight handles: four in the corners and four in the middles of the sides. Two-dimensional objects, such as lines, have only two handles (one on each end of the line).

You may want to review the other chapters in Book IV for more details on moving and resizing objects.

Figure 5-1: Insert objects into your documents.

Inserting Media (Photos and Video)

The first step in inserting media into your iWork document is to obtain the photos or video. You'll need to have the photos or video on your iPad. Move them to your iPad using iTunes as described in Book II, Chapters 3 (video) and 4 (photos).

From then on, it's a simple matter of adding them to your document. Photos are the easiest to add; here's how:

The step list that follows shows you how to add photos to an iWork document. (If you want to insert a video, see the first three steps of this list and all the steps in the step list that follows it.) The figures happen to show a Keynote presentation, but the process is the same for Numbers and Pages.

1. **Open an iWork document (or create one) as described in Book IV, Chapter 1.**

2. **Tap the location where you want to insert the object.** In Pages it's a location in a sentence (by default, it's the current insertion point); in Numbers it's a sheet; and in Keynote it's a slide.

3. **Tap the Insert button on the right side of the toolbar.**

   The Insert popover appears.

4. Tap the Media button in the top-left corner of the popover.

The list of photo albums on your iPad appears.

5. Tap the album you want to use. (See Figure 5-2.)

Figures 5-1 (Pages) and 5-2 (Keynote) demonstrate that no matter which app you're using, you're looking at the same photo albums on your iPad. Note that videos also appear in the list of photo albums. (I'll discuss videos shortly.)

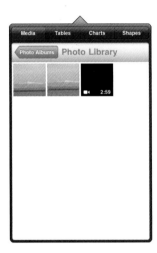

Figure 5-2: Choose the album.

6. Tap the photo you want to use.

The photo is placed on the slide. (See Figure 5-3.) You can now move and resize the photo as you wish.

Videos are a bit more involved, but that's only because they contain more than a single image. Here's how to add a video:

1. Go to the album containing the video, as shown in Steps 1–5 of the previous step list.

When you select the album containing the video you want to use, you see a screen similar to the one in Figure 5-4.

Figure 5-3: Choose the photo.

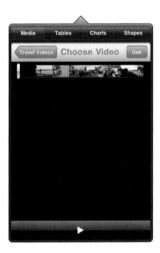

Figure 5-4: Navigate to the video you want to use.

2. **If there's more than one video in the album, tap the one you want to use.**

3. **The movie appears in a horizontal series of a few of its images at the top of the popover. A white and gray vertical bar (the *playback head*) lets you position the movie at a specific point as seen in Figure 5-5.**

The frame under the playback head appears in the center of the popover. The Play button at the bottom of the popover lets you play the movie starting from where the playback head is. In this way you can verify whether or not this is the movie you want to use.

Progress bar   Frame

Playback head

Figure 5-5: Select the video and the starting frame.

4. **Tap the Use button in the top-right corner of the popover.**

The app will compress the video for use in your iWork document. This will take a little time: A progress bar at the bottom of the popover shows you how it's going.

5. **The video is placed in the document once it's compressed.**

You can move or resize the video, as shown in Figure 5-6. Just as with other objects, the app will preserve its proportions.

Figure 5-6: Move and resize the video as you wish.

Inserting Tables

If you want sophisticated and powerful tables, Numbers is for you. But if you want a clean and organized set of data, the tables that you can insert in any iWork app do the trick. One of the key features of tables in Numbers that you don't have in the other apps is formulas and calculations; however, a lot of people don't use those, even in high-powered spreadsheet software such as Numbers and Microsoft Excel.

Even people who are careful to use spreadsheet formulas whenever possible (which is often a good idea) frequently need to create tables that are simple, neat presentations of data. The steps in this section work in any of the apps including Numbers.

Here's how to add a simple table without formulas to any iWork document:

1. **With an iWork document open, tap the Insert button on the right side of the toolbar.**

2. **Tap the location where you want to insert the object.** In Pages it's a location in a sentence (by default, it's the current insertion point); in Numbers it's a sheet; and in Keynote it's a slide.

3. From the Insert popover, tap Tables. (See Figure 5-7.)

You have four layouts (five in Numbers) from which you can choose as shown in Figure 5-7. There are six color-themed variations that you can browse by flicking through them in the popover. These layouts offer these types of tables: with a header row and column in the top-left, a header row in the top-right, no headers in the bottom-left, and a header row and column along with a footer row in the bottom-right.

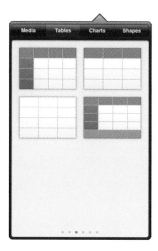

Figure 5-7: Insert a table.

4. Tap the table layout you want to use.

The table is placed in the Pages document.

5. Use the round button at the top left of the table and the handles (see Figure 5-8) to move and reconfigure the table.

As with tables in Numbers, the round button to the left of the column frame selects the table and lets you drag it to where you want it. The handles at the right, bottom, and bottom-right let you resize the table.

6. Use the controls (the circles with the up and down arrows on them) to the right of the column frame and bottom of the row frame to change the number of columns and rows. (See Figure 5-9.)

This part of the interface is different from Numbers.

7. Select a row or column by tapping in the row frame or column frame, respectively. (See Figure 5-10.)

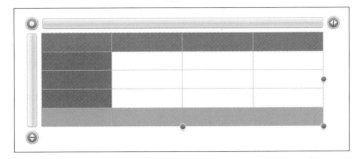

Figure 5-8: Move and resize the table.

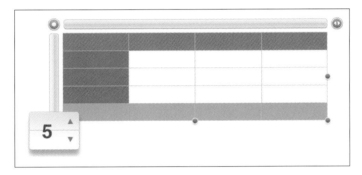

Figure 5-9: Change the number of rows and columns.

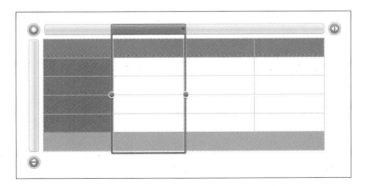

Figure 5-10: Select a row or column.

8. **Expand the selection by using the handles on the sides of the selection. (See Figure 5-11.)**

   The double lines in the top-right corner of the selection let you expand or contract the size of the selected columns. The interface is the same for rows except that it's shown horizontally.

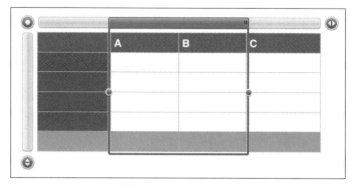

Figure 5-11: Modify the selection.

9. **Drag the selected columns where you want using the column frame. (See Figure 5-12.)**

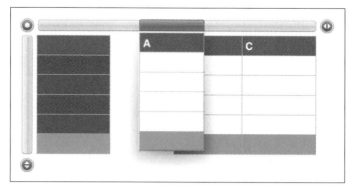

Figure 5-12: Rearrange rows or columns.

Inserting Charts

In Numbers, every chart is related to a range of selected cells in a table. In the other iWork apps, every chart is related to a table that is automatically located on the back of the chart (accessed by double-tapping on the chart).

Because of this difference, these steps apply only to Pages and Keynotes. To add a chart to a Numbers document, refer to Book IV, Chapter 3.

The most important thing to know about charts is that you don't have to draw lines or dots on the chart. You enter data in the table, and the chart puts it in the right place on the chart.

If you want to show extrapolated data, you may have to create a category that will be shown in a different color with estimated data. You'll see how to do this in this section.

Here's how you get started with charts:

1. **Open the iWork document to which you want to add a chart.**

2. **Tap the location where you want to insert the object.** In Pages it's a location in a sentence (by default, it's the current insertion point); in Keynote it's a slide. (See Book IV, Chapter 3, for inserting charts into Numbers documents.)

3. **Tap the Insert button on the right side of the toolbar, then tap Charts, and finally tap the chart type you want to use.**

   Figure 5-13 shows the nine basic chart layouts; as usual, there are six color schemes to swipe through.

   You can change the chart type later, so don't worry if you're not sure which chart type to use.

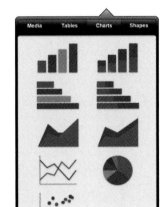

Figure 5-13: Choose a chart type and color scheme.

The chart is added to your document.

4. **You can move and resize the chart by dragging it or using the resize handles. (This is exactly the same process you use for media, tables, and shapes.)**

Also note that the legend can be dragged and resized separately from the chart.

5. **Double-tap the chart to flip it over, view the supporting table (see Figure 5-14), and change the data or row and column headers as you want.**

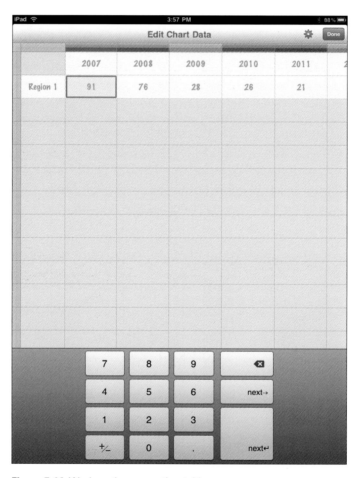

Figure 5-14: Work on the supporting table.

6. **Tap the gear wheel in the top-right corner of the Edit Chart Data dialog to switch the chart's orientation. (See Figure 5-15.)**

That is, whether the data is plotted with the rows vertically or horizontally in a bar or scatter chart. Experiment with the settings to see the result.

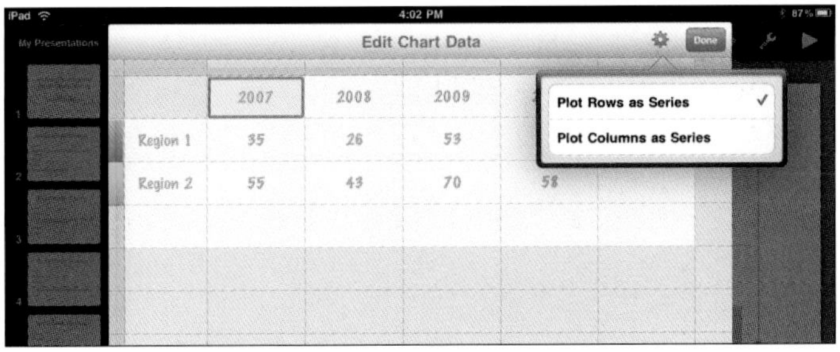

Figure 5-15: Experiment with the chart's orientation.

7. **Tap the Done button to return to the chart.**

8. **If you want to customize the chart's appearance, tap the chart to select it, and then tap the Info button. (See Figure 5-16.)**

The Info popover appears.

9. **Tap Chart at the top left of the Info popover.**

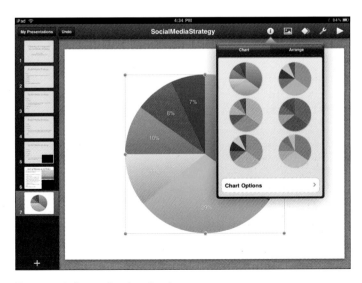

Figure 5-16: Customize the chart's appearance.

10. **Tap the Chart Options button in the Info popover to choose whether or not to show the title or legend, to change the text font and size, to change the chart type, and to chose other options, as shown in Figure 5-17.**

The best way to get to know Info for Charts is to experiment with the settings. This is a very compact and sophisticated tool and you will discover wonderful and intuitive features. For example, in Chart Options, you can choose whether Value Labels are shown or not. (These are shown in Figure 5-16 in the slices of the pie.) If they are turned on, you can specify the number format that is used to display them. If you turn Value Labels off, Number Format disappears from the popover because it's no longer needed.

Figure 5-17: Adjust chart settings and type.

11. **If you want to change the chart type, tap the Chart Options button at the bottom of the popover and choose a new chart type. (See Figure 5-18.) The change is immediate.**

You may want to scroll up or down in the document so that the chart is visible and is not obscured by the popover so that you can see how it looks.

Your data won't be changed, just the type of chart used to display it.

Figure 5-18: Changing the chart type doesn't change the data.

Adding Shapes (Including Text Boxes)

The last inserting technique is for inserting shapes — including text boxes. You probably think this is going to be very complicated. After all, placing text inside objects of all shapes and sizes is really messy, right?

In the iWork apps, adding a shape is actually one of the simplest tasks of all. The reason? There's really nothing new here — if you've read the other sections in this chapter, you already know how to do just about everything in this section.

Though it contains text, a text box is considered a shape in iWork.

To get started adding shapes and text, follow these steps:

1. **Open an iWork document and tap the location where you want to insert the object.** In Pages it's a location in a sentence (by default, it's the current insertion point); in Numbers it's a sheet; and in Keynote it's a slide.

2. **Tap the Insert button on the right side of the toolbar, and then tap Shapes.**

   The popover shown in Figure 5-19 appears.

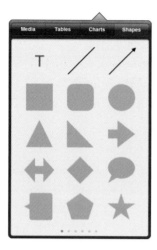

Figure 5-19: Insert a text box.

3. **Tap the T button to insert a text box.**

   The text box is inserted in the spreadsheet.

4. **Double-tap the text box to begin editing the text.**

   You can type anything you want. When you are finished, tap something else to work with it, or just hide the keyboard with the button at the lower right.

You can select the text box with a single tap and resize it appropriately. With the text box selected, you can also tap the Info button on the right side of the toolbar to bring up text editing options. (This selection and resizing behavior as well as the use of the Info button is the same for all embedded objects. The only thing that's different with a text box is that a double-tap brings up the keyboard.)

Try working with a more complex shape. Here's how you customize an arrow and place styled text inside it.

1. **Open an iWork document and tap the location where you want to insert the object.** In Pages it's a location in a sentence (by default, it's the current insertion point); in Numbers it's a sheet; and in Keynote it's a slide.

2. **Tap the Insert button on the right side of the toolbar, and then tap Shapes.**

   The Shapes popover (refer to Figure 5-19) appears.

3. Tap the arrow at the right of the third row.

The arrow is inserted in the spreadsheet, as shown in Figure 5-20.

You can try any shape you want — and you should experiment with a number of them just to get the hang of things.

Figure 5-20: Add an arrow to your document.

4. Resize the shape by tapping and dragging the handles.

You'll notice that shapes resize in different ways. In the case of the arrow, the shaft is lengthened as you enlarge it horizontally, but the shape of the arrowhead doesn't change. (See Figure 5-21.)

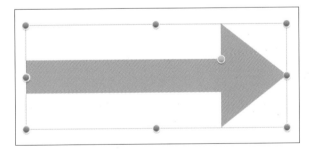

Figure 5-21: Resize the shape.

5. Change the shape's appearance.

Note that some shapes, such as the arrow, have additional handles beyond the eight regular handles at the corners and middles of the shape's edges. In this case, there's a small green handle where the arrowhead joins the shaft; you can drag it (see Figure 5-22) to change the proportions. I used it to widen the shaft of the arrow to make room for the text.

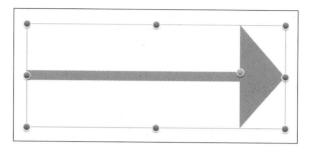

Figure 5-22: Change the shape's proportions.

6. **Double-tap inside the arrow shape to bring up the keyboard.**

   By default, the insertion point will be in the center of the shape.

7. **Type in some text and tap Info to bring up the styling options. (See Figure 5-23.)**

   By default, all the text is selected. If you want, you can use the handles at the edges of the selection to limit your style settings to just part of the text.

Figure 5-23: Add text and style it.

If you want a text box all by itself (that is, with no text inside a shape), tap the T at the upper left of the shapes in the Insert popover shown previously in Figure 5-19. This inserts a text box without an enclosing shape as you see in Figure 5-24. Use the handles to resize it as you would do for any shape, and double-tap in it to bring up the keyboard — again, the same as for any other shape.

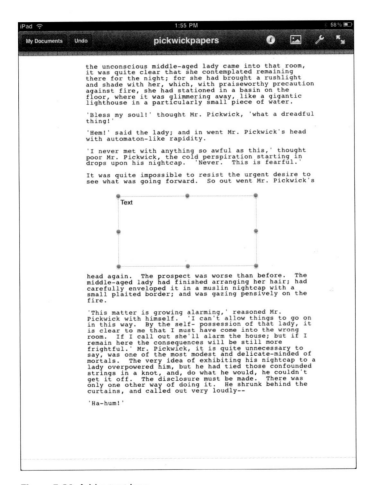

Figure 5-24: Add a text box.

Also, as with any of the other shapes, the text box is added to the insertion point in a Pages document or to the selected spreadsheet in Numbers or the selected slide in Keynote. And, as Figure 5-24 demonstrates, you can insert a text box into a word processing document. This lets you create some sophisticated formatting as you'll see in the following sections.

Layering shapes

Although the iPad is a two-dimensional surface, you can create a sense of depth by moving objects forward and backward. This is accomplished in the iWork apps by making portions of overlapping shapes visible or not to give the illusion of layered shapes.

Layering only matters if two shapes overlap. If you want to adjust layering, select the object you want to move forward or back, tap the Info button, and then choose Arrange. A slider lets you move the objects forward or back as you can see in Figure 5-25.

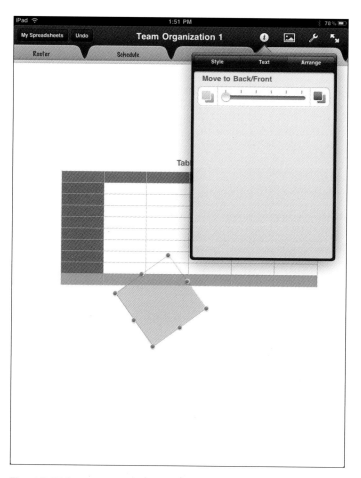

Figure 5-25: Layer a shape.

Rotating shapes

You can rotate a shape as shown in Figure 5-26. Rotating objects on iPad is actually easier than doing so using a mouse on a desktop computer. Do so by selecting the shape and then, with two fingers, rotating it with a twisting motion in your wrist. Give it a try and you'll see how easy it is.

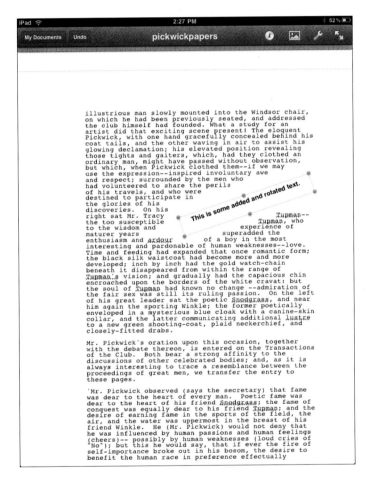

Figure 5-26: Rotate a shape.

Wrapping shapes (Pages only)

In Pages, the text in the word processing document can automatically move aside for a shape as you see in Figure 5-27. (This is called *wrapping*.) You set the wrapping for the embedded object rather than for the word processing document itself. Even though people talk about wrapping the text around the object, the settings are set for the object.

Here's how you wrap text around an object (a text box, a chart, a table, or media).

1. **Select the object you want to wrap text around and open the Info popover.**

2. **Select Arrange at the top right of the popover as you see in Figure 5-27.**

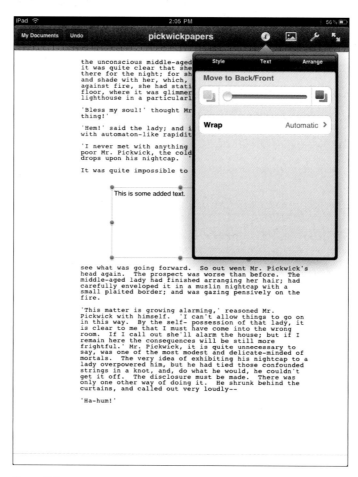

Figure 5-27: Adjust wrapping.

3. **Tap Wrap to open the Wrap settings shown in Figure 5-28.**

   The buttons at the top of the Wrap settings illustrate the three different styles you can choose. The Extra Space slider at the bottom of the popover lets you control the space that surrounds the shape and bumps into the surrounding text.

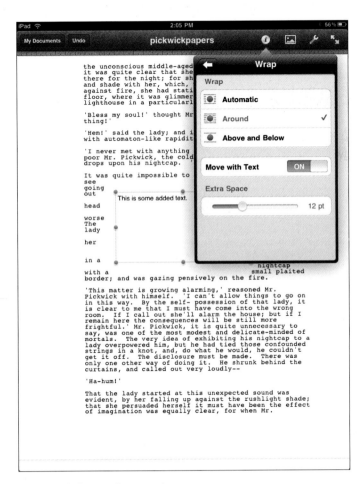

Figure 5-28: Choose the wrapping you want.

Flowing shapes (Pages only)

The Wrap popover shown previously in Figure 5-28 contains the Move with Text control. When it is turned on, the embedded shape moves with the text into which you inserted it. If you add or delete text before the text into which the shape is inserted, that text flows up or down in the document automatically. When Move with Text is turned on, the shape moves as well.

When Move with Text is turned off, the shape is anchored to the page and not to the text. One way to use this is in conjunction with page breaks that you insert yourself. Here's how to use page breaks and shapes that don't move together.

1. **Open or create a Pages document and tap where you want to insert a page break.**

2. **Show the ruler if necessary, and then tap the Insert button in the ruler as shown in Figure 5-29.**

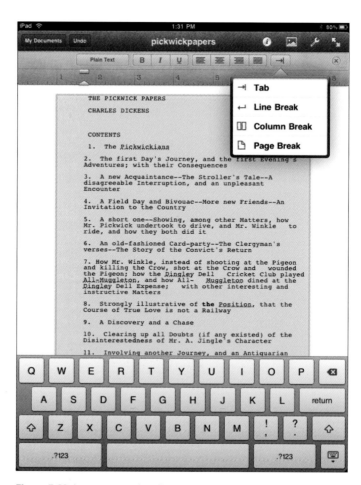

Figure 5-29: Insert a page break.

3. **Insert a shape. You can add text to it if you want. Place it where you want after the page break and then use Wrap settings (refer to Figure 5-28) to turn Move with Text off.**

   The shape will stay where you place it as you add or delete text. Note that this shape is placed on this page only — it's not an element on every page. As shown in Figure 5-30, you can use it as a kind of header or footer, but you can use your own shape and you can place it somewhere other than the top or bottom of the page.

Figure 5-30: Use a shape as a constant element on a page.

Book V
Using iPad to Get Organized

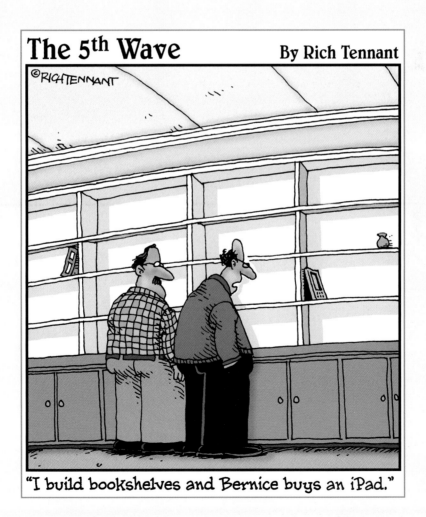

The 5th Wave   By Rich Tennant

"I build bookshelves and Bernice buys an iPad."

_W_e could all use a little more organization in our lives, and iPad is there to help. There's the usual Calendar and Contacts apps to keep your schedule on track and stay in touch with friends and colleagues, as well as a handy Notes app for jotting down quick notes.

In this minibook, you also get information about how to manage your files on iPad: how to sync files to your computer, store things online so you can access them from any computing device, and print hard copies.

Chapter 1: Managing Files and Printing

*O*kay, I'm going to be very upfront about this: Apple has not used a traditional paradigm for moving files to and from your iPad or managing files on the device. In essence, this is partially a chapter about what iPad does differently from traditional file management and how you can get things in and out of the device without a USB port or DVD drive.

The other topic in this chapter is printing, and I'm happy to say that in updating its operating system to version iOS 4.2, Apple did add the capability for wireless printing to the iPad feature arsenal.

In this chapter, I provide you with some ways to manage files in your first generation iPad and take advantage of its wireless printing capabilities.

Finding Your Files

Though there's no Windows Explorer or Documents folder on iPad where you can view all your stored files in one place, iPad does store files. Open up the Photos app, for example, and you see lots of photos, each one contained in a file. iPod contains audio files, Videos contains movie files, iBooks contains e-Book files, if you own Pages it contains word processing documents (as shown in Figure 1-1), and so on.

How did those files get there? You may have created them in iPad (as with the Notes or Numbers apps); you may have downloaded them from the Internet, as with music or video purchases from iTunes; or you may have synced them from your computer, as with music files or photos.

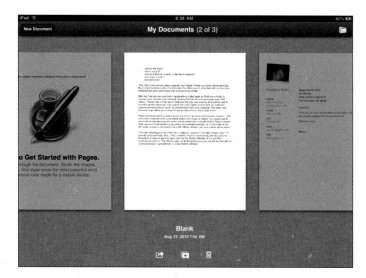

Figure 1-1: Documents stored by Pages.

Depending on the app you open, you may see a My Documents button to display thumbnails of documents, as shown in Figure 1-1, libraries of photos as in Photos, albums of music or individual song files as in iPod (see Figure 1-2), or bookshelves or lists of e-books as in iBooks. Each app offers a slightly different way to find whatever you've created on, downloaded to, or synced to your iPad.

Figure 1-2: iPod shows you files by album, song, or artist.

If you go to iTunes on your other computer, you can see your iPad file structure organized by app. But however the files got in there and however you find them when you open an app, getting them out of your iPad is the next trick I tackle.

See Book II, Chapter 1 for information about buying and downloading content, and Book I, Chapter 4 for information about syncing to your computer and buying apps. Book IV, Chapter 1, gives some details about moving files around for use with iWork products.

Sharing Files

As mentioned in the previous section, iPad doesn't let you get at files the way your computer does with a series of folders and files. You open files in individual applications, such as Photos and Videos. You can't save files to a storage medium, such as a flash drive that you can remove and place in another computing device. Therefore, managing and sharing your files with other devices or other people works a bit differently on your iPad.

You have three options for getting files out of your iPad: e-mail them; sync with a computer to share things like calendar events, contact records, music, or photos, which is covered in Book I, Chapter 4; or use the Safari browser and a third-party service, such as Dropbox, to upload and view files in the Cloud.

Relying on good old e-mail

You can use tools in individual applications to e-mail files to yourself or others. E-mailing files to yourself can be useful if you've worked on a document on your iPad and then want to get a copy of it on your computer. You can't exactly save a copy because (remember) there is no storage medium on your iPad, so you e-mail the file and save the e-mail attachment to your computer hard drive or other storage.

Here's an example of e-mailing from an app, in this case, Photos:

1. **Open Photos and locate a picture you'd like to e-mail.**

2. **Tap the picture to open it, and then tap the Sharing button (it's a little triangle with an arrow popping out of it) shown in Figure 1-3.**

3. **Tap Email Photo and the e-mail form shown in Figure 1-4 appears.**

4. **Fill out the e-mail form and tap Send to get the e-mail on its way to yourself or somebody else.**

Tap the Sharing button

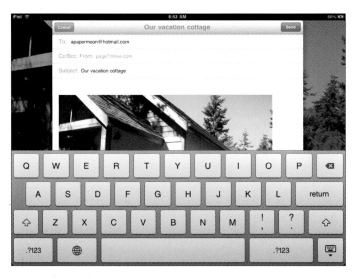

Figure 1-3: Tap the Sharing button.

Figure 1-4: The e-mail form and onscreen keyboard appear together.

Going through the Cloud

Apps such as Dropbox, DropCopy Lite, and FireFly (a wireless file sharing app) allow you to upload files to an online site and, using an app you download to your iPad, access and view those files.

I explain how this works with Dropbox, which is a good free file-sharing app that provides one of the easiest ways to get any and all files to and from your iPad to any and all other computers and devices.

Dropbox is a cloud-based service that allows you to store your files on their servers and access them on any device that's connected to the Internet (Figure 1-5 shows you the Dropbox interface if you surf there on your computer). It directly supports (in the form of dedicated software) Windows, Mac OS X, Linux, Android, BlackBerry, and of course iOS.

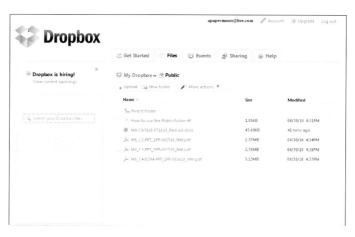

Figure 1-5: Dropbox with files stored in its Public folder.

When you're on a computer, Dropbox works like any other folder on your hard drive. When you open it up, there are all your files for instant access. When you drop something into your folder, it's copied up to the company's servers, and then pushed out to anywhere you've set up with your Dropbox account, including your iPad.

After you download the Dropbox app, you can open a file on iPad and you can view but not edit it, unless you choose the option of opening the document with an app you have on your iPad that would be a logical fit. For example, Figure 1-6 shows the Sharing button, and iPad suggests opening this Word document in Pages, where I can edit it, or PrintCentral, a printing app I cover shortly.

After purchasing and downloading PrintCentral to your iPad, in order to use the app you need to first download WePrint to your computer (there are both Mac and Windows versions available at `http://mobile.eurosmartz.com/print/download.html`). Plug your connector cable into your iPad and computer's USB port. Open WePrint and you can see your server address (see Figure 1-8).

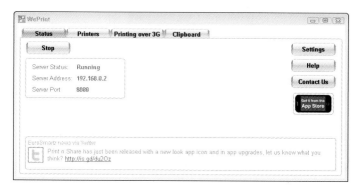

Figure 1-8: The WePrint app on your computer.

Now open PrintCentral on iPad. Tap the Getting Started file listed there to test your printer. Tap the Print icon in the top-right corner, and the Print dialog shown in Figure 1-9 appears.

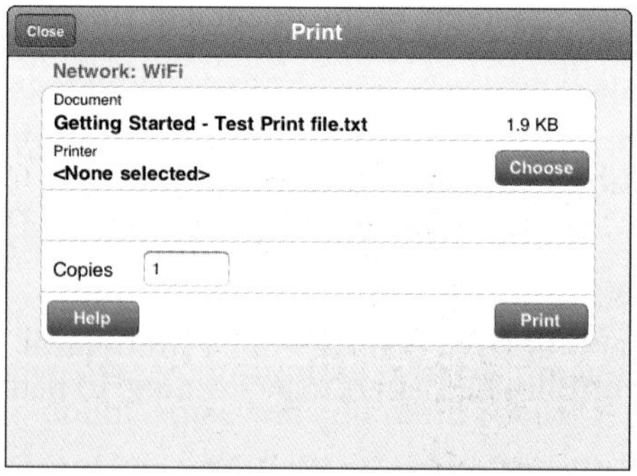

Figure 1-9: PrintCentral's Print dialog.

Tap the Choose button and enter the server address you found in WePrint into the dialog that appears. PrintCentral connects and displays all possible printers (see Figure 1-10). Tap the one you want to use and then tap the Print button in the Print dialog. The test document prints.

Figure 1-10: PrintCentral's possible printers dialog.

After you have it working, you can use the Sharing button from within apps to open a document in PrintCentral and print it. In other apps you can make a copy of a file that places it on your Clipboard, then open the Clip Archive in PrintCentral (see Figure 1-11) and choose the file you want to print and print it.

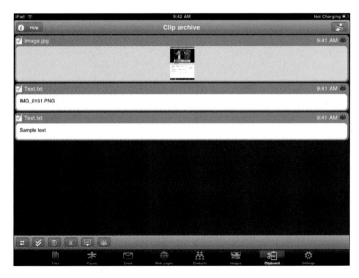

Figure 1-11: PrintCentral's Clip Archive dialog.

Chapter 2: Making Notes

In This Chapter

- Opening a blank note
- Creating a new note
- Using copy and paste
- Displaying the Notes List

*N*otes is a built-in application that you can use to do everything from jotting down notes at meetings to keeping to-do lists. It isn't a robust word processor like Apple Pages or Microsoft Word by any means, but for taking notes on-the-fly or writing a few pages of your novel-in-progress while you sit and sip a cup of tea on your deck, it's a great option.

In this chapter, you discover how to enter and edit text in Notes and manage notes by navigating among them, searching for content, e-mailing them, or deleting a note.

Making Notes

Notes are pretty simple to create — kind of like grabbing a sticky notepad, jotting your thoughts down, pulling off the note and sticking it somewhere, and starting to write the next one. You can use the included editing tools to select, cut, copy, and paste. Notes are saved for you in a list of notes so you can easily find the one you need (covered in the next section).

Opening a blank note

If you have no stored notes, Notes opens with a new, blank note displayed. (If you have used Notes before, it opens to the last note you were working on. If that's the case, you might want to jump to the next section to create a new blank note).

If you have no stored notes and open Notes to a blank document, follow these steps:

1. **Tap the Notes app icon on the Home screen.**

   Depending on how you have your iPad oriented, you see the view in Figure 2-1 (portrait) or Figure 2-2 (landscape).

Figure 2-1: This yellow lined pad format should look familiar to most.

Figure 2-2: Landscape shows you the current note and a list of saved notes on the left.

2. Tap the blank page.

The onscreen keyboard shown in Figure 2-3 appears.

Figure 2-3: Use the onscreen keyboard or your keyboard dock, if you have one.

3. Tap keys on the keyboard to enter text.

If you want to enter numbers or symbols, tap either of the keys labeled .?123 on the keyboard. The numbers keyboard shown in Figure 2-4 appears. When you want to return to the regular keyboard, tap either of the keys labeled ABC.

Figure 2-4: Use this alternative keyboard for numbers and many common symbols.

4. **To capitalize a letter, tap the Shift key at the same time that you tap the letter.**

5. **When you want to start a new paragraph or the next item in a list, tap the Return key.**

6. **To edit text, tap the text you want to edit and use the Delete key to delete text to the left of the cursor or type new text.**

When you have the numbers keyboard displayed (refer to Figure 2-4), you can tap either of the keys labeled #+= to access more symbols, such as the percentage sign, the symbol for euros, and additional bracket styles. With some of these keys, pressing and holding them displays alternate characters. This also works on some keys on the alphabetic (for example N gets you foreign language options such as a Spanish ene) and numeric keyboards (like the exclamation key, which offers an upside down exclamation point used in some languages).

No need to save a note — it's automatically kept until you delete it.

Creating a new note

If you have stored notes, when you open Notes, the most recently used note is displayed. If you then want to create a new note, with one note open, it's a very simple procedure. To create a new note, tap the New Note button (the one with the + symbol on it) in the top-right corner. A new, blank note appears (refer to Figure 2-1). Enter and edit text as described in the previous section.

If you're in portrait orientation and want to see the list of saved notes beside the current note, switch to landscape orientation on your iPad or tap the Notes button at the top left.

Using copy and paste

After you enter content into a note, you may want to modify it. The Notes app includes essential editing tools you're familiar with from other word processors: select, copy, and paste. You can use these to duplicate content, or cut and paste it from one part of a note to another.

To use the copy and paste tools, follow these steps:

1. **With a note displayed, press and hold your finger on a word.**

   The toolbar shown in Figure 2-5 appears.

Press and hold on a word to display this toolbar

Figure 2-5: This toolbar provides selection and paste tools.

2. **Tap the Select button.**

   The toolbar shown in Figure 2-6 appears.

Tap this button

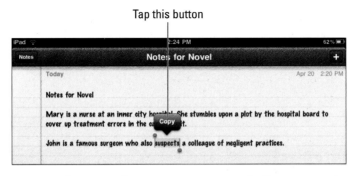

Figure 2-6: Once you select text, you can access the Copy command.

3. **If you want to modify the selection you can tap either blue endpoint dot and drag it to the left or right.**

4. **Tap the Copy button.**

5. **Press and hold your finger in the document where you want to place the copied text.**

6. **In the toolbar that appears (see Figure 2-7), tap the Paste button.**

   The copied text appears.

If you want to select all the text in a note to either delete or copy it, tap the Select All button in the toolbar shown in Figure 2-5. A Cut/Copy/Paste toolbar appears that you can use to deal with the selected text.

Tap this button

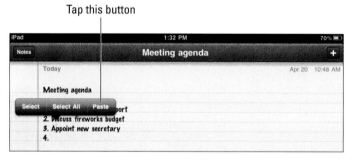

Figure 2-7: Use the press and hold method to again display the editing toolbar.

To delete text, you can use the Select or Select All command, and then press the Delete key on the onscreen keyboard.

Finding Notes

After you've created notes, you are likely to want to find one to open again. You can scan the Notes List to find a note, or use a search tool. You can also use Next and Previous buttons on the Notes pad to move among notes. The following sections help you find and move among notes you've created.

Displaying the Notes List

The Notes List isn't always available in every orientation, but it is the list you need to see what notes you have stored. If you're using landscape orientation, a list of notes appears by default on the left side of the screen (refer to Figure 2-2).

If you're using portrait orientation, you can display this list by tapping the Notes button in the top-left corner of the screen; the Notes List appears, as shown in Figure 2-8.Tap any note on the list to display it.

Tap this button...

to display the list of notes

iPad	1:41 PM	68%
Notes	**Meeting agenda**	+

3 Notes		Apr 20 1:38 PM
Q Search		
Meeting agenda	1:38 pm	
Vacation	12:33 pm	
Notes for Novel	10:57 am	

Figure 2-8: Tap the Notes button to display a list of saved notes.

Notes names your note using the first line of text that you enter. If you want to rename a note, display that note, tap at the end of the first line of text, and tap the Delete key on your keyboard. Enter a new title; it's reflected as the name of your note in the Notes List.

Moving among notes

You have a couple of ways to move among notes that you've created, and they're both pretty simple:

1. **Tap the Notes app icon on the Home screen to open it.**

2. **With the Notes List displayed, tap a note to open it.**

   You can display the Notes List by either turning iPad to a landscape orientation or tapping the Notes button in portrait orientation; see the previous section for more on viewing the Notes List.

3. **Tap the Next or Previous button (the right-and left-facing arrows on the bottom of the Notes pad shown in Figure 2-9) to move among notes.**

Notes isn't a file-management pro; it allows you to enter multiple notes with the same title, which can cause confusion. Be advised, and name your notes uniquely!

Tap either of these buttons

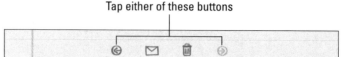

Figure 2-9: Familiar Next and Previous buttons you've used in browsers make navigation easy.

Searching notes

If you're not sure which note contains that very important item, you can search to locate a note that contains certain text. The Search feature only lists notes that contain your search criteria, however; it doesn't actually highlight and show you every instance of the word or words that you enter in each note.

Follow this procedure to use the Notes search feature:

1. **Tap the Notes app icon on the Home screen to open it.**

2. **Either hold the iPad in landscape orientation or tap the Notes button in the portrait orientation to display the Notes List shown in Figure 2-10.**

Tap this button...

to display the list of notes

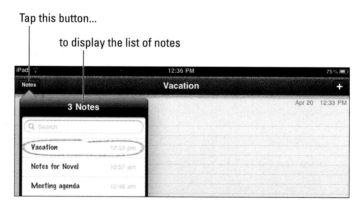

Figure 2-10: The Search feature is located on the Notes List.

3. **Tap in the Search field at the top of the Notes List.**

The onscreen keyboard appears, as shown in Figure 2-11.

Tap here to display the on-screen keyboard

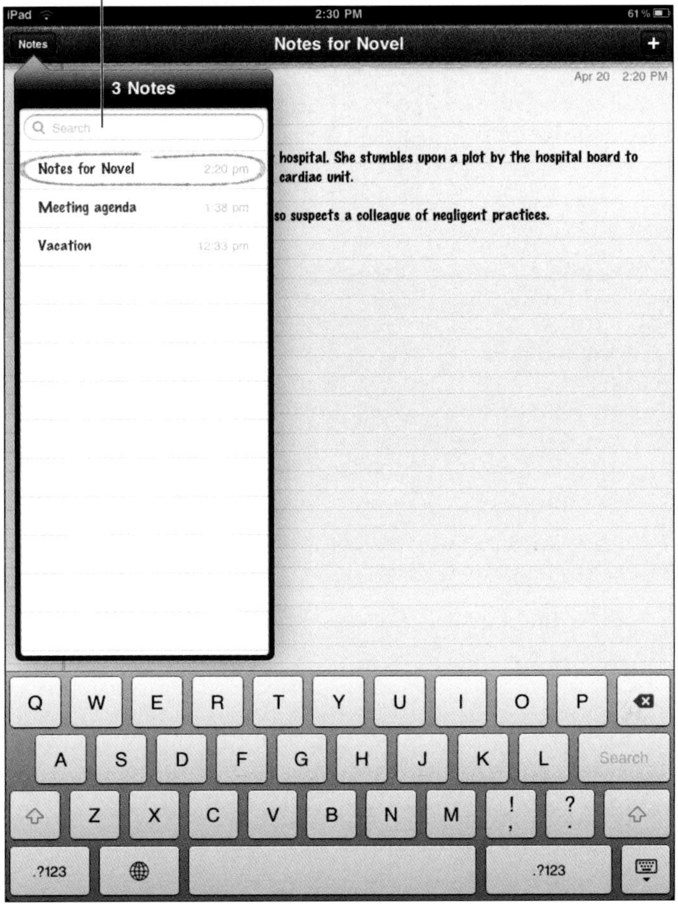

Figure 2-11: Enter search terms using the on-screen keyboard or keyboard dock.

4. **Begin to enter the search term.**

   All notes that contain matching words appear on the list, as shown in Figure 2-12.

5. **Tap a note to display it and then locate the instance of the matching word the old-fashioned way — by scanning through it.**

Figure 2-12: The search feature narrows down by words that match your entry.

TIP

If you want to look for a note based on how long ago you created or last modified it, it might help you to know that notes are stored with the most recently created or modified notes at the top of the Notes List. Older notes fall toward the bottom of the list. The day you last modified each note is also listed in the Notes List to help you out.

E-Mailing a Note

Today it's all about sharing content. If you want to share what you wrote with a friend or colleague, or even access your note on your main computer to move it over into a word processing program and flesh it out, you can easily e-mail the contents of a note using these steps:

1. **With a note displayed, tap the E-Mail button on the bottom of the screen, as shown in Figure 2-13.**

2. **In the e-mail form that appears (see Figure 2-14), type one or more e-mail addresses in the appropriate fields.**

   At least one e-mail address must appear in the To field.

3. **If you need to make changes to the subject or message, tap in either area and make the changes.**

4. **Tap the Send button and your e-mail is on its way.**

TIP

You can tap the button with a plus sign on it in the top-right corner of the e-mail message form to display your contacts list and choose recipients from there. This only works with contacts for which you've entered e-mail addresses. See Book V, Chapter 4, for more about using the Contacts app.

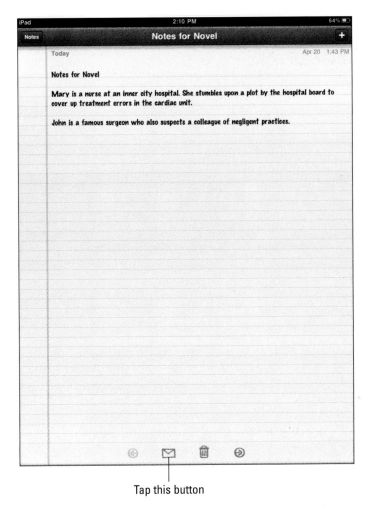

Tap this button

Figure 2-13: Share your scribblings with others through e-mail.

To cancel an e-mail message and return to Notes without sending it, tap the Cancel button in the e-mail form and then tap Don't Save in the menu that appears. To leave a message but save a draft so you can finish and send it later, tap Cancel and then tap Save. The next time you tap the E-Mail button with the same note displayed in Notes, your draft appears.

Enter e-mail addresses here

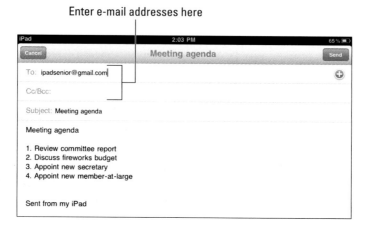

Figure 2-14: You can't save iPad contents to a storage medium, so
e-mail may be your best bet!

Deleting Notes

Over time notes can accumulate, making it harder to find the note you need
in the long list that's displayed. No sense letting your Notes List get cluttered up, or leaving old content around to confuse you. When you're done
with a note, it's time to delete it.

1. **Tap the Notes app icon on the Home screen to open it.**

2. **With the iPad in landscape orientation, tap a note in the Notes List to
   open it.**

3. **Tap the Trash Can button shown in Figure 2-15.**

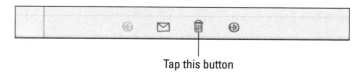

Tap this button

Figure 2-15: With a note displayed, tap the Trash Can button to delete it.

4. **Tap the Delete Note button that appears (see Figure 2-16).**

   The note is deleted.

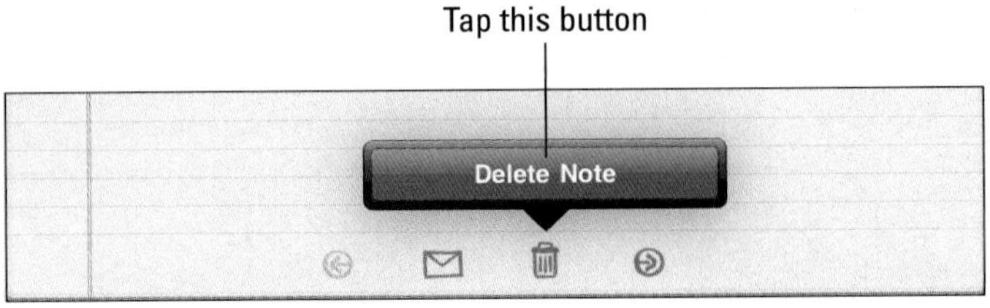

Tap this button

Delete Note

Figure 2-16: Go ahead, delete whatever you don't need with a tap of this button.

Notes is a nice little application, but it's limited. It doesn't offer formatting tools or a way to print the content you enter without a third-party printing app, such as PrinterShare. You can't paste pictures into it (you can, but what appears is the filename, not the image). So, if you've made some notes and want to graduate to building a more robust document in a word processor, you have a couple of options. One way is to buy the Pages word processor application for iPad, which costs about $9.99, and copy your note (using the copy/paste feature discussed earlier in this chapter). Alternately, you can send the note to yourself in an e-mail. Open the e-mail and copy and paste the text into a full-fledged word processor, and you're good to go.

If you want to move beyond Notes and use a note taking app that lets you write with a stylus, check out PaperDesk for iPad ($1.99) or Penultimate ($2.99) in the App Store. Both make drawing and writing handwritten notes pretty easy and fun. Pogo Sketch and Pogo Stylus are two good stylus tools to check out (www.tenonedesign.com).

Chapter 3: Keeping On Schedule with Calendar

In This Chapter

✓ **Viewing your calendar**

✓ **Adding calendar events**

✓ **Creating repeating events**

✓ **Syncing to calendars on other devices**

*M*ost of us have busy lives full of activities that aren't always easy to keep straight. You may need a way to keep on top of all those work-related and personal activities and appointments. The Calendar app on the iPad is a simple, elegant, electronic daybook that helps you do just that.

In addition to allowing you to enter events and view them by the day, week, or month, you can set up Calendar to provide alerts to remind you of your obligations, and search for events by keywords. You can also set up repeating events, such as your weekly staff meeting, a regular social get-together, or monthly flea treatments for your cat. And given that you probably have calendars on your computer and mobile phone, you'll be happy to hear that you can sync your iPad calendar with them using iTunes.

In this chapter, you master the very simple procedures for getting around your calendar, entering and editing events, setting up alerts, syncing, and searching.

Taking a Look at Your Calendar

You've probably used calendar apps in a slew of settings — in your e-mail client, on your cellphone, and even in robust contact management programs. The Calendar app on iPad is more robust than some and less robust than others, but it is a very nicely designed and simple to use program that saves you the cost of buying one app. Calendar offers several ways to view your schedule, so the first step in mastering it is to learn how to navigate those various views.

You get started by tapping the Calendar app icon on the Home screen to open it. Then tap one of the top buttons to change the view. The choices are:

✔ **Day:** This view, shown in Figure 3-1, displays your daily appointments with times listed on the left page, along with a calendar for the month and an hourly breakdown of the day on the right page.

List of the day's appointments

Calendar for the month   Hourly breakdown of the day

Figure 3-1: This shows Calendar in landscape view; in portrait orientation the two pages are narrower.

✔ **Week:** Use the Week view to see all your events for the current week, as shown in Figure 3-2. In this view, appointments appear with times listed along the left of the screen.

✔ **Month:** See one month at a time with and switch among months with the Monthly view (see Figure 3-3). In this view, you don't see the timing of each event, but you can spot your busiest days and what days have room for yet one more event.

✔ **List:** The List view displays your daily calendar with a list of all commitments for the month to the left of it, as shown in Figure 3-4.

The Week button

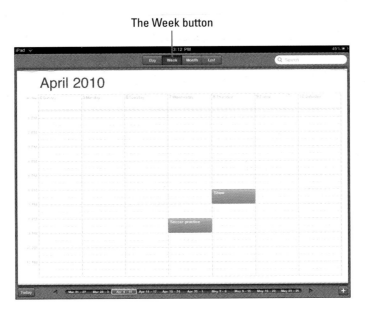

Figure 3-2: Tap another week in the row beneath the weekly calendar to jump there.

The Month button

Figure 3-3: Tap a month along the bottom of the screen to jump to another one.

Search field

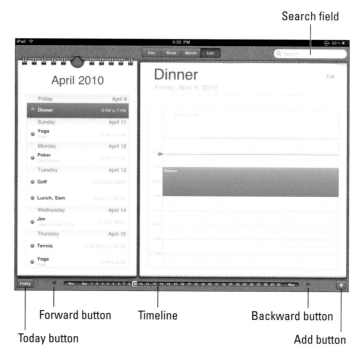

Forward button   Timeline   Backward button

Today button   Add button

Figure 3-4: The List view shows both today and all the days in the month ahead containing events.

To move from one day/week/month to another, use the Timeline displayed along the bottom of every view. Tap a day to move to it, or use the Forward or Backward button to move forward or backward one increment at a time: a day at a time in Day view, a week at a time in Week view, and so on.

To jump back to today, tap the Today button in the bottom-left corner of the Calendar. And now you know the basics about views in Calendar!

For the feel of a real calendar book, rotate your screen when in the Calendar app. It provides a nice book-like experience, especially in the Day view.

If you are looking for a more robust scheduling app, consider buying Pocket Informant for about $6.99. This app is easy to use and has great scheduling tools for your tasks. You can also sync it by using Google Calendar, making a paid-for service, such as MobileMe that coordinates all your device calendars almost superfluous. Also, if you want to use a calendar program for business, check out the app called Shifty, which has tools for managing work shifts that can be very useful to managers and supervisors.

Adding Calendar Events

Events in your life might range from business meetings to Karaoke dates, but whatever the nature of your appointments, Calendar can help you keep them all straight. You can enter single events or repeating events and include alerts to remind you that they're coming up.

Adding one event at a time

If you've used other calendar programs, you know that adding events is usually a pretty simple procedure. It's also easy to add events using iPad's Calendar app, but if you haven't used a touchscreen computer or smartphone before, it's worth a walk through.

Follow these steps to add an event to your calendar:

1. **With Calendar open and any view displayed, tap the Add button to add an event.**

   The Add Event dialog shown in Figure 3-5 appears.

Figure 3-5: Add your event details in this dialog.

2. **Enter a title for the event and, if you wish, a location.**

3. **Tap the Starts/Ends field.**

   The Start & End dialog in Figure 3-6 is displayed.

4. **Place your finger on the date, hour, minute, or AM/PM column and flick your finger to scroll up or down.**

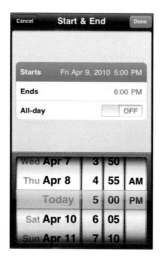

Figure 3-6: Use this cool slot machine-like interface to set up event timing details.

5. **When each item is set correctly, tap Done.**

(Note that, if the event will last all day, you can simply tap the All-day On/Off button and forget setting starting and ending times.)

6. **If you want to add notes, use your finger to scroll down in the Add Event dialog and tap in the Notes field.**

7. **Type your note and then tap the Done button to save the event.**

Note that you can edit any event at any time by simply tapping it in any view of your calendar. The Edit Event dialog appears, offering the same settings as the Add Event dialog shown back in Figure 3-5, minus the ability to assign the event to a different calendar. Just tap the Done button in this dialog to save your changes after you've made them.

Creating repeating events

Many events in our lives happen on a regular basis: that Tuesday evening book club, the monthly sales meeting, or your company's yearly audit, for example. You can use the repeating events feature of the Calendar app to set repeating events.

Here are the steps involved in creating a repeating event:

1. **With any view displayed in the Calendar app, tap the Add button to add an event.**

   The Add Event dialog (refer to Figure 3-5) appears.

2. **Enter a title and location for the event and set the start and end dates/ times as shown in the previous section.**

3. **Tap the Repeat field.**

   The Repeat Event dialog in Figure 3-7 appears.

Figure 3-7: You have to use preset intervals, but there are several.

4. **Tap a preset time interval: Every day, week, 2 weeks, month, or year.**

5. **Tap Done.**

   You return to the Add Event dialog.

6. **Tap Done again to save your repeating event.**

Some other calendar programs may seem to give you more control over repeating events; for example, they might enable you to make a setting to repeat an event every Tuesday. To do this in iPad's Calendar app, simply add the first event on a Tuesday and make it repeat each week.

If you have a MobileMe account, your iPad recognizes and supports all the calendars you've compiled there as well as those you've synced and the iPad calendar.

Adding alerts

Back in the day, a helpful assistant would set a printed schedule for the day's activities in front of his or her boss to remind that person of prior commitments. Today, I'm not sure anybody but the most senior manager gets such service. Instead, we all get to set up alerts in calendar programs to remind ourselves of where to be, and when.

Luckily, in the iPad Calendar app, it's easy to set up alerts by following these steps:

1. **Tap the Settings icon on the Home screen and choose General, and then choose Sounds.**

2. **If Calendar Alerts is not on, tap the On/Off button to turn it on.**

3. **Now create an event in your calendar or open an existing one for editing (see the preceding sections).**

4. **In the Add Event dialog (refer to Figure 3-5), tap the Alert field.**

   The Event Alert dialog appears, as shown in Figure 3-8.

Figure 3-8: Use these preset intervals to set up alerts.

5. **Tap any preset interval, from 5 minutes to 2 days before.** (Remember, you can scroll down in the dialog to see more options.)

6. **Tap Done to save the alert and then tap Done in the Add Event dialog to save all settings.**

7. **Tap the Day button to display the Day view of the date of your event; note that the alert and timeframe are listed under the event in that view, as shown in Figure 3-9.**

It's important to know that, if you are on the road and change time zones, iPad may not recognize the local time, which could cause your alerts to become useless. You can adjust the time of your iPad manually by using the Date and Time feature in Settings to avoid this problem.

An event's alert and timeframe

Figure 3-9: An alert is noted along with the appointment in your calendar.

If you work for an organization that uses a Microsoft Exchange account, you can set up your iPad to receive and respond to invitations from others in your company. When somebody sends an invitation that you accept, it appears on your calendar. Check with your company network administrator (who will jump at the chance to get his/her hands on your iPad) or the iPad User Guide to set this up if having this capability sounds useful to you.

Working with Your Events

After you have some events entered in Calendar, you can use features to search for events, sync your events with other calendars on other devices, or delete events that have been cancelled.

In this section, you work with the various events on your calendar to keep things up to date and organized.

Searching calendars

Displaying events by day or week and scrolling through the pages is one way to look for appointments, but if you need to find a particular event and can't remember the timeframe, you can use the Calendar search feature to do so.

Follow these steps to search for events in Calendar:

1. **With the Calendar open in any view, tap the Search field in the upper-right corner (refer to Figure 3-4).**

   The onscreen keyboard appears.

2. **Type a word or words to search by and then tap the Search key on the onscreen keyboard.**

   As you type, a Results dialog appears, as shown in Figure 3-10.

Figure 3-10: Every instance of an event including your search term is displayed.

3. **Tap any result to display it in the view you were in when you started the search.**

   A box appears with information about the time of the event and an Edit button you can use to make changes, if you want, as shown in Figure 3-11.

Working with multiple calendars

You can choose a calendar for each of your events — for example, Business, Personal, Parties, Classes, and Volunteering. If you're synchronizing your calendars with your Mac or PC or through MobileMe, Google, Microsoft Outlook, or AOL, each source can have its own calendars. On your iPad, tap Calendars at the top left of the screen in the Calendar app. Each calendar's events are shown in a different color.

You can choose to display the events from several calendars at once including your iPad calendar and calendars you sync with from your PC, only your PC calendars, or only your iPad calendar. With the Calendar app open, click the Calendars button and in the Calendars dialog tap to select or deselect the calendars you want to display: All from My PC, My Calendar, On My iPad, or Birthdays. If you have synched to other source's calendars you can choose them here; for example, tap All MobileMe to show all your MobileMe calendars. Tap Done and your chosen calendar displays. When you add a new event, use the Calendar field to choose the calendar you want to add the event to.

Figure 3-11: Tap an event and use the Edit button to make changes to it.

If you've got lots of events, in the Calendar app you might want to tap Hide All Calendars and then tap the one or two you're interested in right now so that you can quickly find their events.

Deleting events

Let's face it, things change. When an event you thought was going to happen is cancelled, you need to reflect that change in Calendar by deleting it. Here's how:

1. **With Calendar open, tap an event.**

   Then tap the Edit button in the information bar that appears (see Figure 3-12).

2. **In the Edit Event dialog, tap the Delete Event button (see Figure 3-13).**

   Confirming options appear.

Tap this button

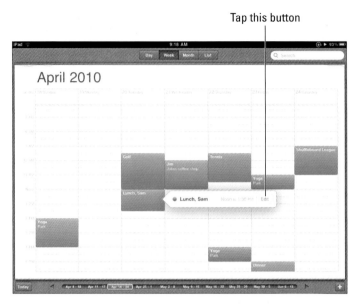

Figure 3-12: To delete an event, use the Edit function.

Tap this button

Figure 3-13: Get rid of an event you no longer need by tapping Delete Event.

3. **If this is a repeating event, you have the option of deleting this instance of the event or this and all future instances of the event (see Figure 3-14). Tap the button for the option you prefer.**

The event is deleted and you're returned to the Calendar view.

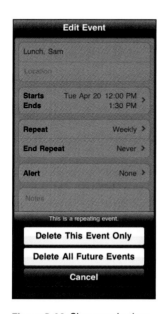

Edit Event

Lunch, Sam

Location

| Starts | Tue Apr 20 12:00 PM |
| Ends | 1:30 PM |

| Repeat | Weekly |

| End Repeat | Never |

| Alert | None |

Notes

This is a repeating event.

Delete This Event Only

Delete All Future Events

Cancel

Figure 3-14: Choose whether to delete one instance of a repeating event or all.

If an event is moved but not cancelled, you don't have to delete the exiting one and create a new one; simply edit the event to change the day and time in the Edit Event dialog.

Subscribing To and Sharing Calendars

If you use a calendar available through an online service, such as Yahoo! or Google, you can subscribe to that calendar to read events saved there on your iPad. Note that you can only read, not edit, such events.

1. **Tap the Settings icon on the Home screen to get started.**

2. **Tap the Mail, Contacts, Calendars option on the left.**

3. **Tap Add Account.**

The Add Account options shown in Figure 3-15 appear.

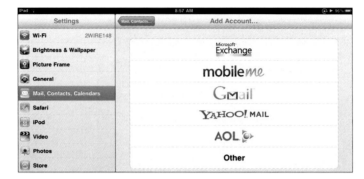

Figure 3-15: Select your e-mail of choice.

4. **Tap an e-mail choice, such as Gmail or Yahoo! Mail.**

5. **In the dialog that appears (see Figure 3-16), enter your name, e-mail address, and e-mail account password.**

Figure 3-16: Enter your email settings here.

6. **Tap Save.**

   iPad verifies your address.

7. **Your iPad retrieves data from your calendar at the interval you have set to fetch data. If you wish to review those settings, tap the Fetch New Data option in the Mail, Contacts, Calendars dialog.**

8. **In the Fetch New Data dialog that appears (see Figure 3-17), be sure that the Push option's On/Off button reads On and then choose the option you prefer for how frequently data is pushed to your iPad.**

Make sure this is set to On

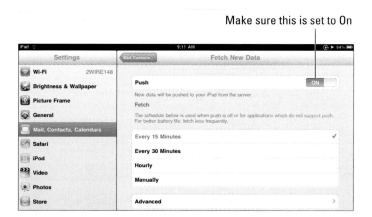

Figure 3-17: Choose how often to fetch new data here.

You can also have calendar events sent if you subscribe to a push service, such as MobileMe. If you choose to have data pushed to your iPad more frequently, it may cause your battery to drain a bit faster.

Syncing with Calendars on Other Devices

Many people today have several computing devices they use to keep track of events. Now that you have an iPad as well, you don't want to have to enter and edit events one by one on it, your mobile phone, desktop computer, and laptop computer, right? That's where syncing comes in handy.

If you use a calendar feature, such as Microsoft Outlook or Apple iCal on your main computer, you can sync that calendar to your iPad calendar via iTunes. You do this by modifying the iPad settings in iTunes to manage sync settings when your iPad is connected via the Dock Connector to USB Cable.

To make calendars in your other accounts available to your iPad you need to subscribe to and share the calendars first. If you have not done this see the "Subscribing To and Sharing Calendars" section earlier in this chapter before proceeding.

Now it's time to sync your calendars. Follow these steps to sync Calendar information using iTunes:

1. **Open iTunes and sign in.**

2. **Connect your iPad using the Dock Connector to USB Cable.**

3. **When your iPad appears in the Library list on the left side of the screen, click on it.**

4. **Click on the Info tab as shown in Figure 3-18, and check the Sync Calendars with check box.**

5. **Click the arrows to display a list of accounts, and click on the one you want to sync with, such as Outlook or iCal.**

6. **To sync with all calendars, click the All Calendars check box.**

   If you don't want older appointments synced, select the Do Not Sync Events Older Than check box and set the number of days (30 days by default).

7. **To sync with just selected calendars, click the Selected Calendars check box and choose the calendars with which you want to sync.**

8. **Click Apply.**

9. **Click the Sync button, and your Calendar settings will be shared between your computer and iPad (in both directions).**

Find out more about working with iTunes to manage your iPad content in Book I, Chapter 3.

Figure 3-18: The iTunes Info tab.

MobileMe syncs your calendars automatically on all your devices without having to place your devices in docks and sync them using your computer. For more about MobileMe, go to www.apple.com/mobileme.

Chapter 4: Managing Contacts

In This Chapter

✔ **Adding contacts**

✔ **Syncing contacts using iTunes**

✔ **Assigning a photo to a contact**

✔ **Addressing e-mails using Contacts**

✔ **Sharing contacts**

ontacts is the iPad equivalent of your address book on your cellphone and, in fact, if you own an iPhone, it's identical to your Contacts app. The Contacts application is simple to set up and use, and it has some powerful little features beyond simply storing names, addresses, and phone numbers.

For example, you can pinpoint a contact's address in iPad's Maps application. You can use your contacts to address e-mails quickly. If you store contact records that include a Web site, you can use a link in Contacts to view that Web site instantly. And, of course, you can easily search for a contact.

In this chapter, you discover the various features of Contacts, including how to save yourself time entering their information by syncing your e-mail contacts list to your iPad.

Populating Your Contacts with Information

Contacts entire purpose is to store contact information and make it available to you, but first, you have to make that information available to it. You can do that by manually adding records one at a time, or syncing via iTunes to bring over your contacts instantly.

Adding contacts

You can, of course, enter your contacts the old fashioned way, by typing in their names, addresses, phone numbers, and so on in a contact form. Follow these steps to create a new contact record:

1. **Tap the Contacts app icon on the Home screen to open the application.**

   If you haven't entered any contacts yet, you see a blank address book like the one shown in Figure 4-1.

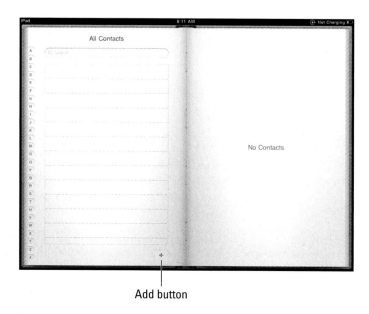

Add button

Figure 4-1: Tap to add a new contact.

2. **Tap the Add button (the button with a small plus sign on it).**

   A New Contact page opens and the onscreen keyboard is displayed, as you can see in Figure 4-2.

3. **Enter any contact information that you wish.**

   Only a first name in the First field is required.

4. **To scroll down the contact page and see more fields, flick up on the page with your finger.**

5. **If you want to add a mailing or street address, you can tap Add New Address, which opens up additional entry fields.**

6. **To add an additional information field, tap Add Field. In the Add Field dialog that appears (see Figure 4-3), choose a field to add (you may have to flick the page up with your finger to view all the available fields).**

Figure 4-2: Enter as much information as you wish about your contact.

Figure 4-3: Round out your contact's information by adding more information fields.

7. Tap the Done button when you finish making entries.

The new contact appears in your address book. Figure 4-4 shows an address book with several entries added.

If you're entering a phone number in a contact record that requires a pause, as when accessing an outside line at a company, simply enter a comma at the place in the number where you require the pause to occur.

Figure 4-4: A list of your contacts arranged alphabetically.

If your contact has a name that's difficult for you to pronounce, consider adding the Phonetic First Name or Phonetic Last Name fields to that person's record (refer to Step 6).

If you have set up an LDAP account on iPad that allows you to connect with your school or company, you may able to access their directories via Contacts. See Book III, Chapter 1, for more about setting up an LDAP account.

Syncing contacts using iTunes

You can use your iTunes account accessed from your computer to sync contacts between your e-mail accounts (such as the one shown in Figure 4-5) and your iPad Contacts application. This sync works in both directions: Contacts from iPad are sent to your e-mail account and contacts from your e-mail account are sent to iPad.

Make sure that you have the most recent version of iTunes before syncing with your iPad. If you use a PC, open iTunes and choose Help➪Check for Updates. On a Mac, choose iTunes➪Check for Updates.

Here are the steps for syncing contacts between your e-mail and your iPad:

Figure 4-5: A Gmail account with contacts displayed.

1. **Connect your iPad to your computer with the Dock Connector to USB Cable.**

2. **In the iTunes window that opens on your computer, double-click the name of your iPad (such as Earl's iPad), which is now listed in the iTunes source pane.**

3. **Click on the Info tab, shown in Figure 4-6.**

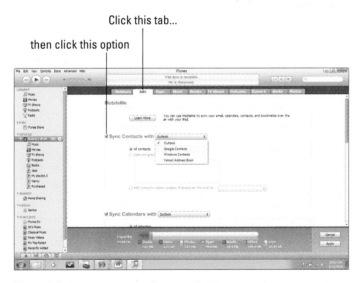

Figure 4-6: Choosing to sync Contacts in iTunes.

4. **Click to select the Sync Contacts check box, and then choose your e-mail provider from the drop-down menu (Windows) or pop-up menu (Mac).**

You may be required to agree to share your contacts and provide your username and password for the e-mail account.

5. **If you want to replace the information on your iPad with the e-mail account information, scroll down and in the Advanced section, click to select the Contacts check box.**

   Next time you sync your iPad contacts will be replaced.

6. **Click the Apply button in the lower-right corner.**

   The first time you do this, a dialog appears asking if you want to Merge or Replace contacts on the iPad.

7. **Click the option you prefer.**

   After any changes are applied, the Apply button turns into the Sync button, and your iPad screen changes to show that syncing is in progress.

8. **When the sync is complete, open Contacts on your iPad.**

   All contacts have been brought over to it.

9. **Unplug the Dock Connector to USB Cable.**

You can also use a MobileMe or Microsoft Exchange account to sync contacts with iPad, but MobileMe charges a subscription fee. Microsoft Exchange may, for example, be what a company uses for its networked e-mail accounts, so if you're not working for a big company, this may not be an option.

Assigning a photo to a contact

It's always good to associate a face with a name. With Contacts you can do just that by adding a person's photo to his contact record. You add photos from the Photos app albums which you have saved from a Web site, uploaded from a digital camera, received as an e-mail attachment, captured as a screenshot, or synced from photo collections stored on your computer. (See Book II, Chapter 4 for more about working with the Photos app).

Follow these steps to add a stored photo to a contact record:

1. **With Contacts open, tap the contact to whose record you want to add a photo.**

2. **Tap the Edit button.**

3. **In the Info page that appears (see Figure 4-7), tap Add Photo.**

Tap here...

then tap on the photo's location

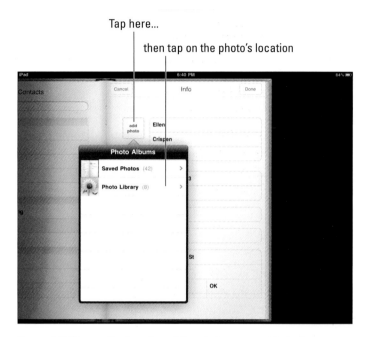

Figure 4-7: Choose the location of the photo you want to include.

4. In the Photo Albums dialog that appears (refer to Figure 4-7), tap either Saved Photos or Photo Library, depending on where the photo is stored.

Saved photos are ones you've downloaded to your iPad or taken using the screen capture feature; the Photo Library contains photos synced from your computer.

5. In the photo album that appears, tap a photo to select it.

The Choose Photo dialog shown in Figure 4-8 appears. If you want to modify the photo, move the image around in the frame with your finger, or shrink or expand it by pinching your fingers inward or outward.

6. Tap the Use button to use the photo for this contact.

The photo appears in the contact Info page (see Figure 4-9).

7. Tap Done to save changes to the contact.

Figure 4-8: Select or edit the photo you want to include.

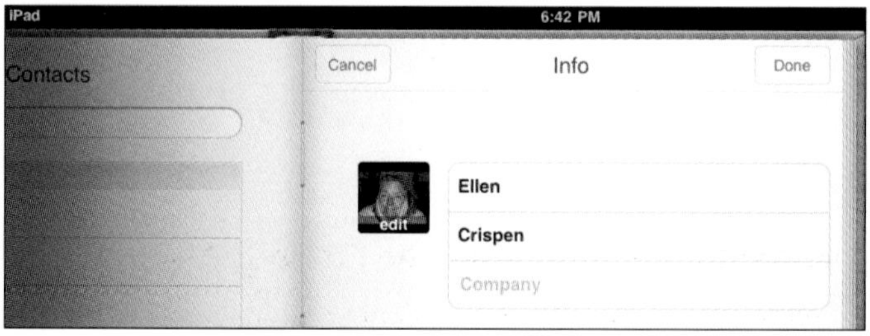

Figure 4-9: A photo displayed with a contact in iPad.

You can edit a photo you've added to a contact record by simply displaying the contact information and tapping it. Choose Edit Photo from the menu that appears, and then in the dialog shown in Figure 4-8, use the described gestures for moving and scaling the image, clicking Use when you're done to save the changed figure.

If you want a more powerful contact-management app, check out Contact Journal, iPad Edition. It syncs with your Contacts app content and can also sync with a computer contact-management program such as Outlook. But the nicest feature for a road warrior is how it keeps a record of who you've visited and when you've e-mailed them.

Finding Contacts

You can use a search feature to find contacts in the Contacts app, using that person's first or last name or a company name. This one is pretty much like every search feature you've ever used, though it's a simple feature compared to some, since you can only search for names and there are no advanced search techniques available.

Here are the steps to search for a contact:

1. **With Contacts open, tap in the Search field at the top of the left-hand page (see Figure 4-10).**

   The onscreen keyboard opens.

Tap in the Search field

Figure 4-10: Easily search for contacts.

2. **Type the first letter of either the first or last name.**

   All matching results appear, as shown in Figure 4-11. In the example, typing "N" displays Nancy Boysen, Nellie Dillon, and the Space Needle in the results, which all have an "N" starting their first or last name.

3. **Tap a contact in the results to display their information on the right page (refer to Figure 4-11).**

Search results

Figure 4-11: Search results narrow down as you type.

You can't search by phone number, Web site, or address in Contacts at the time of this writing. We can only hope that Apple adds that functionality in future versions of the app!

You can also use the alphabetical listing to locate a contact. Tap and drag to scroll down the list of contacts on the All Contacts page on the left. You can also tap any of the tabbed letters along the left side of the page to quickly scroll to the entries that start with that letter (you can see this in Figure 4-10).

Using Contacts Beyond Your iPad

Contacts isn't just a static database of names and addresses. After you've got contact information in the app, you can use it to reach out to people in several useful ways. You can jump to the contact's Web site to see what he/she or a company is up to online; use a contact's e-mail information to quickly send an e-mail message; share the contact information with somebody else; or find the physical address of the contact using the iPad Maps app.

Going to a contact's Web site

Everybody's got a Web site today, so whether your contact is a person or an international conglomerate, there's likely to be an associated Web site you might want to access now and then. You can do that from your iPad using the Contacts app.

If you entered information in the Home Page field for a contact, it automatically becomes a link in the contact's record. With Contacts open, tap a contact to display their contact information on the right-hand page, and then tap the link in the Home Page field (see Figure 4-12).

Tap this link

Figure 4-12: Tap to go to a Web page related to a contact.

The Safari browser opens with the Web page displayed (see Figure 4-13).

Figure 4-13: Visit contact Web sites to check up on their latest info.

There is no way to go directly back to Contacts after you follow a link to a Web site. You have to tap the Home button and then tap the Contacts app icon again to reenter the application. Maybe in the next generation iPad?

Addressing e-mails using contacts

If you entered an e-mail address for a contact, it automatically becomes a link in the contact's record that allows you to open an e-mail form and send a message. It's a handy shortcut for getting in touch:

First, be sure you've entered an e-mail address in the contact's record and then follow these steps:

1. **Tap the Contacts app icon on the Home screen to open Contacts.**

2. **Tap a contact to display their contact information on the right-hand page and then tap their e-mail address link (see Figure 4-14).**

   A New Message dialog appears, as shown in Figure 4-15.

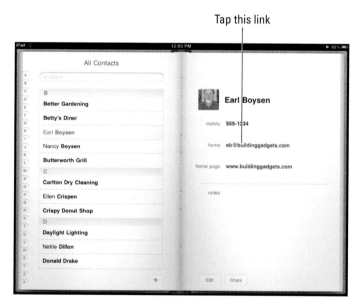

Figure 4-14: Tap to open a new e-mail message.

3. **Use the onscreen keyboard to enter a subject and message.**

4. **Tap the Send button.**

   The message goes on its way!

Figure 4-15: A new e-mail message form.

Sharing contacts

After you've entered contact information, you can share it with others through an e-mail message. Sharing is especially handy when you've got locations in contacts, such as your favorite restaurant or movie theater.

Here's how to share your contacts' information:

1. **With Contacts open, tap a contact name to display its information.**

2. **On the information page, tap the Share button (see Figure 4-16).**

   A New Message form appears.

3. **In the New Message form shown in Figure 4-17, use the onscreen keyboard to enter the recipient's e-mail address.**

4. **Enter information in the Subject field.**

5. **If you like, enter a message and then tap the Send button.**

   The message goes to your recipient with the contact information attached as a `.vcf` file (the vCard format which is commonly used to transmit contact information).

When somebody receives a vCard containing contact information, he or she need only click on the attached file to open it. At that point, depending on their e-mail or contact-management program, they can perform various actions to save the content. Other iPhone or iPad users can easily import `.vcf` records into their own Contacts apps.

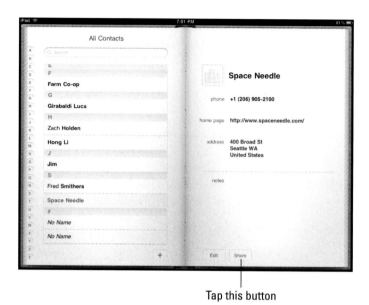

Tap this button

Figure 4-16: Easily share contact information with others.

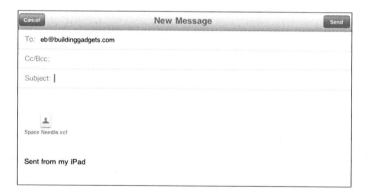

Figure 4-17: If you like, enter a subject and message.

Viewing a Contact's Location in Maps

If you've entered a person's street address in Contacts, you have a shortcut for viewing that person's location in the Maps application. Once again, this is useful for places you need to visit for the first time such as several clients' offices on that next business trip.

Follow these steps to pinpoint your contacts in iPad's Maps app:

1. **Tap the Contacts app icon on the Home screen to open it.**

2. **Tap the contact you want to view to display his or her information.**

3. **Tap the address.**

   Maps opens and displays a map to that address (see Figure 4-18).

Figure 4-18: Click this information bar to view more details in the Maps app.

After you jump to a contact's location in Maps, you may want to use the features of Maps to display different views, figure out what the traffic is like on that route, or calculate the route between two locations. For more about using the Maps application, see Book III Chapter 2.

Deleting Contacts

Remember that iPad's memory is limited compared to your standard computer. Though a contact record is tiny compared to a TV show, there's no sense keeping lots of old records around when you no longer need them. When you need to remove a name or two from your Contacts, doing so is easy. Follow these steps:

1. **With Contacts open, tap the contact you want to delete.**

2. **On the information page on the right, tap the Edit button at the bottom of the page.**

3. **On the Info page that displays, drag your finger upward to scroll down and then tap the Delete Contact button (see Figure 4-19).**

   The confirming dialog, shown in Figure 4-20, appears.

4. **Tap the Delete button to confirm deletion.**

Tap this button

Figure 4-19: Tap this red bar, and your contact record is gone forever.

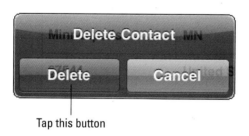

Tap this button

Figure 4-20: Tap the Delete button to confirm.

During this process, if you change your mind before you tap Delete, tap the Cancel button in Step 4. But be careful because after you tap Delete, the only way to put it back is to resync with your computer, assuming you haven't deleted it there!

Book VI

Must-Have iPad Apps

*O*ne of the great things about the iPad are all the cool apps available on Apple's App Store (more than 35,000 as of this writing!). At the same time, however, it can be hard to sift through all those apps to find the best ones to suit your needs.

That's where this part comes in, because I've spent a lot of time with many of these apps, and I show you what I think are the best of the best. I show you what you can do with them and explain why I think you'll want to put them on your iPad. Some are genre defining, some set the bar in the user interface department, some help you be productive and do things you wouldn't otherwise be able to do on your iPad, and some are just plain cool.

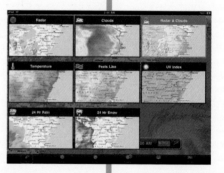

Chapter 1: Business Apps

In This Chapter

*O*ne of the most compelling strengths of all of Apple's iOS devices is the App Store and the thousands of apps that allow you to do just about anything you might want to do. (Remember that iOS is the name of the operating system that runs the iPad, as well as the iPhone and iPod touch.) In this chapter, I show you some of the best apps for business, including some of the great productivity apps that are available. I talk about what makes the app good and tell you what you can do with it so that you can decide if you need it on your iPad.

Many of the apps I talk about in this chapter are apps that were written for the iPad. Some apps, however, have been written by the developer to run as native apps on both the iPad and iPhone (or iPod touch). These are called *hybrid* apps, and you'll find "Hybrid" next to the price for those apps. Hybrid apps have the advantage of allowing you to buy once and use on whatever iOS device you have. For the latest iPad updates, be sure to check out my Web site at www.iPadMadeClear.com.

...il you what, Pages is the bee's knees. I listened to Apple e... Pad would fulfill most people's computing needs in the future, i got my hands on this app. I don't think we're there yet, but th... might get there.

So if you're new to the worl... software, Pages is the Com... Microsoft Word on the Mac everything Word does, and ... consumers than Word is. M... everything it does do it doe...

Letters, resumes, thank you newsletters, proposals, rep... posters and flyers...these ar... Pages does well, and it mak...

pretty darned easy.

The key to that is the work Apple put into reworking the user interface. This was on... the first iPad apps released, and I think Apple really wanted to show other develope... what could be done. The result is that thanks to some great use of gestures you do... need a mouse.

...ther key ingredient to Pages is making context king. The tools that are availa... ...reen depend entirely what it is you are doing or have selected, and that k... ...n becoming cluttered.

Pages

by Apple, Inc.

$9.99

 Pages is Apple's advanced word processor for the Mac, and now the iPad. I think it's one of the best apps available for the iPad in terms of demonstrating how a touchscreen interface can be used to get things done. In fact, I suspect that's why Apple developed Pages, Numbers, and Keynote, to set the bar for other developers.

I should probably stress right off the bat that Pages is not "Microsoft Word for the iPad." On the Mac and PC, Word is a heavy-duty word processor with all kinds of tools for business, publishing, and other serious needs. Oh sure, people type up letters and resumes on it all the time, but it's made with much more in mind. Pages for iPad was built from the ground up to create letters, resumes, thank-you notes and cards, newsletters, proposals, reports, term papers, and even posters and flyers. It's the word processor for the rest of us.

Everything in this app was designed to be accomplished with gestures (pinch, zoom, tap, and swipe) and the onscreen keyboard, including layout, formatting, and placing graphics like photos, charts, and graphs. It comes with 16 templates and a library of tables, customizable charts, and shapes. You can also add photos from your photo libraries, as I did in Figure 1-1, including any images you may have created in another iPad app and saved to your photo library.

One of the coolest things about Pages is the way objects work. Once you drop, say, a photo into your document, you can move it, resize it, change the presentation style, or even rotate it, and the text will just autoflow around it in real time. It makes it so easy to do layout and design on your iPad that you may have to try it to truly appreciate it.

Pages works with Apple's free iWork.com site, which means you can share your Pages documents directly on the Web.

Pages is a great app for small business and home office users; students; neighborhood associations, church groups, and other organizations; and anyone looking to create and edit word processing documents on the go.

What you can do with it: write letters and reports and create resumes and a variety of other professional-looking documents.

For more on the Pages app, see Book IV, Chapter 2.

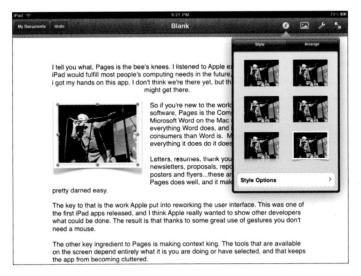

Figure 1-1: Picking a style for the inserted photo.

Numbers

by Apple, Inc.

$9.99

Numbers is a spreadsheet app, and it's also part of Apple's iWork suite for iPad. It, too, is aimed at a different kind of user than Microsoft Excel. It's a great app for small business and home office spreadsheets, for keeping budgets and logs, and organizing teams and other group competitions. It's an even better app for turning your spreadsheets and data into gorgeous charts and graphs that you can use to make your reports, presentations, and other documents look great.

Just like with Pages, everything in Numbers was designed to be done with gestures. Filling in data in a spreadsheet, changing colors, adding a chart or graph, resizing . . . All of these things can be done super fast and easy on your iPad. You can see a sample chart and data set in Figure 1-2. Some things are even easier and faster to do with this app on the iPad than you could do them on your desktop computer with a full-blown spreadsheet application.

Like Pages, Numbers also works with Apple's iWork.com Web site for document sharing.

Numbers comes with 16 templates (checklists, budgets, invoices, schedules, rosters, and so on), and the library of charts and graphs contains nine different varieties for you to use. Each of those nine different types comes with several different color palette choices that can then be edited further still. The same is true for the included shapes — you can edit the color, style, and other attributes with a few taps.

Spreadsheets have come a long way from being the sole domain of the accountant, and Numbers for iPad makes it easier than ever for you to use them. Whether you have a small business or are organizing a PTA event or working to manage your household budget, Numbers is a must-have on your iPad.

What you can do with it: create and manage spreadsheets, make gorgeous charts and graphs from that data, and then format your document as needed.

For more on the Numbers app, see Book IV, Chapter 3.

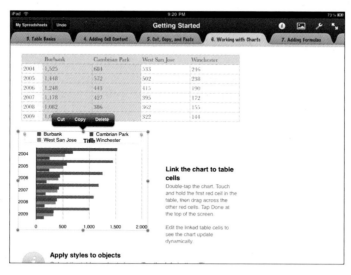

Figure 1-2: Double-tap an element in your spreadsheet to pull up resizing handles and the Cut/Copy/Delete menu.

Keynote

by Apple, Inc.

$9.99

PowerPoint may rule the business world, but Keynote makes the best-looking presentations. There, I said it! What's weird is that Keynote on the iPad is just as capable as Keynote on a Mac (which in my opinion makes it better than PowerPoint for Mac or Windows). It's perfect for anyone wanting to work on a presentation on the go, and many may find they never bother with PowerPoint or Keynote on their desktop computer again. It really is that good!

Like Apple's other iWork apps, Keynote comes with 16 templates that look terrific. Each of those templates includes several different premade slides that comport to a different theme (Modern Portfolio, Showroom, Chalkboard, and Photo Portfolio, which you can see in Figure 1-3, as well as others). You can create your own presentation without a template, of course, but if you want to start with a style all laid out for you, try the templates.

Most of the time, presentations are displayed on projectors or some kind of large display, but if you have a small group (say a couple of customers or your boss), you can just make and display your presentation right on your iPad with Keynote!

Once you're working on a presentation, you'll have access to awesome transitions and effects, each of which has options and controls that are a breeze to understand and use. You can add photos and images from your photo library, and the app has the same charts, graphs, and shapes that come with Pages and Numbers. Creating new slides is easy, and editing them is even easier. Seriously, this is an amazing app to use, and it makes such great-looking slides and presentations that some people will wonder who your advertising agency is.

Whether you give a monthly or quarterly presentation to your peers at work, train people, make sales pitches, have a school report to present, or give keynote speeches at major industry events (you know, like a certain iCEO of one of the world's largest corporations), Keynote should be on your iPad.

What you can do with it: make gorgeous, professional-looking slides and full-blown presentations.

For more on the Keynote app, see Book IV, Chapter 4.

Figure 1-3: Choosing a transition in a Keynote presentation.

Quickoffice Connect Mobile Suite for iPad

by Quickoffice, Inc.

$14.99

This is the app for people who are more comfortable in Microsoft Word and Excel than with Apple's iWork approach. Quickoffice Connect Mobile Suite for iPad is built on the same paradigms as Word and Excel — in fact, its *raison d'être* is to view, create, and edit files in Microsoft Office file formats. That means you can go back and forth between your Mac, PC, and iPad with your Word and Excel files (you can only view PowerPoint files with Quickoffice as of this writing), so long as you use DOC, DOCX, TXT, XLS, XLT, and XLTX file formats. Until and if Microsoft brings the real deal to iOS, Quickoffice is the best way to work on your Office files on the iPad in an Office-y kind of way.

Another great thing about Quickoffice is that it has Dropbox support built right into it. I talk about Dropbox in the next section, but the short version is that Dropbox is a great utility that gives you access to files on a variety of devices, including iPad. With Dropbox support in Quickoffice, you can create a Word document on your PC at work and put it in your Dropbox. Then when you're at the coffee shop that afternoon and you need to edit it, just open it from your Dropbox in Quickoffice on your iPad. Once you get home to your Mac, you can open it from Dropbox there, too! If for some bizarre reason Dropbox just doesn't float your boat, Quickoffice also supports Google Docs, MobileMe, and Box.net.

This app offers a nifty navigation tool, too. If you press and hold the right margin in a multipage document, you'll get a thumbnail view of all the pages in your document, as you can see in Figure 1-4. Just slide your finger down the page until you get the thumbnail of the page you want to jump to, and you're there. It's a nifty feature.

Quickoffice doesn't have a lot of fancy formatting tricks like Pages and Numbers, but I think it's the best app for those who either have to, or are accustomed to, working with Microsoft Office, OpenOffice, or the other Office-like productivity suites on the market.

What you can do with it: create and edit word processing and spreadsheet documents in Microsoft Word and Excel formats. You can also view PowerPoint files, but you can't edit them.

Figure 1-4: Using the cool thumbnail navigation feature to go to another page.

Dropbox

by Dropbox

Free — Hybrid

Okay, I can't wait any longer — I have to tell you about Dropbox now. If you are doing serious work on your iPad, be it for business or other tasks, you need Dropbox because it's the easiest and best way to get any and all files to and from your iPad to any and all other computers and devices.

Let me back up a bit. Dropbox is a *cloud-based service* that allows you to store your files on the provider's servers and access those files on any device that's connected to the Internet. Dropbox directly supports (in the form of dedicated software) Windows, Mac OS X, Linux, Android, BlackBerry, and of course iOS. Even if you are using some other OS (webOS? Windows Mobile? Sun Solaris?), or if you don't have Dropbox installed on the device you are using right now, you can access your files through a Web browser.

When you're on a computer, Dropbox works like any other folder on your hard drive. When I open it, I see all my files there for instantaneous access. When I drop something into my folder, it's copied up to the company's servers, and then pushed out to anywhere I've set up a Dropbox account, and that includes the iPad.

Dropbox folders can be selectively shared with other Dropbox users, making it a great tool for any sort of collaborative project.

This is key because Apple doesn't make it all that easy to move files to and from your iPad. You can sync photos, music, and video files through iTunes, and some apps support Apple's iTunes File Sharing, but even that requires you to sync your iPad to your computer. As a power user, what you need is Dropbox.

Dropbox works on your iPad in two ways. The first is with the free app you can download from the App Store. In that app, you'll find all your Dropbox files and folders. With iOS's Open With feature, you can tap a file to select it, then tap the file-sharing icon in the upper right, as you can see in Figure 1-5, to choose which supporting app to send your file for editing or other work.

Dropbox has a great file preview feature that will show you the contents of the file you have highlighted, as you can see in the figure below. It supports most of the major file formats and makes it easy to pick the right file you want to work with on your iPad.

In addition to the Dropbox app, iOS app developers can add Dropbox functionality directly to their apps, like the Quickoffice folks did in the app I discuss in the preceding section. This makes it even easier to work with your files in those apps, and I hope to see more and more apps take advantage of what this service can do for users.

If you want to easily move files on and off your iPad, Dropbox is currently the very best way to do so.

What you can do with it: access your important files on your iPad anywhere you have an Internet connection.

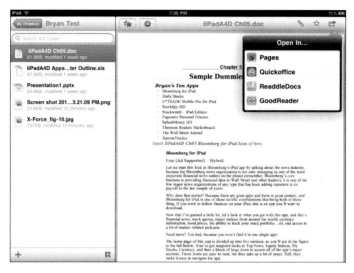

Figure 1-5: Using the Open With feature in iOS to open a Pages document in my Dropbox with the Pages app.

OmniGraffle

by The Omni Group

$49.99

OmniGraffle is expensive as far as iPad apps go, but it's worth it if you need to make flowcharts or diagrams. This app is just as intuitive as the apps in Apple's iWork suite, and it's a breeze to work with. It comes with a wide array of customizable tools that allow you to make anything from a very basic flowchart to complex drawings, like the full espresso machine that The Omni Group includes in one of the example charts that comes with the app. I think that anyone for whom flowcharts, process charts, diagrams, and other such charts are important will find that OmniGraffle on the iPad makes them rethink what they can do with a tablet device.

You can also open OmniGraffle apps created with the Mac version of the software on your iPad, or vice versa!

iThoughtsHD (mindmapping)

by Craig Scott

$7.99

iThoughtsHD is a dedicated mind-mapping app for the iPad. For those not familiar with the concept, mind mapping is using a diagram to show the structure of an idea or plan, and showing the relationships between different aspects of that idea or plan. There are many mindmapping apps for Mac and Windows, but only a few (so far) on the iPad — and iThoughtsHD is the best one I've found so far. It has easy-to-use tools for quickly developing your own maps, and I think this is one area ideally suited to the tablet-in-your-lap form factor.

iAnnotate PDF

by Aji, LLC

$9.99

If you want to be able to just view PDF files on your iPad, check out GoodReader for iPad. It's just 99 cents, and it's a great app. If you need to be able to annotate or mark up PDF files on your iPad, however, you'll want iAnnotate PDF. This app allows you to quickly and easily highlight text, add notes, draw lines, strike out or underline text, or even just doodle in the margins if that's your thing. There are a lot of professions where the ability to annotate a PDF file is needed, and this app makes doing so on your iPad so easy that you might move all of those tasks to this device and off your computer.

PrintCentral for iPad

EuroSmartz Ltd.

$9.99

PrintCentral is the third-party printing app I recommend. It has a file browser and e-mail reader that allows you to access anything on your iPad, and it allows you to print to a network printer across your Wi-Fi network. If you install a free printer server provided by EuroSmartz on your Mac or PC, you can even print to your printer remotely through a 3G connection on iPad with Wi-Fi + 3G. (I recommend installing the print server anyway, as it also gives you more printing options.)

Prompster and Teleprompt+ for iPad

by Dante Varnado Moore and Gene Whitaker (respectively)

$14.99 and $9.99

In addition to all the other things your iPad can do, it can also be a portable teleprompter, which is great for giving speeches and other presentations. There are two apps I'd like to recommend, Prompster and Teleprompt+ for iPad. Prompster allows you to record your speech right there on your iPad as you're giving it, and it has great onscreen controls. Teleprompt+ for iPad has more and better options for controlling your speech, but it doesn't include a recorder function as of this writing. If you want more control over timing, the display colors, and other aspects though, it's a better pick.

**Book VI
Chapter 1**

Business Apps

Chapter 2: Travel Apps

In This Chapter

- Kayak Explore + Flight Search
- Wikihood Plus for iPad
- Urbanspoon for iPad
- ZAGAT TO GO
- FlightTrack Pro – Live TripIt Flight Status Tracker by Mobiata
- Inrix Traffic! and Inrix Traffic! Pro
- World Customs & Cultures
- The World Clock
- World Atlas HD
- WiFiGet HD

I love to travel, but I'll be the first to tell you that I'm not very organized before or during (or after!) my outings. Fortunately, there are a lot of iPad apps that can help me with that. There are apps for booking travel and accommodations, apps to show you where to go, apps for tracking flights, and even apps for helping you find local services and other information. In this chapter, I show you some of these apps so you can use your iPad to make your trips more fun, more efficient, and maybe even hassle-free. (But don't hold me to that last one!)

Many of the apps I talk about in this chapter are apps that were written for the iPad. Some apps, however, have been written by the developer to run as native apps on both the iPad and iPhone (or iPod touch). These are called *hybrid* apps, and you'll find "Hybrid" next to the price for those apps. Hybrid apps have the advantage of allowing you to buy once and use on whatever iOS device you have.

Kayak Explore + Flight Search

by Todd Barnes

$5.99

You may be familiar with Kayak as an online travel service. Or you may have used the company's iPhone apps, but either way, you should check out Kayak Explore + Flight Search for iPad. This app offers the standard flight search features, but it also has some cool features like Explore that may help you have a little fun, too.

Let's look at the mundane stuff first, though. Kayak claims to offer the fastest flight search in the world. I can't speak to the claim of fast*est*, but it's definitely fast. The interface is straightforward and easy to use and understand. Plug in your From and To airports, your Departure and Return dates, number of passengers, class of flight (Economy, Business, First), and whether you prefer nonstop flights, and then tap Search. On the left side of Figure 2-1, you can see that I was looking for some flights from San Francisco to New York City in September, and in the Search History pane, you can see past searches. That's very handy if you're comparing prices between different date ranges and/or locations. You'll also see a map of my route. (In Landscape mode, you also get a separate pane for recommended hotel deals.)

Figure 2-1: Search results for a cross country flight (left) and the Explore interface for finding flights to destinations around the world (right).

There's also a pane called Hot Searches from *Your Departure City* that shows some great deals to random cities from the departure city you entered. These are deals that other Kayak users found, and you never know when you might see a destination or killer price that strikes your fancy.

When you perform a search, you get a list of all the flights from the major airlines that service that route. A progress bar lets you know the status of your search. You can order the search results by Price, Airline, Stops, Duration, and Class (some search results may include a mix of Classes, even though you specified a particular class). You can also toggle any particular airline (or other factors) on or off from a list on the right side of the screen.

Under the Filter pane, tap the Price tab to get a slider that limits your search results from the cheapest flight in the list to a maximum price. This can limit the amount of scrolling you need to do.

I like this interface for searching and filtering my results, and I bet you will, too. You can also search for cars and hotels, and there's a Deals section that includes various vacation packages and other travel deals to and from different cities around the world. The Deals section is really a Web page being served up through an in-app browser, and these pages include sponsored links to vacation packages and flights and those sponsored links were not generated by the Kayak engine, so be careful about what you tap on in the Deals page if you want to limit yourself to Kayak-searched results.

But let's talk about that fun feature I mentioned. It's called Explore, and with it you can choose your departure city and quickly get flight destinations to cities all over the world. It works like this: Set your city, and you'll get a map of the planet with orange dots all over it, as shown on the right side of Figure 2-1. Each of those dots represents a flight. Pinch and zoom in far enough, and those dots become red rectangles with prices in them. Tap a rectangle (or a dot), and you get a little pop-up window with the name of the destination city and a date range that the price represents. Tap that square, and you're taken to the Flights search page so you can see all Flights to that city.

But it gets even cooler because there are three tabs at the bottom of the screen, as you can see on the right side of the figure. The When tab lets you specify a date range; What lets you specify activities (Golf, Beach, Gambling, Skiing) and a temperature range (how cool is that?); and the Flight tab lets you specify whether you want nonstop flights and a maximum travel time. Tweak these as you want, and the dots (or rectangles) are filtered accordingly!

I realize that this isn't a great feature for planning a business trip, but how about for planning a vacation or a get-away-from-it-all trip? I think it's just great for finding a place to visit that you might not otherwise have considered.

If you don't want to browse restaurants from a map, tap the icon that looks like six little boxes at the bottom of the screen to browse local restaurants in list form. You can sort by food, décor, and service ratings, by cost, or alphabetically. Just swipe the screen to go to the next page, and tap any of the eight listings on each page to get the full-screen workup I mentioned previously.

Note that you'll need a connection to the Internet to make the most use of this app, as it pulls reviews from the company's servers. This will ensure you have the very latest information and most up-to-date reviews. You can, however, view reviews in your History and Favorites without a connection.

ZAGAT TO GO is the app for foodies or anyone who is interested in getting a more formal, organized, and edited approach in a restaurant guide. Whether you're traveling for business or pleasure, if you care about where you eat, take ZAGAT TO GO with you.

What you can do with it: find nearby restaurants that have been reviewed and rated by ZAGAT. You can get directions, hours of operation, features of the restaurant, contact information and the menu, and many restaurants have links to their Web sites.

FlightTrack Pro – Live TripIt Flight Status Tracker by Mobiata

by Ben Kazez

$9.99 — Hybrid

Ignore the long name and call this app what everyone else calls it, FlightTrack Pro. This app is great for when you're traveling, but it's also a good app to have when you're expecting friends, family, or business associates who are traveling to you! With it, you can track flights all over the world on a map, and you can do it in real time, too. In addition, it has integrated support for TripIt, which makes tracking those flights super easy.

I don't have any upcoming flights to show you of my own, but FlightTrack Pro has a fun little feature that allows you to shake your iPad to find a random flight. To be honest, this fun feature is easier to use on the iPhone, but it's still a great way to show off the app to your friends. You can also add flights by hand if you know the flight number, or search for them by route if you don't.

You can also make an in-app purchase for $3.99 to add the ability to search for flights according to the departing airport. Most users aren't likely to need that ability, but if you're a flight junkie — and there are flight junkies out there, let me tell you — you won't want to miss it.

On the left side of Figure 2-5, I've picked several random flights in the U.S. The pop-up window lists all the flights I am tracking, and I can remove any individual flight by tapping the little eyeball icon underneath the date. You can see take-off and landing times, status (the top flight is en route), and I can delete a flight by tapping the Edit button.

Figure 2-5: Monitoring several flights in the Continental U.S. (left) and a push notification about a flight I was monitoring (right).

Now, on the map you'll see green and red squares, and an airplane icon and line representing each of the routes. The red squares are destinations, and the green ones are departure cities. If you tap those squares, you'll get a pop-up window with information and any warnings regarding that specific airport.

Tap a jet, and you'll find additional information about that flight. The pop-up window includes take-off and landing times, on-time status, and if I scroll down, I get total air time, elapsed time, the remaining time for the flight, a weather forecast, and other information.

The mapping service is provided by Google, and it includes an overlay of live weather information, as you can see on both sides of the figure.

Most people aren't going to fire up this app just to watch random flights. Its main use is to monitor flights you actually care about. There are two key features that make this app very convenient for this use. The first is support for TripIt, a third-party service that monitors your flights for you. You can use

TripIt to get e-mail notifications of status updates for your flight, and with support for the service in this app, you can use it to make entering your flight information easy. TripIt, which is free (there's a paid Pro level that FlightTrack Pro currently doesn't support), allows you to simply forward your itinerary to the company, and then they automagically grab all your flight (and other data) for you. When you enter your TripIt account information in FlightTrack Pro, it automatically looks to TripIt for any flights you are taking, and presents them to you on a silver platter. No muss, no fuss!

The other key feature is the way the app uses Push Notification Service to send you any updates on the flights you are tracking. On the right side of Figure 2-5, you see a Push notification for a new arrival time for one of my flights. These Push notifications show up even if you don't have the app open, meaning you get those status updates without having to go look for them! And since this app is a hybrid app that works on your iPhone, iPod touch, and iPad, you're a lot more likely to find out when your wife is landing early or when your boss's flight has been canceled. Believe you me, this is a great feature, especially if you have to travel frequently or work with people who do.

You can e-mail flight information directly from the app, too. You'll appreciate this when you get a Push update that a flight has been delayed and need to send it to your coworker or family member who is picking someone up.

FlightTrack Pro is gorgeous, and tracking a flight is fun (to me) even if I'm not involved with it. To me, it's a must-have app for anyone involved with any sort of semi-regular travel. It's more convenient on your iPhone when you're in the car, but it looks so great and is so much easier to use on your iPad that you'll use it there whenever you can.

What you can do with it: track flights all over the globe. With integrated TripIt support, entering your flight information is super easy.

Inrix Traffic! and Inrix Traffic! Pro

by INRIX, Inc.

Free; $9.99 per year or $24.99 for life

When you're traveling to another city, one thing you're not likely to have much knowledge of is local traffic. Of course, if you have to commute for 45 minutes each way just to get to work, you might consider that "travel," too. Whatever the case, Inrix Traffic! and its Pro counterpart can provide you with the kind of real-time traffic data that could be the difference in getting to that wedding, business meeting, dinner reservation, or maybe just your job, on time. The free version works well enough for most people, and it displays real-time conditions in Google Maps in a straightforward and easy-to-follow way. (It shows green lines for normal traffic, orange for slow, and red for heavy traffic.) The Pro version, which costs $9.99 per year or $24.99 for a lifetime subscription, offers you fastest-route information, expected travel time (and ETA), directions, the best time to leave, traffic cameras, and the ability to save frequent destinations. Try out the free one, and if you like it, you'll probably want the Pro version.

World Customs & Cultures

by Hooked In Motion, LLC

Free

Pay attention because this is the only iPhone app that hasn't been updated for the iPad that I am recommending in this entire book within a book! World Customs & Cultures is a fantastic guide for local customs, attitudes, and other things (like taboos) that you'll need to know when traveling to another country. Greetings, Communication Style, Personal Space & Touching, Eye Contact, Views of Time, Gender Issues, Gestures, Taboos, and Law & Order information is offered for 165 countries! I wish I had this when I first went overseas, let me tell you! This app might also help you when dealing with foreign nationals visiting you. Sure, they should be learning your customs just like you're learning theirs, but understanding something like the fact that direct eye contact, in some cultures, is considered threatening can make a world of difference (Get it? *World?*) in helping to understand your foreign friends.

The World Clock

by Orlin Kolev

99 cents

Have you ever been traveling and picked up your phone to call your wife, husband, friend, or coworker without realizing it was midnight where they are? Or maybe you've been on the other side of that, and someone who is important to you is traveling — and you just can't for the life of you remember what time it is in Japan? There are several apps for that, but my favorite is The World Clock. It shows up to 12 clocks at a time (they scale according to how many you choose), and you have lots of options for what is displayed. You can have the faces of the clocks indicate daylight/nighttime or business hours, and each clock can provide additional information, including local date, sunrise/sunset times, and more. It also features a beautiful map of the planet with real-time daylight and nighttime markings. Lastly, you can choose from two analog clock styles and one digital clock.

World Atlas HD

by National Geographic Society

$1.99

 Admittedly, this app will probably be of more use to you before you travel than when you are traveling, but it's so cool that I'll take any excuse to talk about it. World Atlas HD is produced by The National Geographic Society, so you know it has quality maps and information about countries around the world. It comes with a global map that you can pinch and zoom around to look at whatever part of the planet you care to check out. It features an Executive map, a Political Map, and a Satellite map. The first two are really just different styles for displaying countries, while the satellite map shows pictures of the areas as they appear from satellites orbiting the globe. With these maps, you can tap and hold a country to get some information about that country. You can tap the + button to bookmark that country, and that also places a pin on the map, which is handy for seeing which countries you have and haven't read about. All of these maps are available for online browsing, but you can also download them for offline (and faster) viewing, which I recommend.

WiFiGet HD

by WiTagg, Inc.

$2.99

 If you're traveling with an iPad, you should probably know where you can get a Wi-Fi hotspot. WiFiGet HD can tell you. It comes with 150,000 known free hotspots preinstalled, which means you can browse them even when you don't have a connection. If you have a connection but need to find a different hotspot, or you're planning ahead, you can access the company's online database of more than 200,000 free or paid hotspots. The app allows users to add hotspots they find (hopefully it's not the poor schmuck living near the coffee shop who didn't protect his network), or update known hotspots if their status changed. Wi-Fi is becoming more and more common, but it isn't yet ubiquitous. If you're traveling to a place you don't know well and plan to use your iPad, you should probably take this app with you.

Chapter 3: Educational Apps

In This Chapter

- NASA App HD
- Star Walk for iPad
- Science Glossary
- Art Authority for iPad
- abc PocketPhonics: letter sounds & writing + first words
- PopMath Maths Plus
- Merriam-Webster's Collegiate Dictionary, Eleventh Edition
- Animals' Matching HD
- Fish School HD
- The Elements: A Visual Exploration

The iPad is a great educational tool, and I think that in the next few years we're going to see it play an increasingly important role in the classroom. For now, though, there are already apps for kids, college students, and adults to learn more about just about anything. In this chapter, I show you some of my favorite educational apps and include some good learning games for kids. I even found some apps that some people just shouldn't be without.

Many of the apps I talk about in this chapter are apps that were written for the iPad. Some apps, however, have been written by the developer to run as native apps on both the iPad and iPhone (or iPod touch). These are called *hybrid* apps, and you'll find "Hybrid" next to the price for those apps. Hybrid apps have the advantage of allowing you to buy once and use on whatever iOS device you have.

NASA App HD

by Todd Barnes

$5.99

Don't worry. That giggling sound you hear is just me playing with NASA's brand-new iPad app, NASA App HD. It was released just a few days before I started writing this chapter, so I'm even more excited to be able to tell you about it. NASA App HD is part NASA propaganda (in the nonpejorative usage of that term) and part education map, but it's definitely 100 percent cool, at least to a geek-nerd like me.

This app works in portrait mode, but don't bother. It belongs in landscape mode, where it was designed to be used.

In Figure 3-1, you see the gorgeous home screen for the app. It features the solar system, including the Sun, our Moon, the International Space Station, and all eight planets. Tap one of these ten bodies, and you'll pull up a marvelous information page about it that includes a lot of text and a few pictures. I wish there were more photos, and I wish you could tap all of them to get a larger version — but it's still a great resource to learn a lot about our solar system.

Figure 3-1: The home page of NASA App HD, including the solar system.

When was it discovered? By whom? What's the planet composed of? How big is it? Does it have any moons of its own? Oh, really? Then how'd they get there? All these and many more questions are answered, and I found myself getting lost reading all the great information. At the bottom of every entry is a list of key dates for scientific discovery about that body, too.

Oh no! There are only eight planets — where's Pluto? A few years ago, Pluto was downgraded to the status of "dwarf planet" by the various powers that be in the world of astronomy. That means, buckaroos, that we have eight planets in the solar system (as of this writing), and that Pluto isn't one of them. Accordingly, there are eight planets on the home screen of NASA App HD.

The information about the solar system alone would have made me include it, but there's a lot more to it, too. In fact, let's look at the NASA Image of the Day (IOTD) link you see in the lower-left corner in Figure 3-1. This feeds my jones for more photos, as does the Astronomy Picture of the Day (APOD) tab next to it. Both tabs have gorgeous photos of our planet and the heavens, along with good descriptions explaining what they are. They look great on your iPad, and if you're like me, you'll spend a lot of time paging through them and examining them closely. Note that you can pinch and zoom in on these photos — but the images are provided in the iPad display's native resolution, and there's a limit to the clarity when you zoom in.

Next to the two photo tabs is a tab labeled NASA TV that provides a current stream of NASA's cable TV broadcast. This can be hit and miss, but real space geeks will love it. In a similar vein, there's a tab called Videos that provides archival footage from NASA TV, and other videos produced by NASA. Yeah, there are some dry interviews in this collection, but there's also some really cool stuff, too.

NASA App HD also provides access to all of the various NASA Twitter accounts. You can find a lot of news, announcements, and links to photos, videos, and news accounts in these feeds, and the app makes it easy to follow NASA's efforts at social networking. The app also includes the ability to e-mail, tweet, or post images and articles from the app to Facebook.

You can even save photos to your Photo Roll on your iPad from the social networking buttons. I know; saving a photo isn't social networking, but it's an awesome feature!

The last tab on the bottom of the screen is for monthly Featured content. When I was writing this, for instance, September's Featured content was Women in Space, and it included a look at key and influential women in the U.S. space program, and in astronomy in general. It was good reading, and I look forward to future Featured content.

I'm still not done, though! There are navigation icons at the top of the screen that change according to where you are in the app. On the home page you see buttons for learning about NASA's facilities around the world, news articles organized in several categories, a NASA calendar, and a button for reading up on more than 60 of NASA's satellites! That's cool!

The big downside of this app is that the navigation is poor, and sometimes links or videos don't even work. It's still early in this app's life as I write this, though, and I've little doubt that these deficiencies will be corrected, maybe even by the time you read this.

That said, the content is so cool that it warrants inclusion in this book, despite the glitches I've encountered. If you're a space nut, science geek, or just like gorgeous pictures of the solar system, you should check out this app.

What you can do with it: with this app, you get NASA, NASA, and more NASA! There are cool photos, great stories, in-depth information, videos, and more.

Star Walk for iPad

by Vito Technology, Inc.

$4.99

While I am getting my space geek on, let's look at another cool app, Star Walk for iPad. A purely astronomy-oriented app, Star Walk brings the heavens straight down to your iPad. It has several features, but when you first open it, you'll be asked for your current location. Once you've given the app permission to use Location Services, you're presented with a map of the stars that moves as your iPad moves! Wondering what star (or planet) you're looking at? Point your iPad at it and you can get the star's name and see if it's part of a constellation. Tap the i button to zoom in on the star and get detailed information about its makeup, historical information on how cultures have viewed it or named it (where applicable), how far away it is, and more! If that's not blow-your-mind cool to you, you should maybe skip on down to the next app.

This feature is called Star Spotter, and it works by tapping into your iPad's GPS, compass, and accelerometer abilities. I think it's super cool!

Of course, you can also just touch and drag this map around to look for and examine whatever stars (and planets) you'd like. And if you want to be shown a particular constellation, tap the magnifying glass in the lower-left corner of the screen, as you can see on the left side of Figure 3-2. Constellations that are visible (in the visible sky in your hemisphere) are highlighted with brighter text. The constellations listed in grey text aren't visible, but Star Walk will still show them to you.

Figure 3-2: Visible constellations are listed in white text (left), and the Picture of the Day with information about the currently selected image (right).

Do you see that horizontal red line on the left side of the figure? That's the horizon. Stars below the horizon aren't visible to you, while those above are. Well, more or less. Intervening buildings, hills, mountains, and even trees, might limit what you can see, but the horizon line is updated in real time just like the rest of the night sky.

You can pinch and zoom in on this map to get a closeup view of stars you'd never be able to see with your naked eye. If you can see it in Star Walk, though, you can get at least some basic information, like its name, position, visual magnitude, and so on.

In the lower-right corner of the Star Walk screen is an index-like icon, and that's where you access the rest of this app's features. For instance, Live Sky gives you sunrise and sunset information, a track of the moon's current, recent, and near-future phases, and rising and setting information for any planets that will be visible in the sky today. Tap the arrow keys next to today's date and you can go backward and forward in the calendar for historical and future information.

My second favorite feature in this app (after the Star Spotter display) is The Picture of the Day. This is a gallery of astronomy photos taken from the Hubble space telescope, radio and other earth-based telescopes, and sometimes just from the ground by an amateur astronomer. They're all gorgeous on your iPad's display, and they come with varying amounts of information to tell you more about what you're seeing. The app uses Apple's Coverflow interface to show you the images, as you can see on the right in Figure 3-2, and you can save the images to your photo library or share them via e-mail, Twitter, or Facebook.

Other features include the ability to take a snapshot of the night sky and save it as a bookmark, and you can also find your position on Earth with the Location feature.

This is a great app for astronomy fans and space nuts alike. If you've ever been even a little curious about the stars you can (hopefully) see in the night sky, you should get this app. It's a lot of fun, informative, well designed, and it looks great, too.

If you like this app, check out Solar Walk for iPad ($2.99), a similar app from the same company. It focuses exclusively on the solar system (the Sun, planets, asteroids, and so on). If I thought I could get away with it, I'd have included it in this chapter, too! One more astronomy app worth your while is SkyVoyager ($14.99) from Carina Software.

What you can do with it: see the night sky in real time, get information about the stars you can see (and some you can't), view the Picture of the Day, and learn about the constellations that stargazers have identified throughout history.

Science Glossary

by Visionlearning, Inc.

Free — Hybrid

 I love language, and the use of language. I love the way words can be used to convey emotion, information, events, and the way even a slight alteration in your choice of words can profoundly change the meaning of what you are saying or writing. I guess it's a good thing that I write for a living, given this obsession of mine, but I mention it here in an effort to point out the value of having a good vocabulary. This is just as true in the sciences as it is in liberal arts, and the next app I want to show you, Science Glossary, will help improve your vocabulary and give you a broader knowledge of science.

Science Glossary is a standalone app filled with definitions and biographies of important scientists and historical figures from the world of science. It also ties into the company's online site, VisionLearning.com. You won't need to access anything at that site if you don't need to, but it's free if you do want to explore these external links.

Let's look at a definition, then, shall we? In Figure 3-3, you can see a list of terms on the left and a definition for one of them, greenhouse gas, on the right.

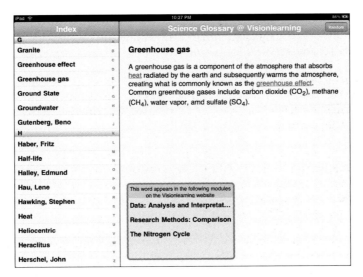

Figure 3-3: The definition of "Greenhouse Gas."

**Book VI
Chapter 3**

Educational Apps

Words and phrases that are underlined in blue in the definitions are links to other definitions in the app. Words and phrases that are listed in the pullout box, like the one in the figure, are links to VisionLearning.com. Tap the blue links and you immediately pull up the new definition. Tap the words in the box and you'll leave Science Glossary and be taken to VisionLearning.com in Safari.

As you can see, the definitions are succinct and they include everything I need to know to understand the term. If I want more, I can tap the blue links for an additional definition, or tap through the terms in the box for more detailed articles at VisionLearning.com.

See that button in the upper-right portion of the screen, labeled Random? That's just what you think it is: a button for pulling up random definitions and biographies. I'll be honest; I've spent more than my fair share of time tapping that button to see what I might learn. For instance, that's how I learned the definition of *lenticular* (having a lens-like shape) and how I found out just precisely what a *nonpolar molecule* is. (You know — a molecule that has an equal distribution of bonding electrons.) Fun stuff!

One shortcoming of this app is that although you can do a search at the top of the list of definitions, that search is only for titles, and not the content of the definition itself. I'd like to see that feature added, but it's still a great app.

If you work in, with, or for anything even vaguely scientific in nature, this app will prove a good resource that you might be surprised how often you utilize. I suspect most people use it to look up terms they aren't familiar with, but I also know some of you will use it just to learn.

What you can do with it: look up science definitions and find short biographies for important people in the world of science.

Art Authority for iPad

by Open Door Networks, Inc.

$8.99

 It's hard to believe I can carry this much art around with me and not get arrested for art thievery. I like the Art Authority app a lot, probably because the iPad has such a great display. There are several art-related apps in the App Store, but I think Art Authority for iPad is the best of the lot.

What you get with this app is pictures of art from more than a thousand artists. Seriously, there are more than one thousand artists represented in this app! All told, there are pictures of more than 40,000 paintings and sculptures, making for 10GB worth of images optimized for your iPad.

 Wait, what was that about "optimized for your iPad?" What that means is that each of the images looks great at full screen on your iPad, but that also means that while you can zoom in, the images become pixilated. I'd love to have at least the option to download high-resolution images so that I could really zoom in and check out some of the small details, even if it was an in-app purchase option.

These works of art are divided into eight categories, as you can see on the left in Figure 3-4: Early, Renaissance, Baroque, Romanticism, Impressionism, Modern, Contemporary, and American. You can tap a category to see its "room," as the app uses a museum metaphor for displaying the art. In that room, each category is then divided further into subcategories.

For instance, Modern art is divided into ten categories, with an eleventh category for sculpture. Tap one of those subcategories, and you'll get a pop-up window offering you an overview tour or direct links to each artist in that category. With more than a thousand artists represented, each subcategory is broadly represented.

Figure 3-4: The main room, where you can delve down into specific periods and styles of art (left), and viewing a specific painting (right).

If you like an image, you can save it to your photo library or use it as wallpaper on your iPad.

On the right side of Figure 3-4, I've gone to the Abstract Expressionism subcategory and selected *The Liver is the Cock's Comb* (1944) by Arshile Gorky. I know that because I tapped the image to make it display full screen, and then tapped the globe icon so I could view the Wikipedia entry for the painting. There are also some additional viewing options, and you can watch everything in the overview as a slide show, with or without the Ken Burns effect turned on.

The *Ken Burns effect* is a way of using panning and zooming when showing still photos. It's a technique developed by director Ken Burns (a funny coincidence, no?) to impart the impression of motion where there is none, and it can make for a great way to view paintings in this app.

Back to the figure with Gorky's painting, I can scroll through the thumbnail images on the right side of the screen to jump to a particular painting, or I can just swipe through each painting one by one. I can also pull up a navigation pop-up window by tapping the gear icon in the upper-right portion of the screen. If I want to learn more about this subcategory, tapping the nameplate at the top of the screen brings up an About This Artist subcategory pane that pulls more information from Wikipedia.

There's a Getting Around plaque that you can tap in the main room (the home screen) that has directions and tips for making the most of the app.

I should note that you'll need an Internet connection to view all the images. When the app launches for the first time, it will tell you that it's downloading and installing images, but don't be fooled into thinking that it's downloading everything in the app. In fact, it's just the category images that are getting downloaded. Once you've viewed an image, however, you can then view it offline.

Art Authority is an app that art fans, students, and anyone interested in art history can appreciate. It looks great, the paintings and sculptures look great, and it's fun.

What you can do with it: view more than 40,000 images of paintings and sculptures from more than 1,000 artists, ranging from contemporary artists to ancient art from Chinese, Egyptian, Greek, Roman, Japanese, and other ancient cultures.

abc PocketPhonics: letter sounds & writing + first words

by Apps in My Pocket Ltd

$1.99 — Hybrid

I'll be the last person to claim to be an expert on child education, but I like this app. It's based on a teaching method called *synthetic phonics,* which teaches children to associate letters with sounds and then learn how to combine those sounds (and therefore letters) into words. I'll leave the debates to the experts out there, but parents looking for an app that will engage their young children and teach them something at the same time will like this app.

abc PocketPhonics (PocketPhonics from here on out) offers two learning games for kids. One is called Letter Sounds and Writing, and the other is simply Word Game.

Starting with Letter Sounds and Writing, the app displays six letters (s, a, t, p, i, and n). Tap one of those letters, and the game starts. Starting with *s,* I get a screen with a blue letter *s,* with a woman narrator's voice making an *essss* sound for me and asking me to say it, too. I'll be honest: I was pretty good at this game and took to it right away! But seriously, after pronouncing the letter and asking me to say it (note that the app does not actually listen and grade the user's pronunciation), the app asked me to write the letters while the blue example is traced for me in green, as you can see in Figure 3-5. Once I'm shown how, a green dot pulsates where I should start my own tracing. If I can properly trace the letter, two pencil characters pop up, and I am rewarded with kids applauding and cheering. Then we move on to the next letter. Complete all six, and I'm taken to the next set of letters and sounds. Some sounds are combinations of two letters, and there are 64 such sounds all told.

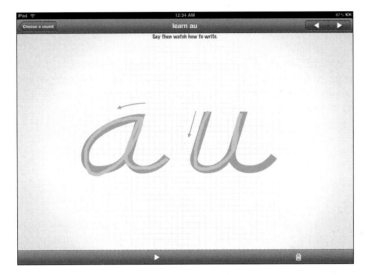

Figure 3-5: Learning how to write and say the "au" phonic.

Tap the Play forward arrow at the bottom of the screen to hear the sound repeated.

That's all there is to this first game, but it's comprehensive in its coverage of the sounds in American English, and I think it will keep kids engaged. It offers a nice combination of reward and correction for mistakes.

Kids can repeat any of the games they want, or repeatedly go through them all as many times as they want.

The second game is more complex in that it challenges children to match these newly learned sounds and letters with actual words. The narrator makes a sound and asks the child to pick the letter or letter combo that the sound represents. If you pick correctly, it is filled into one of the hangman-like slots on the screen for each syllable in the word. Once you fill in all of the syllables, the narrator puts the pieces together for you, pronouncing each sound individually, and then the completed word.

Most words have an image, once you've completed the exercise, that appears as the narrator pronounces the word. This should further help the child associate the sounds, letters, and word with the concept it represents.

My only criticism of this app is that while there are 64 sounds in the Letters game, there are only eight games in the Word Game portion. I'd like to see just as many words for kids to practice and learn!

Still, this is a good app if you want your children to learn the synthetic phonic method, which is singled out in the No Child Left Behind Act, for what that's worth. PocketPhonics will keep kids engaged, and they can go through the games with or without your help.

What you can do with it: kids learn sounds and letters and associate the two together. They then learn how to form those letters and sounds into words.

PopMath Maths Plus

by Laurent Denoue

99 cents — Hybrid

Tee hee hee! PopMath is fun even for us old fogeys, but it's intended for young people wanting to improve their basic math skills. The idea is to put several math problems in colored balloons that float next to other colored balloons that contain answers. Tap a problem, and then its answer (or vice versa), and those two balloons disappear. If the second balloon doesn't match the first one you tapped, you get an error sound, like two balloons rubbing together, and they both remain on the screen. Once you clear the last two balloons, you're told how long it took (with a descriptor based on how quickly you did it, like "Phenomenal" for 4 seconds, "Great" for 10-12 seconds, and "You did it!" for anything over 15 seconds), and how many mistakes you made (if you made any). As you progress to each new screen, the problems get more complex, and you can limit that complexity to a smaller set of numbers or just one kind of problem. Games with timers have always made me want to try to be faster, and I suspect it will work on students, as well.

Merriam-Webster's Collegiate Dictionary, Eleventh Edition

by Paragon Technologies GmbH

$24.99 — Hybrid

 If you have a college student in the family, get this app for her. If you *are* a college student, convince someone in your family to buy this dictionary app for you. That's because it's $24.99, and that's a lot of tacos and espressos, right? And for $24.99, it isn't even a good-looking app, but it contains some 250,000 words and phrases and their definitions, something that most college students need frequently and often. At least it's a hybrid app, so the same $24.99 will work on your iPhone, iPod touch, and iPad. This app will do something a printed dictionary won't do, too, and that's allow you to do wildcard searches. You can use question marks (?) to substitute for specific letters you aren't sure about, and you can use an asterisk (*) to substitute for an unknown number of words. If you're my age, I bet you wish you'd had that sort of tool when you were in school! The app also allows you to search for similar words, though it doesn't contain an actual thesaurus. Lastly, you can make in-app purchases to get additional Merriam-Webster dictionaries in English, French, and Spanish.

Animals' Matching HD

by Alexandre Minard

$1.99

 Here's another learning game for young kids. Matching games, like playing Concentration with a deck of cards on your living room floor, are always fun, especially when you can just start a new game instantly! The point of Animals' Matching HD is to pick two cards. If they match, they are removed from the playing field. If they don't, they are turned back over, where you will hopefully remember them for when you need them. Animals' Matching HD is merely one among many such games in the App Store, but I think it has good graphics that will appeal to kids — and it also adds animal sounds with each card as it's turned over. The audio component adds an extra clue for each card, which helps players remember what was where, and from the kid's point of view, it has the added bonus of sounding like a cacophony to any nearby adults!

 Have a pair of headphones on hand for your young one if he's going to play this game in the company of others!

Fish School HD

by Duck Duck Moose, Partnership

$1.99

I wanted to offer one more app for young children, so let's look at Fish School HD, a fun game that will help your kids learn the alphabet, colors, pattern matching, and more through different games. For instance, it starts with a game called abc, which is identified in a bubble in the lower-left corner of the screen. Fish swim out and form a letter *A,* while a voice actor sings that letter. (Strung together, it becomes the melody known as "The Alphabet Song.") Tap the screen, and a new school comes out to make a *B,* and so on. If you tap the bubble labeled abc, the app switches to 123, which is the numbers version of the game. (It covers 1-20.) Tap it again, and kids get Play time as a reward. In this game, they can tap and hold to cause a fish to grow really big. Tap the bubble again, and they get Shapes, and one more time to get the full alphabet song. The app also includes a Colors game and a game where kids have to pick out which fish on the screen is different from all the others. There's a lot here, and I think most kids will find it very engaging.

The Elements: A Visual Exploration

by Element Collection

$13.99

The Elements is such an awesome app! It's a periodic table of the elements app, but it's amazing looking and contains a lot of detailed information on each of the elements, along with very professional photography. The home screen is the full periodic table, complete with an image for almost all of the elements. (The theoretical elements don't have pics, for instance.) Some of the images are of their discoverer, others are images of the element in its raw form, while others are finished products made from that element. And most of them are 360° rotating images! Tap an element, and you're taken to a page with a larger version of the image, the element's atomic weight, other atomic-specific information, a temperature scale, and more. Tap the Forward arrow button at the bottom-right side of the screen, and you get a detailed write-up about the element, including history and other information. Plus, if there's a photo of the element on this page, you can even spin it with your finger! Yay! I love this app!

You can hear the great 1959 song by Tom Lehrer called "The Elements" in the app, too, complete with a visual tour of each element as he names them.

Chapter 4: News and Weather Apps

In This Chapter

- Pulse News Reader
- Instapaper
- NPR for iPad
- BBC News
- The Weather Channel Max for iPad
- Weatherbug Elite for iPad
- WeatherStation Free and Weather for iPad
- Reeder for iPad
- Wall Street Journal
- USA TODAY for iPad

From what I've been hearing from our readers at The Mac Observer — not to mention all the anecdotal evidence I see at my local coffee shops — reading on the iPad is one of the most popular activities for iPad users, especially when it comes to catching up on the news. There are a lot of different newspapers, magazines, and RSS news readers in the App Store, however, and in this chapter I show you some of the best of them. Don't tell anyone, but I also throw in some cool weather apps, just for good measure.

Many of the apps I talk about in this chapter are apps that were written for the iPad. Some apps, however, have been written by the developer to run as native apps on both the iPad and iPhone (or iPod touch). These are called *hybrid* apps, and you'll find "Hybrid" next to the price for those apps. Hybrid apps have the advantage of allowing you to buy once and use on whatever iOS device you have.

Pulse News Reader

by Alphonso Labs, Inc.

$3.99

Alphonso Labs' Pulse News Reader is one of the most interesting apps to come out of the iPad ecosystem yet. Pulse is an *RSS news reader*, but rather than presenting those feeds as straightforward lists, Pulse presents them as graphically rich blocks that look almost like a filmstrip, as you can see in Figure 4-1. If the RSS feeds you are following include images with them, those images are displayed by the text, making it a lot easier to get the gist of each article, and it certainly makes scrolling through your feeds more interesting.

RSS stands for Really Simple Syndication, and it's another way for a Web site to serve up new articles, stories, or other forms of content, usually with a headline link to the full article, a teaser, and sometimes an image. An RSS news reader is an app that displays RSS feeds from one or more sites. It's just another way to read a Web site.

Figure 4-1: Pulse News Reader's home screen.

If you follow a lot of RSS feeds (more than 20), Pulse may not be the best news reader for you. As of this writing, it's limited to 20 RSS feeds and 5 custom feeds called Pulses that you or your friends create (for 25 total feeds). If you're a news junkie with more than that, you'll want to look at NetNewsWire, Reeder (which I tell you about later in this chapter), or some other RSS news reader.

Each of your feeds is featured as a horizontal strip, with the newest article to the left. You can swipe up and down to see more of your feeds, and you can swipe from side to side to scroll the articles in a given feed. It's pretty simple. When you see an article you want to read, just tap its box (articles you haven't read yet are brighter than articles you have already read), and it gets pulled up in its own pane. If your feed offers entire articles, you'll get the whole thing right there. Most RSS feeds (in my experience) offer teasers, though, and for those you'll get the title, the teaser, and any images included. Tap the title, and you're taken to the full Web page via the in-app browser.

You can also tap the Web button in the upper-right corner of the screen and automatically open the full article every time you tap a block! To go back to reading just the RSS feed, tap the Text button.

One of my favorite things about this app is a real help to a lot of users. RSS readers allow you to add feeds by adding in the direct URL of that feed. That's great on a computer where you have a mouse, cut and paste, and can have two apps open side by side. On iPad, however, it's a little harder. You can copy a URL to your clipboard in one app and then go back to Pulse and paste it, or you can memorize it and type it by hand. Or, and this is that cool feature I mentioned, you can enter a search term, say *The Mac Observer*, and Pulse will give you a list of links it believes contain an RSS feed for that term. Choose the one you want, and boom! It's added! It's a great feature, and I won't be surprised if it makes its way to other news readers sooner, rather than later.

Lastly, there's a social networking component in Pulse. When you see an article you like, you can tap the Heart icon and add it to your own Pulse. This is basically an RSS feed that you create that has only those articles you pick. You can have up to five Pulses, as mentioned in the Tip above, and your friends can follow them. I'd personally trade these Pulses for more standard feeds, but that's just me.

Pulse is a really cool news reader for casual RSS users, and it offers a much more aesthetically pleasing way of viewing your feeds than any other reader out there.

What you can do with it: you can follow up to 20 RSS feeds, or create your own Pulses for others to follow. Because each article in a feed is displayed along with any images in the feed, it offers a more graphically intense way of viewing your news.

Instapaper

by Marco Arment

$4.99

Instapaper has been . . . dare I say it? An insta-hit! This app taps into one of the fundamental side effects of the information blitz that makes up a big part of our digital lives today, and that's managing all the cool things we see but don't ever get around to actually reading. Instapaper allows us to tag articles, Web sites, Flickr pics, and just about everything else on the Web for viewing later when you have a moment to spare. You can even view your tagged content offline, when you're not connected to the Web. You can do it from within the Instapaper app, but there are currently several dozen iOS apps that have added support for Instapaper, too!

To help you understand how cool this is, let me paint a scenario for you. You're catching up on tweets from your friends and some of the cool guys over at The Mac Observer (TMO). One friend links to a hilarious picture of her kitten that can't figure out how to get out of a box, and then another friend has a link to an article with tips on how to get the most out of your iPad. And then there's an editorial over at TMO about how Apple's strategy in the tablet market has thrown the netbook market into disarray. And then . . . well, you probably know just what I mean. We see all these things when we're reading tweets, looking at RSS feeds, or sometimes just reading our e-mail, and we usually don't get around to reading very much of it.

But let's back up a little bit and look at the app itself. As you can see in Figure 4-2, the app allows you to browse RSS feeds, each with its own folder. When browsing your feeds, you can either read the articles right then and there or save them to your Read Later folder.

You can also Star articles as a favorite. Tapping the star saves the article, but Instapaper also allows users to follow the Starred folders of their friends. (You have to do this on the service's Web site.)

If you're in one of those other apps that supports Instapaper — say Twitter for iOS — when you're finding all those cool things that I mentioned previously, you can add items to your Read Later folder from within those apps. This is handy for offline viewing, but it's especially great if you're going through a lot of tweets and want to be able to gather everything together at one time, and then read it later.

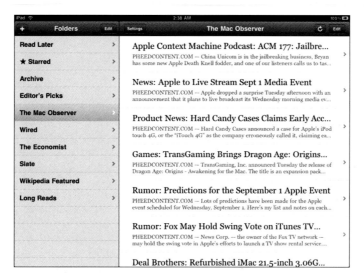

Figure 4-2: On the left are the RSS feeds I've added to Instapaper. On the right are the articles found in The Mac Observer's RSS feed.

Check out the Editor's Picks folder for some interesting articles you might not have otherwise found!

What I don't like about Instapaper is that the app takes content produced by others, usually content paid for by display advertising, and then presents that content without the ads. Some will delight in this, but that's only because they don't understand, or maybe just don't care, that it's the advertising that pays for what they are consuming. Still, each article in Instapaper has a link to the original posting on the Web, allowing users to view the article with its original formatting and layout, including any ads that paid for it. I'll be the first to admit that your mileage will vary on this issue!

Instapaper is a capable RSS news reader, but most users like it for its offline capabilities and the ability to gather lots of material from browsers and other apps for reading all at one time.

What you can do with it: browse RSS feeds, get articles and other Web pages from within other apps, save favorite articles, share articles with others through your Starred list, and view articles offline.

NPR for iPad

by NPR

Free

NPR (that stands for National Public Radio) for iPad is one of those best-in-class iPad apps in terms of its user interface. More importantly, it offers you access to just about everything NPR produces, including written stories, radio news stories, and a broad selection of the entertainment and informational radio shows.

You can browse NPR's content in several ways. The home screen features three scrollable timelines, one each for News, Arts & Life, and Music, as you can see in Figure 4-3. These three streams are all stories and articles produced by the NPR news organization — the different radio programs are offered separately. You can swipe through these three streams from left to right, and once you tap a story that interests you, it takes over the screen, with the category stream at the bottom.

Figure 4-3: The main screen for NPR for iPad.

Some of these articles are offered up in text only, but most of them have an accompanying radio report embedded right there. You can listen to the audio report from the home screen by tapping the speaker button in the teaser, or by tapping the Listen Now button in the full article. Better yet, you can queue up stories in a Playlist for later listening. It's a great way to make sure you're hearing all the articles you want to listen to.

Most of these articles have pictures in them. (Tap a pic for a full-screen version.)

NPR for iPad also offers up about twenty of its radio programs, from *All Things Considered,* to *Fresh Air,* to *Science Friday,* to *On the Media.* If you tap the Programs button at the bottom of the screen, you get a pop-up window with each program listed. Tap a show and you get a list of current and recent episodes you can play or add to a Playlist. If it has a podcast version on iTunes, you'll find a button for getting it there, too!

Any show currently being aired somewhere in the world has an On Air label. You can tap into these shows live.

Lastly, the app lets you find local public radio stations that offer NPR content, and you can stream that station's broadcast directly to your iPad! This is a great way to listen to your local station, or to listen to what used to be your local station before you had to move. If you're in one of those few places without a public radio station, this makes it easier than ever before to find and listen to a station.

NPR for iPad is a must-have app for any fan of NPR's awesome news and entertainment shows. It looks great, and it's so easy to use that you may find yourself using it more than your radio.

What you can do with it: read articles and listen to news reports from NPR's news arm, find and stream public radio stations, and listen to many of the organization's entertainment radio programs.

BBC News

by BBC Worldwide Ltd.

Free — Hybrid

The BBC is one of the most respected news organizations in the world, and it's also one of the largest. The BBC News app for iPad brings that news to you, including written news reports and BBC radio, too. Some articles even have video additions that include background interviews for added color, broadcast TV reports, and more.

One of the coolest things about the BBC News app is that it is highly customizable. The home screen of the app shows several rows of news articles, with each row representing a different category of news. You can swipe up and down to scroll through these categories, or right to left to scroll through the individual stories in a category.

The app defaults to featuring Americas, Technology, Features & Analysis, and Business, as you can see in Figure 4-4, but there are many more categories available, including Science & Environment, Europe, UK, and several other global regions. The featured categories are expanded to show individual stories, and while you can tap any other category to expand it, you can also define which categories are featured by tapping the Edit button at the top of the screen. This is great for expats who want to start off with news from home, or anyone who is interested in a particular category of news. In addition to being able to decide what is featured, you can also reorder the categories as you see fit.

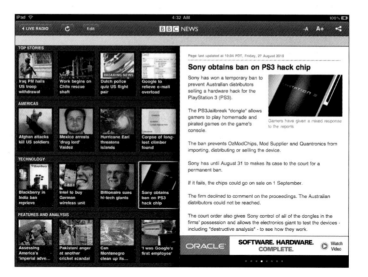

Figure 4-4: The BBC News app.

BBC News even offers news in several languages other than English, including Mundo, Brasil, Chinese (Traditional), Chinese (Simple), Russian, Arabic, Persian, and Urdu. You can find the stories offered in those languages at the bottom of the category list.

The other great thing about this app is that it offers one-tap access to the BBC's great radio news coverage. Just tap the Live Radio button at the top of screen (make sure to wait a moment while the app buffers the stream), and you'll have whatever is being streamed by BBC Radio delivered straight to your iPad. This will be even more cool once Apple brings multitasking to the iPad so that you can stream BBC Radio in the background while using other apps.

Just below the red title bar with the navigation buttons is a Latest News ticker. This lets you quickly see whatever has come in recently from BBC News. I wish you could tap the ticker to go straight to the article currently being shown, but this is still a great way to see if there's anything new that you want to read.

Just about every single story has an accompanying photograph or other image, but some stories come with a video component instead, as I mentioned previously. You'll know which is which because the videos have a big label that reads Tap to Play. Follow those directions, and a video player takes over your screen. I've found those videos to be of high quality — they aren't full HD-quality, but they look good on your iPad. Note that because they are high quality, you'll want a good connection to the Internet to watch them without interruption. If your connection is slow, you'll want to let them load before playing.

There's one more cool feature of this app I want to mention: Once you're in a story, you can swipe from left to right to navigate to other stories in the same category.

The biggest advantage this app has over some of the other news apps is the BBC's focus on global news. It's well designed, and the developers made great use of the iPad's screen real estate in creating this app. If you have an interest in what's happening outside the borders of the U.S., you should try out BBC News on your iPad.

What you can do with it: the BBC News app offers you news content from all over the world, as well as one-tap access to BBC Radio.

The Weather Channel Max for iPad

by The Weather Channel Interactive

Free

I'm a bit of an information junkie, and I regularly check the weather forecast with Apple's Weather app on my iPhone. There is no default weather app on the iPad, for some mysterious reason unknown to me, but (or maybe because of this) there are some great options for you to choose from in the App Store. Now, I'll point out right up front that weather apps are one of those things that people take pretty seriously, and what works for me may not work for you. But for my money (Okay, it's a free app), The Weather Channel Max for iPad is one of the best of the bunch.

The Weather Channel Max for iPad is basically like having a big slice of The Weather Channel itself. It has forecasts, weather maps, warnings, and even some of the TV station's video reports. It also has ads . . . a lot of them. This turns some people off, but you're getting a lot of content that is otherwise free. And it's those ads that pay for all that content.

That out of the way, let's look at the app! When you first launch it, it asks if it can use your current location (assuming you have your iPad set to ask for that permission). If you tap OK, you'll see a Google Maps display of your local area, and six buttons for you to choose different features of the apps: Maps, Local, Video, Severe, Social, and On TV.

I think the way The Weather Channel — let's call it TWC from here on, okay? — offers up maps is very cool. Some of the other weather apps give you different views (radar, satellite, temperature, and so on), but TWC's app gives you an overlay with all eight types of maps it offers, including Radar, Clouds, Radar & Clouds, Temperature, Feels Like, UV Index, 24 Hr Rain, and 24 Hr Snow. This overlay has example map slices, as you can see in Figure 4-5, which helps you quickly understand what you're picking and what it's going to show you. I like this feature.

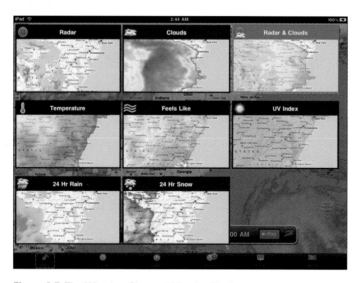

Figure 4-5: The Weather Channel Max for iPad app.

Some of the map views have the ability to play through the observed weather for the last two hours, or the forecast for the next four hours. I'm enough of an information junkie to think that's super cool.

The Local pane is what most people use the most, I think. In one view, it offers current weather conditions and the forecast for the next ten days. (Swipe sideways to scroll through all ten days.) With a tap, you can also get an hourly forecast through the next 24 hours, along with four-hour forecasts for the 12 hours after that, and then daily forecasts for the next eight days. There are also mini panes for the other major features (swipe to scroll through them), as well as a pane for ads. Other apps do a better job of displaying just current conditions or a forecast, but there's enough here to satisfy most weather junkies.

The Video pane offers local weatherperson forecasts, regional forecasts, national forecasts, travel forecasts, storm watch videos, weather-related news stories, and other content from TWC's TV network. And you can display these videos full screen, though it's not HD quality. There's a lot here to watch, and I'd call it a premier feature of the app.

Now let's scoot over to the Severe pane, where you can get local and national severe weather warnings. When I was writing this, there was a local Bay Area warning about unexpectedly hot temperatures for the next two days, and a National warning about Hurricane Earl heading toward the U.S. If you live in a place where severe weather can occur, you'll find this a great resource for keeping abreast of these warnings.

The Social pane offers you direct access to TWC-related Twitter feeds, for what that's worth, and the On TV pane is just a one-touch way to get to the video feature stories I mentioned previously.

There's a lot here for the weather junkie, including lots of video content, great map views, and a passable local weather display. If you want a simple display of current conditions and the forecast, look to one of the apps I highlight in the next sections, but if you want to dig around in detailed weather information, try this free app.

What you can do with it: view several weather maps, get local conditions and forecasts, watch TWC video content, read severe weather alerts, and follow TWC-related Twitter accounts.

Weatherbug Elite for iPad

by AWS Convergence Technologies, Inc.

Free

 Weatherbug Elite is a different kind of weather app. It offers a map view with several overlay options (Temperature, Pressure, Humidity, Wind Speed, I.R. Satellite, Visible Satellite, Radar, Worldwide Satellite, and forecast overlays for Tomorrow's High and Low Temperatures. One quarter of the screen is dedicated to really cool panes with current conditions, different weather camera views, a daily forecast, an hourly forecast, weather alerts, and a video pane offering a weatherperson's national forecast. These panes are large enough to read if you're close to your iPad, but if you tap them, they expand over to the map portion of the screen. Just tap outside an expanded pane to send it back to its place. The weather map info is supplied by Bing, and what I don't like about this app is the way some of the fonts are fuzzy when you pinch and zoom in and out on the map.

WeatherStation Free and Weather for iPad

by Bigsool and Presselite (respectively)

Free and 99 cents

Here's another approach to a weather app: WeatherStation Free is a single-page app that gives you big readouts of current conditions and the forecast. That's it. If you want to leave an app up on your iPad all the time, this might be the app for you. WeatherStation Free comes with a dozen different themes, in case you don't like the default color scheme, but that's about the only thing you can change.

Another simple display app is Weather for iPad, by Presselite. This is a very simple and colorful app that offers large text displays of the current temperature with a pleasing, but unchangeable, blue (sky) and green (rolling hills) background. A moon or sun icon in the middle of the screen tells you if it's day or night. There's not a lot here, but if you want a very casual weather display, you should check it out.

Reeder for iPad

by Silvio Rizzi

$4.99

Reeder is an RSS news reader that is designed to work exclusively through Google's Reader service. In fact, I'll say that if you use Google Reader but want to follow your feeds on the iPad, this is the only solution you should consider. With it, you can browse your Google Reader news feeds by feed or folder, manage starred items, and share stories through e-mail and Twitter. It also supports Instapaper, ReadItLater, Delicious, and Pinbard, and it allows you to open articles directly in Safari. It uses a binder theme for browsing through your RSS feeds, and all your controls are conveniently lined up on the left. The only thing I don't like about this app is that you can't add new feeds to Google Reader, but for all I know, that's Google's issue.

Wall Street Journal

by Wall Street Journal

Free (subscription required)

News Corp. has brought *The Wall Street Journal* to the iPad, and in a big way. CEO Rupert Murdoch has talked about the future of newspapers being on devices like the iPad, and the company was among the first to invest major resources in developing a dedicated app for the new device before it was even released. What you get is a sort of print newspaper look on your iPad display. Swipe and scroll, tap, pinch, and zoom, and you can navigate through individual stories and different sections of this business publication. It's not the best iPad app out there, but it's really good. And I personally think *The Journal*'s business coverage is top-notch. One thing about pricing: News Corp. has been experimenting with how to monetize this property online. As of this writing, the iPad app is free with an online subscription, which is where I imagine it will stay, but you should check before you download it.

USA TODAY for iPad

by USA TODAY

Free

USA TODAY was one of the first, if not *the* first, national daily newspaper in the U.S., and it was one of the first newspapers with a dedicated app for the iPad. Published by Gannett Company, USA TODAY for iPad offers a mix of national, regional, and local news coverage, sports scores, weather reports, and a lot of color photos. (In addition to the photos in many of the stories, there is a daily gallery of the day's best photos that I enjoy.) Navigation is easy, and the app has a clean layout and design that any iPad user will find familiar and easy to use. You can also share articles via e-mail, Twitter, and Facebook. If you're into online polls, check out the USA TODAY Snapshot, a poll of your fellow *USA TODAY* readers. If you like *USA TODAY*'s coverage, reading it on the iPad will be a pleasure.

Chapter 5: Financial Apps

In This Chapter

- StockWatch – iPad Edition
- Bloomberg for iPad
- SplashMoney for iPad
- PowerOne Financial Calculator
- Daily Stocks
- QIF Entry
- QuickTimer
- Quick Sale for iPad
- Pageonce Personal Finance
- E*TRADE Mobile Pro for iPad

Each of us is likely to think of something different when we hear "financial app." There are apps to balance your checkbook or home budget, apps to buy stocks, banking apps, invoicing and billing apps, apps to read up on financial news, and even a few combinations of all those features. In this chapter, I show you some of the best of them so that you don't waste your finances having to try them all!

Many of the apps I talk about in this chapter are apps that were written for the iPad. Some apps, however, have been written by the developer to run as native apps on both the iPad and iPhone (or iPod touch). These are called *hybrid* apps, and you'll find "Hybrid" next to the price for those apps. Hybrid apps have the advantage of allowing you to buy once and use on whatever iOS device you have.

StockWatch – iPad Edition

by Todd Barnes

$5.99

 Let's start our look at financial apps with an all-around stock app called StockWatch – iPad Edition. This is a great app for people who want to monitor one or more stock portfolios and follow news pertaining to those stocks or the broader markets. It can be particularly handy for those with investments across multiple brokerage firms.

One of the things I like most about this app is something I'm a little persnickety about, the fact that it's a good-looking app with a good interface. Okay, fine — I'm a lot persnickety about those kinds of things; it's true. It has a color scheme that's muted and easy on the eye; navigation is intuitive; and the app works in both portrait and landscape modes, though I prefer landscape mode for this app. It also has all of the features you'll need to monitor your portfolios, making it a one-stop shop for most users.

There are two main tabs in this app, Watchlist and Portfolios. As the name suggests, Watchlist is for setting up a list of individual stocks you want to watch. This is useful for individual companies you want to monitor from your portfolio, or for watching a company you're considering adding to your portfolio. This tab offers a snapshot current status for each of the stocks you're watching, and it includes the name of the company (or index), its ticker symbol, the last trade, and the change that trade represents (green for up and red for down). The middle pane offers you details about the stock in the list you have selected, as well as a chart for the stock. The third pane offers you a list of recent news articles pertaining to the stock or index you have selected in your list.

 Tap the chart to get a larger version, along with different viewing options from which to choose. These include the type of chart (line, bar, candlestick), the time frame (from one day to five years to max), and the different values you want to see in the chart.

The other main tab is the one labeled Portfolios. In this tab, you can set up one or more portfolios and monitor both their individual and collective performance. This is useful if you have a broad portfolio and want to be able to monitor it by sector (or whatever other breakdown you fancy) or if you have your investments spread out amongst multiple brokerages. In Figure 5-1, you can see that the view for this tab includes a pane that shows the value of all your portfolios, another pane for the portfolio you have selected, and a third pane for the individual stocks in that portfolio. The middle of the screen shows detailed information on the day's trade and a chart, just like the Watchlist tab has. The third pane is for news relating to the individual stock you have selected.

Figure 5-1: Viewing a sample portfolio.

There are a lot of preference options in StockWatch, and they're useful options. There are three date formats to choose from, the ability to set your default tab, preferences for setting your default chart range, and more. Poke around in the Settings tab to see everything you can tweak.

You can set an app-specific passcode if you wish to prevent other users of your iPad from accessing the information in this app. You can find this in the Settings tab.

You'll see another tab in Figure 5-1, called Sync Data, that allows you to sync your data between your iPad and iPhone. Set up your Portfolios and Watchlist once, and then manage them on whatever device is convenient at the moment.

E*TRADE customers should use that company's iPad app (and I tell you about it later in this chapter), as I think it is even better than StockWatch, but StockWatch is a must-have app for anyone else looking to monitor her portfolios or set up stock watchlists. Its great design, awesome features, and intuitive interface make it a pleasure to use.

What you can do with it: monitor one or more stock portfolios, set up stock watchlists, and access financial news relating to specific stocks or the broader markets. You can also sync your portfolios and watchlists with other devices running StockWatch.

Bloomberg for iPad

by Bloomberg LP

Free

 I'm a big fan of Bloomberg's financial news coverage, and I'm a bigger fan of this app. For one thing, it offers instant access to all of that great news coverage, and it provides stock and index data like you'd expect. It also provides currency, commodities, and bond data — one of the few iPad apps I've seen that does so. For some icing on this cake of financial goodness, it offers direct access to a number of Bloomberg-produced podcasts that will be invaluable to traders and investors wanting to learn more about the markets.

Let's start with the home screen (accessed by a button simply labeled Bloomberg when you're in another tab). In Figure 5-2, you'll see that it offers you all the top financial news of the day and snapshots of the major global indices (DOW JONES, S&P 500, FTSE 100, and NIKKEI 225), two of the stocks in a watchlist you set up, current data on the U.S. dollar, and tappable links to the different tabs in the app.

Figure 5-2: Top News in the app, along with snapshots of the major indices.

Like many other iPad apps I talk about, Bloomberg works in both landscape and portrait mode, but I think it looks best in landscape mode. For instance, in the figure, the buttons at the bottom of the screen are laid out nicely in landscape mode, but in portrait mode they take up one-third of the screen because they're stacked three deep.

The best thing about this app to me is all the Bloomberg news articles. In the News tab, you get all of Bloomberg's news coverage divided into many categories over seven swipable pages. The first page has panes for Worldwide news, the Most Read stories of the day, Bonds, Commodities, and the company's Exclusive content. Swipe to the left, and you get a new page of Currency news, Economy Emerging Markets, Energy, and Funds. Another swipe, and you get five more categories, and so on. You can edit the order of all these categories, making this a convenient place to catch up on the news that's important to you.

The Equity Indices, Currencies, Commodities, Equity Index Futures, and Bonds tabs all contain simple, scrollable lists of those markets. You can't customize them; but these are finite lists to begin with, so that's not a big deal to me. Having quick and easy access to them is what I think is important.

The other big feature of this app is all the Bloomberg podcasts you listen to on your iPad. Yeah, you can get these podcasts from iTunes, but Bloomberg for iPad gives you easy access to the lot of them without you having to monitor and manage podcast subscriptions. There are podcasts for News, Economics, Politics, and the Markets, and all the ones I have listened to are high-quality, professionally produced programs suitable for broadcast radio. You can also listen to them even while you are messing around in other parts of the app.

Lastly, I'd be remiss in my duties if I didn't point out that some people are put off by the black background with orange or white text theme of this app, but I personally like it. It makes for easy reading, in my opinion.

There are better apps (like StockWatch, covered earlier in the chapter) if you just want to monitor your stocks, but Bloomberg is the app for people who want to monitor the markets as a whole. The company's financial news coverage is among the best, and access to all of the markets outside of the usual stock markets is convenient.

What you can do with it: monitor your stocks, as well as all of the world's major equity indices, global currency markets, commodities, futures, and bonds. You also get all of Bloomberg's extensive financial news and several of the company's financial podcasts.

**Book VI
Chapter 5**

Financial Apps

SplashMoney for iPad

by SplashData, Inc.

$4.99

 Most of us need help when it comes to managing budgets, and the reality is that different things work for different people. I know people who know how much they have in their checking account to the penny, but have never recorded a check in the ledger or balanced their checkbook, not even once. On the other end of the spectrum, I know people who spend lots of time and effort in planning their budget, balancing their checkbook, and trying hard to be on top of their spending, and yet nothing seems to work for them despite their best efforts. Most of us fall between those two extremes and just need a little extra help in watching what we spend and seeing where our money goes. If that's you, SplashMoney for iPad might be the app for you.

SplashMoney HD is a money-management app for the iPad that allows you to monitor online banking accounts (checking, savings, and so on) and credit cards, create budgets, and track your actual spending. You can sync data between the iPad app and the Mac or Windows version of the company's software, too, which is very handy. You can also directly download online banking information from a list of a couple of hundred banks and online banking services, including most of the major banks. The app is designed well, colorful, and provides attractive and informative graphs to help you visualize what you are doing with your money. It also includes an app-specific password option for additional security.

Setting up this app takes some work, but once you do that initial setup, it's pretty easy to work with on a day-to-day basis. The key is to simply make sure you keep up with it. It comes with a few default accounts, including Checking, Savings, and three credit card accounts. In Figure 5-3, I added a couple of other accounts, and then added a bunch of (fake) transactions under my (fictional) checking account. When I set up each account, I named it, picked an icon, and established a beginning balance. Then when I make payments, write checks, buy things with my debit card, or make deposits, I just enter each one as I go. I can assign categories, the payee, enter the date, and assign it as either a personal transaction or business transaction.

 Once you've entered a transaction assigned to a particular payee, the next time you select that payee for a new transaction, the category, payment type, and other things you selected are autofilled from the previous transaction. This is a handy timesaver, especially for those transactions you conduct frequently, like buying gas or groceries. You can also set up recurring transactions with reminders, and who doesn't need that kind of help!?

Figure 5-3: Viewing a sample checking account with recent checking activity on the right.

If you're like me, I wouldn't worry about trying to backdate a bunch of transactions when you first start using the app. Instead, just set your starting balances properly and focus on entering new transactions going forward!

Once you've set up all the proper accounts and have some transactions under your belt, you get reports that show you where your money is going. You can view these reports in list form or as a pie chart, and doing both might really change the way you think about how you spend your money. For instance, it turns out that I spend a lot of money on books and games like World of Warcraft. Who knew?

If you're really ambitious, you can even establish budgets for each and every category you want to track. Need to cut back on how much you spend on movies, or maybe coffee? Establish a budget and monitor it throughout the month. SplashMoney will show you what your budget is, what you've actually spent, and the difference. I think a lot of people will appreciate that feature, and most of us should probably use it!

There's a lot to this app, and it's up to you how much you take advantage of all these features. I think that people who are comfortable with (or need to be more comfortable with) maintaining detailed financial records to manage their budgets are going to like this app. It's not what I would call a perfect app, but it's very good, and it's getting better with each update.

One more note: PocketMoney from Cantamount Software ($4.99) is another great entry in this category of personal finance apps.

What you can do with it: manage your household budget, download your banking transactions, track your spending, and get charts and reports showing you where your money goes.

PowerOne Financial Calculator

by Infinity Softworks, Inc.

$5.99 — Hybrid

Do you remember the days when the math and engineer guys proudly walked around with their calculators from TI and HP? Uhhh . . . yeah, me neither . . . I'm not that old, either. Okay, I'll admit it; I had one back in the 70s, but I had no idea how to use it! I'm not sure if that's a mitigating piece of evidence or if I'm just embarrassing myself further, but it might help explain why I like PowerOne Financial Calculator so much. This app does super complex finance-related calculations for you, but with the included templates, you don't have to really know what you're doing to get the right answers for a lot of things — I call that a score.

For instance, when you're shopping for a car it's sometimes hard to get a straight answer out of the salesperson regarding how much your car is going to cost. Many dealerships like to try to sell you a car based on the car payment, and that can make it hard to understand how much you're really paying! At the same time, if you're price shopping for a car and know the total price, you do still need to know what your monthly payment is going to be. PowerOne has a template called Auto Loan that will get you the information you need. As shown in Figure 5-4, you enter the price, sales tax, any fees you might need to pay, the interest rate on your loan, down payment, and the number of months you intend to carry the loan, and you can get your monthly payment with a simple tap.

You can work backward, too: Say you want to change what you want your payment to be. If you enter that, you can tap the equal sign next to any of the other categories and get that figure. For instance, if you want to pay a certain amount per month, you can see how many months you'd need to carry the loan to hit that target. Or if you know how much you can pay per month and how long your bank will carry your note, you can quickly get the figure for how much of a down payment you'd need to make, or how much you can spend on your car. If you're working on your taxes (or someone else's taxes), the same template will also give you amortization figures.

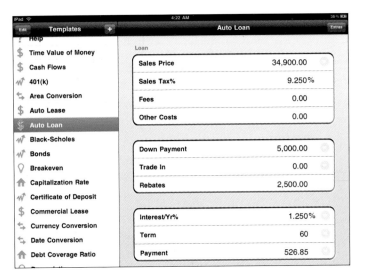

Figure 5-4: Figuring out the specifics of a car loan with the Auto Loan template.

Don't worry. There is, of course a standard calculator in this app. Just choose the Calculator template to get a calculator with both math and trig functions, as well as a history. You can tap away on this like you would any ol' calculator.

But this app isn't just about car loans. There are more than fifty templates included in this app, some for traders, some for accountants, some for super math people, and some that are for us mere mortals. I like the Area Conversion that allows me to fill in one of eleven measurements and with a single tap get that converted to the other ten measurements. There's also a currency converter that uses the most recent exchange rates (if you have a connection to the Internet when you use it). There's a depreciation template, an inflation calculator, several loan-related calculations, mortgage tools, a sales-tax template, and much more. There's even a tip calculator that will divide your bill among multiple people!

For sure, a lot of what this app offers is pretty specialized, but I'd hazard that many of us will be glad we have this app on our iPad if we need it just once. If you do financial transactions for a living, however, this might be a must-have app for you. Real estate agents, accountants, investors, bankers, and anyone on the other side of those transactions will find it useful.

What you can do with it: you can do a variety of complex calculations with it, and it includes many easy-to-use templates for commonly used equations in the world(s) of finance.

Daily Stocks

by 13apps

$19.99

 Let me show you another specialty app for investors, called Daily Stocks. This app provides the user with technical scans of the market (up to 91 such technical scans as of this writing), and is designed to highlight trends in the marketplace based on some highly technical analytical techniques. Those trends, in turn, can help investors identify both opportunities and risks in the markets. This kind of information is mainly the domain of fairly serious traders, so if your eyes start to glaze over as I talk about it, I understand! I think it's important to talk about it here, however, as it is an example of an iPad app for serious investors.

Daily Stocks works just fine in landscape and portrait mode, but landscape mode shows you a little more information. As you can see in Figure 5-5, the left side of the screen offers charts for the three major U.S. indices and five global indices.

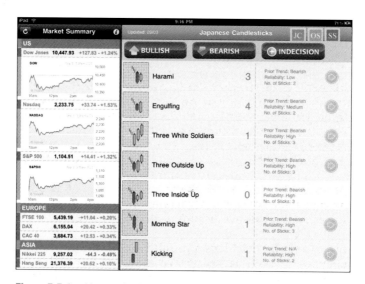

Figure 5-5: Looking at the Japanese Candlestick tab.

It's the right two-thirds of the screen, however, that is dedicated to the real purpose of this app. At the top of the screen in the green bar are three tabs, labeled JC (Japanese Candlesticks), OS (Overextended Stocks), and SS (Stock Scans). These are three different styles of reports, and each offers very different information.

A *candlestick* in the trading world is a kind of bar graph. It shows the opening price of a stock and its closing price, with the color telling you if it was a winning day (opening on the bottom, closing on the top), or a losing day (opening at the top, closing at the bottom).

In Daily Stocks, a red candlestick represents a losing day, and a green candlestick represents a winning day. Simple, eh? And more informative to traders than other graphs.

The JC tab offers ten Bullish trends, ten Bearish trends, and three Indecision trends. These are all attempts to understand where the market is headed based on patterns that have been identified in the past. In other words, they are far from perfect (but their adherents tend to feel strongly about them). Those names you see, like Falling Three Method or Engulfing, are all English approximations of the original Japanese names the patterns were given.

In any event, the trends with more information are shaded darker grey, and a tap gives you a new screen with a definition of what the trend is supposed to identify and a list of the stocks that matched the pattern to begin with.

Overextended Stocks (OS) are stocks that have broken above their resistance levels (Overbought) or below their support levels (Oversold) or that have traveled beyond their Simple Moving Average (SMA). The OS tab gives you a list of the ten most oversold or overbought stocks compared to their SMA over the last nine to 200 days. You can tap through one of those ten stocks in any of the SMA views to get several graphs and charts.

Lastly, the Stock Scans (SS) tab gives you more than 50 reports of stocks that have met some specific criteria (such as new 52-week high or low, various volume levels, crossover reports, and many more).

These are all very technical reports and scans, and if you're not an active — and frankly a serious — trader, you probably don't need this app. Most of this stuff is over my head, and I've been covering (Apple-related) stock news for more than thirteen years. If you are a serious trader, however, you should check out Daily Stocks.

What you can do with it: get a variety of daily technical reports and scans for the markets.

QIF Entry

by Edwin Hou

$2.99

Intuit has a pretty bad track record of supporting Apple's platforms, especially iOS. Why don't we have Quicken for iPad and iPhone? Who knows, but fortunately, there is still an app for that (managing personal finance). Firstly, Quicken is Intuit's personal finance solution for Mac and Windows. QIF Entry allows you to enter transactions on your iPad that you can then send to your Mac or PC and import into Quicken. That might sound kind of kludgy, but as of this writing, there's no other way that I could find for doing much of anything with Quicken on your iPad. Even then, there are some limitations, most notably that it works only with Quicken 2002 for Windows and Quicken 2007 for Mac and Windows. On the other hand, it has built-in support for Dropbox, making getting your files on and off your iPad a breeze. (I tell you about Dropbox in Book VI, Chapter 1.)

QuickTimer

by William Modesitt

$8.99

While I'm ragging on Intuit, it would seem a propitious time to point out that there's no QuickBooks for iOS, either, unless you want to use QuickBooks Online, which isn't accessible if you don't have a connection to the Internet. QuickTimer is a third-party app that allows QuickBooks users to enter time-tracking data into their iPads in a format that they can then import into QuickBooks. This is crucial for anyone using QuickBooks who wants to be able to use the iPad as an on-the-go solution, and the developer of this app has done a very good job with it. Users can export the data in other formats, too, including comma and tab delimited, and even HTML. That means you can also import data from this app into Excel and other applications that read those formats.

Quick Sale for iPad

by IntelliXense

$9.99

Quick Sale for iPad is a handy app for anyone who needs to do invoicing on the go (at street fairs, at a client's location, on a business trip, at a trade show, and so on) or, for that matter, anyone who wants to interface with customers with an iPad in his hands instead of a computer. It is the future, after all. In any event, Quick Sale for iPad is a fairly complete invoicing solution for your iPad. It offers unlimited inventory items and services (including photos for each one, if you want) that you can organize by category. It also offers reports, the ability to e-mail reports and invoices, and integrates with Credit Card Terminal from Inner Fence for conducting credit card transactions!

Apple is adding print services to iPad in November of 2010, but until then, you can use PrintCentral for iPad — which I talk about in Book VI, Chapter 1 — to print invoices directly from your iPad.

Pageonce Personal Finance

by Pageonce, Inc.

Free — Hybrid

Pageonce Personal Finance is a personal finance service for the mobile market. This is a free, ad-supported, hybrid app that will work on both iPhone and iPad. It allows you to track your bills and expenses, monitor your credit cards, check your bank account status, check in on your stocks, and even track your frequent flyer mileage programs. The company also offers the ability to remotely destroy your data through the service's Web site if you ever lose your iPhone or iPad. There's a Premium version of the app ($6.99) that is ad-free and offers additional features. If you like the free version, you'll probably be willing to pay for the paid version.

E*TRADE Mobile Pro for iPad

by E*TRADE FINANCIAL

Free

E*TRADE Mobile Pro for iPad is that company's conduit to all of its online brokerage services. The thing I love most about this app is that it's one of the best designed iPad apps that has yet to hit the App Store. The developers made great use of the iPad's screen real estate, and they put a lot of thought into arranging the app's information panes to match the way people will actually use them. That's a touch I really appreciate. When it comes to using the app, you can buy and sell stocks and options, get financial news, watch the indices, and monitor your portfolio. The only thing that's wrong with this app is that most of its services are accessible only by E*TRADE customers. If you're not an E*TRADE customer, check out the StockWatch app I talk about earlier in the chapter.

Chapter 6: Entertainment Apps

In This Chapter

- Emoti HD
- Netflix
- TabToolkit
- Pandora Radio
- AmpliTube for iPad
- Seline HD
- Acrobots
- IMDb Movies & TV
- Koi Pond HD
- Gravilux/Uzu

Finally! Finally, we're going to get some entertainment on the iPad! I've shown you some great iPad apps, but I saved the best, or at least some of the most fun apps, for last. Entertainment is another one of those broad topics that means a lot of different things to different people, and so in this chapter, I picked several different kinds of apps that I think are entertaining. I've got a social networking helper, several music apps, a way to watch movies and TV on your iPad, some relaxing fish (no, really), and a couple of super cool apps that might even entertain your inner nerd!

Many of the apps I talk about in this chapter are apps that were written for the iPad. Some apps, however, have been written by the developer to run as native apps on both the iPad and iPhone (or iPod touch). These are called *hybrid* apps, and you'll find "Hybrid" next to the price for those apps. Hybrid apps have the advantage of allowing you to buy once and use on whatever iOS device you have.

Emoti HD

by nodconcept, LLC

$2.99

Facebook is probably one of the most popular forms of entertainment on the planet today. The company has more than half a billion members these days, and a lot of us waste — I mean spend — countless hours every day posting updates about ourselves and reading up on what our friends and family are doing. I thought it would be a good idea to kick off this chapter with an app that can make this form of entertainment even more entertaining. Emoti HD is an app that allows you to post great-looking emoticons in your Facebook posts, images that can be informative for those reading your posts, but images that can also simply draw more attention to your posts.

In case you've been hiding in a cave for the last 10 or 15 years before you popped out to pick up an iPad and this book, an *emoticon* is one of those little sideways faces you can make out of text characters, like :) for a smiley face, or :(for a sad face. Emoji, on the other hand, started in Japan as a system for including actual images for smiley (and other) faces through SMS text messages. Emoti (for iPhone) and Emoti HD's name is a juxtaposition of the two concepts.

As of this writing, Emoti HD has 186 emoticons. These high-quality images were custom made by nodconcept, the app's developer, and they look absolutely great. They're colorful, and they just pop off the screen on both your iPad and on Facebook in your browser. The app includes all the basic emoticons for happy, angry, sad, ecstatic, crying, proud, goofy, surprised, in love, and even sleeping. But there's much more, too. There are sports and thank-you emoticons, emoticons to denote that it's raining, snowing, hot, or cold. There are military emoticons, food, music, gambling, and religious emoticons. There are gay-pride, graduation, and baby emoticons (It's a boy! It's a girl!), and even emoticons for the major holidays. That's a lot of emoticons, but the developer says that more are coming!

You can also use Emoti HD to post to Facebook without using an emoticon, too, making this app a one-stop shop for posting. On the first page of emoticons, you'll find a dotted box with the text "no emoti" in it. Tap that, make your post, and your post will have no image and look like a normal Facebook post.

On the left side of Figure 6-1, I'm making a post to my Facebook account about my current favorite band, The Spyrals, out of San Francisco. I could have used one of the music-themed images, but I chose one of the thumbs-up emoticons, instead. It's kind of like having my own personal Like and Dislike tool.

Figure 6-1: Making a post to Facebook with Emoti HD (left) and rearranging the sheets of emoticons by tapping and holding one of the sheets (right).

To make a post, tap an emoticon and you get a keyboard and a spot to write your post. Write the post, tap the Share button, and you're done! On your first post, you'll have a Facebook Connect button you tap to log into Facebook from Emoti HD. If you need to change accounts, you can log out of the current account by tapping the From field in a new post. You can pick your destination (your own Wall, a friend's Wall, a Group, a Page, or a Fan Page) by tapping the second field (Wall in Figure 6-1). It's very easy to use, and it may even be the most direct way to make a Facebook post on your iPad.

There's one more cool feature in Emoti HD that I want to show you. In the upper-right corner of the display is an icon with nine little squares. Tap that and you get all nine pages of emoticons so you can quickly jump to the one you want. This is a cool navigation feature that I wish was in more apps, but nodconcept upped it a notch by adding the ability to rearrange the pages so that you can put them in the order you want. If you tap and hold one of the pages in this view, like I did on the right in Figure 6-1, they start shaking just like apps do when you want to rearrange their order on your iPad or iPhone. Just tap, hold, and drag a page to the position you want it! For instance, I'm not a big soccer fan (and the World Cup is over), so I moved that page of emoticons to the end. That's pretty slick!

All in all, this is a cool app with great-looking emoticons. If you post on Facebook and want a way to make your posts stand out, or if you just want to be able to better illustrate your point, Emoti HD is for you.

What you can do with it: make posts to Facebook with bright, colorful emoticon images to illustrate your mood or some other aspect of your posts.

Netflix

by James Odell

Free (Subscription Required) — Hybrid

Wooohoooo! TV and movies on your iPad! You can watch video content of all sorts on your iPad. You can buy and rent TV shows and movies through Apple's iTunes Store, too. There's also YouTube content, videos you get from your friends and family, and movies that you might have bought on DVD and transferred to your computer and iPad. Some Web sites offer video content, as well, though much of that is currently Flash-based and therefore unwatchable on your iPad. Netflix, however, is another great choice, but I guess I should begin with a basic look at what exactly Netflix is.

Netflix started life as a mail-based DVD rental service. For a monthly subscription, you can get DVDs of TV shows and movies delivered to your house. Once you've watched them, you can return them, and Netflix sends you another DVD. Since you're paying a flat fee, the faster you watch and then return your Netflix DVDs in the mail, the more video entertainment you get for your dollar.

Netflix is a great way to catch up on TV shows you either got behind on or were late watching in the first place. Go back to the beginning of *Breaking Bad*, for instance, or *Mad Men*, or even whole TV shows that went off the air years ago, like *Buffy the Vampire Slayer!*

From there, Netflix started adding other services, including streaming movies and TV shows across the Internet. You can watch TV shows and movies on your Mac or PC, and with the Netflix app on your iPad, you can even watch them on your iOS device, so long as you have an Internet connection. In Figure 6-2, I've got the Bruce Willis flick, *Surrogates*, pulled up. I can add it to my Instant Queue (a queue for those shows I want to stream), add it to my DVD queue (the queue for getting DVDs mailed to my house), or I can just Play it right now. I can also read up on the show, get cast information, and more.

Figure 6-2: On a movie or TV show's entry, you can watch it instantly, add it to your DVD queue, or add it to your Instant Queue (where available).

 Another very cool tool for using Netflix is the ability to rate movies. The company uses proprietary algorithms to suggest movies and TV shows you might like based on the shows that you've rated. The system works, more often than not, and gets better as you give it more information.

The video quality looks great on the iPad's display, and I think it's a great way to rent movies and TV shows. Even if you just want to manage your physical DVD queue on your iPad, however, the app is a better experience than using the company's Web site in Safari. It's a hybrid app, too, and it works just as well on your iPhone.

Another option for watching TV shows and movies on your iPad is Hulu Plus. It's a free download, but it requires a $9.99 monthly subscription. As I write this, Hulu Plus is in beta, though anyone can download the Hulu app. It's just not very useful without a Hulu Plus account. Yet another good TV solution for Mac users is EyeTV ($4.99) from El Gato, which allows you to stream TV from your Mac to your iPad, though it requires additional hardware on your Mac.

What you can do with it: you can stream TV shows and movies for instant viewing on your iPad, and you can also manage your Netflix account and queue. But note that you'll need an Internet connection for both features.

TabToolkit

by Agile Partners

$9.99 — Hybrid

I play guitar. Not all that well, but I play. In fact, once a year I get to play with writer extraordinaire Bob "Dr. Mac" LeVitus, Dave Hamilton of The Mac Observer, long-time Mac author Chris Breen, IDG VP Paul Kent (he runs Macworld Conference & Expo), columnist Chuck La Tournous, and Mac IT expert Duane Straub in a cover band called The Macworld All Stars. We play at a party during Macworld, and our running joke is we practice once a year, whether or not we need it, and then play that party. It's lots of fun (some of those guys are ringers), but it's a lot of songs to learn for one night of playing. Fortunately, the Internet has a ton of guitar tabs out there that make it a lot easier to learn a new song. TabToolkit for iPad makes that process even easier, especially if you need to learn a song on the go.

Tablature (usually called *tab* or *tabs* for short) is a musical notation system popular with guitarists and bassists. Rather than writing notes on a staff, you note which string on which fret is being played. A lot of us don't read sheet music, and tabs have become the most common way to write solos and chords in songs.

TabToolkit's most basic function is to organize and display your tabs. The app doesn't come with any tabs as of this writing, but it's easy enough to find billions of tabs on the Internet. You can get them into this app in three ways, too, which is very cool. The first is to simply browse for them in the in-app browser. Search for a song's name with *tab* at the end, and you'll likely find the right song right away. If TabToolkit detects a tab when you visit the page, it will tell you so — and with one tap, you can import it into the app! Pretty easy! There's also a very cool file transfer system the company developed. If you have tabs on your computer you want to transfer, and both your iPad and computer are on the same network, you can tap the Upload & Download button, shown on the left side of Figure 6-3, to get a URL. Open that URL on your computer, click the Add Files button to navigate to where you have them, select them, and they're added to your app! The third way is to use this same special Web page to simply copy and paste text-based tabs into the app.

Power Tab is software for Windows for creating and editing tabs, while Guitar Pro is a Mac and Windows app that you can use to write, edit, and even play back tab files on your computer.

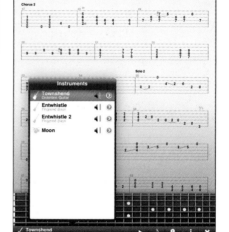

Figure 6-3: The list of songs I have loaded in Tab Toolkit (left) and playback of a song, including the pop-up window for choosing which instruments you want to hear (right).

If you can, though, find tabs that are in Guitar Pro and/or Power Tab formats, because then you'll see the real power of TabToolkit. With these files, which often also include MIDI information for other instruments, TabToolkit will play them so that you can play along. You can select which instruments you hear, and you can control the speed of playback. (That can be crucial for learning a hard-to-play passage!) You can use a metronome, and you can display a fretboard that lights up the strings and frets that are being played, a great visual learning tool!

Lefties aren't left out of this fretboard feature. When you're in a song, tap the gears icon and you can toggle a preference for displaying the left-handed or right-handed fretboard.

On the right in Figure 6-3, I have "I Can't Explain," one of my favorite tunes from The Who. It's a simple song, but even in his early recordings, Pete Townshend had some interesting ways to play chords. I wanted to see if I could improve the way I play it. You'll see that I have his part selected (I could have standard notations displayed, too, but I turned that off), and in this tab file, there are two parts for the bass and one for drums that I could also switch to. The red bar denotes where I am, and the fretboard at the bottom of the screen lights up as the notes are played.

If you play guitar or bass and like to learn cover songs, you'll think this app is the bee's knees! It's great for learning solos from the greats (and not-so-greats), and its playback features and tempo controls make learning even the hardest parts easier than you can imagine.

What you can do with it: manage and display guitar and bass tab files. You can download tabs from the Internet directly in the app, or you can transfer them from your Mac or PC through a special file-transfer system the app offers. If you have Power Tab or Guitar Pro file formats, you can play them back, control which instruments you hear, and adjust the tempo.

Pandora Radio

by Open Door Networks, Inc.

Free — Hybrid

Pandora Radio is the self-titled app that brings the Pandora streaming radio service from your browser to your iPad (and iPhone). If you like music but don't know what Pandora is, I want you to stop reading, put this book down, and go download it from the App Store right now! Go on; I'll wait.

So I'm guessing that if you're still reading, you either already had it or have installed it now, so we can all be on the same page, right? Excellent! There are a lot of streaming radio stations on the Internet, but Pandora came up with an approach of offering a wide variety of music to people in a way that they actually wanted to listen to it. Imagine that!

Here's how it works, in the online service as well as the iPad app: When you first launch Pandora, you're prompted to sign in with an existing account or create a new one. Once you're signed in, you can Create a New Station by simply searching for a band (or song or artist). When you do, Pandora starts playing a song by that band, a song that you can then give a thumbs up or down to. Pandora then looks at the songs you like (and don't like), and plays other songs it thinks you will like based on what people with similar tastes have said they like. This allows you to train your stations to play music you're probably going to really enjoy!

You should rate as many songs as you can. The more data Pandora has, the more you'll like your stations!

You can create as many stations as you want, each one starting with an artist, song, or composer. If a station gets out of control for you, delete it and start a new one. In Figure 6-4, I've got stations for The Brian Jonestown Massacre, The Who, The Beatles, Led Zeppelin, Black Rebel Motorcycle Club, The Church, and a band called Jucifer. (A band I was in opened for Jucifer a couple of years ago, and I wanted to hear if their studio stuff was as chaotic as their live sound — it wasn't.)

Figure 6-4: Several radio stations set up (the list on the left) with information on the current song playing on the right.

In that figure, you'll see that I'm listening to "This Is The First Of Your Last Warning" from The Brian Jonestown Massacre. The album cover of that song is highlighted, and you can see the album covers of the songs that played before, allowing you to tap any of them to find out more. You'll see that I gave this song a thumbs up, from the icon next to the name of the band. If I hit the Menu button directly below it, I can bookmark the song or artist, and I can also get taken straight to the song or artist in iTunes!

Which brings me to why I think Pandora is so cool. The stations and song ratings allow me to train those stations to play only songs I'm likely to like, but I'm still going to hear songs and bands I've never heard before! It's like having a personal DJ! I've found lots of new bands this way.

When you give a song a thumbs down, Pandora immediately skips to the next song.

Another feature I really like is the band histories you get with each song — I just love learning more about bands.

Pandora is free, but the free service limits you to 40 hours of listening per month, a limit relating to a royalty agreement between the station and rights holders. For most users, 40 hours per month will probably be enough, but for $36 per year you can have unlimited listening time, no ads, and a desktop app for listening to Pandora without a browser on your Mac or PC. The only real advantage to iPad users is the lack of ads and the unlimited listening; plus you're supporting a cool service (and the rights holders of all those songs).

As I said previously, if you like music, you should have Pandora on your iPad. It offers you a great way to hear favorite and new music alike, and you can build stations around all your favorite bands.

What you can do with it: Pandora offers live streaming radio through stations you set up around bands, songs, or composers.

AmpliTube for iPad

by IK Multimedia

$19.99

While I'm talking about music, I'll show you another great tool for guitarists and bassists. AmpliTube for iPad is an amplifier and effects modeling package that turns your iPad into a mobile guitar rig! I mean it: Plug your guitar into your iPad (I tell you how to do that next), launch AmpliTube, pick an amp, lay down some effects pedals, and your guitar sounds like you're playing up on a stage somewhere with a full rig behind you. Since most of us don't have roadies in real life, the cool thing is that you can switch pedals and amps with just a couple of taps until you get the sound you want!

To use AmpliTube for iPad, you need an audio interface like AmpliTube iRig ($39.99) or GuitarConnect ($29.99) from Griffin Technology to be able to plug your guitar into your iPad. It's worth it to have so much power in such a small, easy to use package.

AmpliTube for Mac and Windows has been around for several years now, and the iPad app is derived from the same technology that makes the desktop software powerful enough to use with desktop recording. I've even seen it used in a live setting.

One thing you should note is that AmpliTube for iPad works only in landscape mode, but I think that's an acceptable choice the developers made for maximum practical usability. In Figure 6-5, you can see that I chose a Crunch amp, with 4 x 12 inch speaker cabinets and a Shure 57 microphone that IK Multimedia doesn't call a Shure 57.

In fact, nothing gets a brand label, despite the obvious products from Marshall, Fender, Ibanez, and other manufacturers these models are based on. You'll be able to quickly figure out what's what, though, or at least what you like.

Figure 6-5: I've got four pedals, my amp, a cabinet, and my microphone picked — I'm ready to rock out!

Above the amp in my setup are four pedals (Noise Filter, Delay, Fuzz, and Overdrive), and I can swap out any of the pedals from the eleven that are listed in the pull-down menu on the left side of the screen. The Delay and Fuzz pedals are on (the red light is the indicator), while the Overdrive pedal is off (the Noise Filter is behind the pull-down menu). You can adjust all of the knobs just by touching them and moving your finger, exactly like you'd expect. The same goes for the controls on the amps.

The app includes a built-in tuner and metronome, as well as backing tracks you can play on top of, which is very cool. You can also play on top of full songs, but you'll have to add those songs to the app through a file-transfer browser feature similar to the one I describe in the earlier "TabToolkit" section. It would be nifty if AmpliTube would just access the iTunes song library already on my iPad, but the file-transfer mechanism isn't hard to use. Lastly, there are twelve presets you use for amp, cabinet, mic, and pedal combinations that you really like. It comes with nine of them already set up, and three empty ones, but you can change all of them as much as you want.

There's a free version of AmpliTube called AmpliTube FREE for iPad. It has just two amps, three pedals, and two mics for you to use, but it's a great way to make sure you're going to like the app before you plunk down $19.99 for the full version. You can add individual cabinets, amps, and pedals to the free version through the in-app store, but if you're going to buy more than a couple, you'll save money by buying the full version.

AmpliTube for iPad is the app that any guitarist or bassist should have if he wants to have a portable rig with him on his iPad. If you have musicians in your life, consider giving it to them as a gift — before they ask to borrow the money from you anyway! Bada bing! Hey, I kid, my fellow musicians.

What you can do with it: play your guitar or bass through your iPad with full amp and effects models. It's like having a portable guitar rig with you, and with headphones, no one has to hear the ear-splitting volumes you're playing at.

Seline HD – Music Instrument

by Ilya Plavunov

$8.99 — Hybrid

There are apps like AmpliTube that are intended to be used with traditional analog instruments, and there are also virtual pianos — and there's even a virtual Ocarina for the iPhone (a cool 99 cent app). There are turntables and DJ solutions, and loop mixers galore, too. I picked Seline HD – Music Instrument to show you because it's one of the first musical instrument apps that takes a totally new approach to turning your iPad into an instrument. Rather than trying to bring an analog instrument to your digital iPad, Seline HD is played on an interface designed from the ground up for the iPad, called ioGrid. It allows you to play melodies with your hands while automatically generated backing tracks drone underneath what you are playing. The app has two effects, 20 main instrument voices (plus nine drone voices), and you can record what you play! It's fun, it's cool, and I recommend it.

Acrobots

by Vectorpark, Inc.

99 cents — Hybrid

Come on! Acrobatic robots? What's not to like? I'll tell you; there's nothing not to like about this app, and plenty to just absolutely adore! Acrobots are three-legged things that have suction cups for feet. Those suction cups are attracted to other Acrobots and to the walls, and only momentum and what seems to be a desire to move keep them from huddling in a corner of your iPad's screen in a giant clump. Actually, you tweak their size, gravity, balance, stickiness, speed, and even the amount of air drag they are subjected to, so it's possible to make them clump together. You can tap and drag to toss individuals around your screen, or tilt your iPad to make gravity do your dirty work. But either way, they're just super fun to watch. There's a preset called Spazz that I particularly enjoy because it keeps them moving on their own without any intervention from me. This is a fun, entertaining app, and you should check it out.

IMDb Movies & TV

by IMDb

Free — Hybrid

I use IMDb all the time. The abbreviation stands for Internet Movie Database, but the site includes information about movies and TV shows, and the actors, directors, and even crew who make those shows for us to watch. I watch a lot of TV while I work, which means I watch on my computer. I often see someone and wonder where I saw the actor, or struggle at coming up with the actor's name, and I can look on IMDb to find out. I've also settled any number of bets (or at least debates) with friends and family by looking someone or something up on the service.

With IMDb for Movies & TV on your iPad, you get the enormous amount of data about TV and movies, but you get what I think is a huge bonus: an interface that's far superior to the service's browser-based home. While the IMDb app will take you to the Web site if you ask it to, the reality is that it's easier to use the context-oriented menus and buttons on the iPad than it is to click around in a browser on your computer. It's a free hybrid app, too, so you can't really go wrong with it.

Koi Pond HD

by Brandon Bogle

$1.99

I originally came to this app on the iPhone, but I love it on the iPad even more. Koi Pond HD is just what it sounds like: a virtual Koi Pond for your iPad. And I don't know if it's so much entertaining as it is relaxing, though there should be at least some times when the two are the same, right? In any event, when you launch the app, your iPad's display is transformed into the surface of a pond with rocks, lily pads, turtles, and Koi. Everything looks very realistic, like you're truly looking down into a Koi pond! If you tap the screen, you're tapping the water, and that startles the fish. (Turtles retreat inside their shells.) Shaking your iPad drops food into the pond, and your fish will dart to eat it up, just like the real thing. You edit your ponds, apply different themes, adjust the type and numbers of fish and contents, and more. Also, the environmental sounds are very high quality, and this app will serve well for people who are looking for a white noise generator.

Gravilux and Uzu

by Scott Snibbe and Jason K Smith (respectively)

99 cents — Hybrid

 Gravilux and Uzu are two particle visualizers for the iPad (Gravilux is a hybrid app for iPhone, too), but they both work in different ways, and they're both too cool for words. With Gravilux, you "draw with stars" as your finger becomes the very embodiment of gravity itself. Where you touch your iPad's screen, the stars must react to your immense gravitational pull.

 With Uzu, particles careen around on your screen, but they obey rules and patterns according to how many fingers are touching it. (There are ten sets of parameters for up to ten fingers, not all of which have to be your own!)

On the other hand, Gravilux has more settings for you to toggle on and off. (Double-tap a corner of your screen to pull up the settings bar.)

Both apps look great on your iPad, and both are frightfully fun. If you download them, just be sure not to forget to feed your pets and/or kids, and you should be fine!

Index